People Power and Political Change

This book examines the upsurge in mass popular protest against undemocratic regimes. Relating early revolutions to recent global trends and protests, it examines the significance of 'people power' to democracy.

Taking a comparative approach, this text analyses unarmed uprisings in Iran in 1977–9, Latin America and Asia in the 1980s, Africa in 1989–92, Eastern Europe in 1989 and ex-Soviet states after 2000, right up to the 2011 'Arab Spring'. The author assesses the influence on people power of global politics and trends, such as the growth of international governmental organizations and international law, citizen networks operating across borders, and emerging media (such as Twitter and Wikileaks). Although stressing the positive potential of people power, this text also examines crucial problems of repression, examples of failure and potential political problems, disintegration of empires and the role of power rivalries. Drawing from contemporary debates about democratization and literatures on power, violence and nonviolence, from both academic sources and media perspectives, this text builds an incisive analytical argument about the changing nature of power itself.

People Power and Political Change is a must read for students and scholars of democratic theory, international politics and current affairs.

April Carter is Honorary Research Fellow at the Centre for Peace and Reconciliation Studies, Coventry University, UK.

People Power and Political Change
Key issues and concepts

April Carter

LONDON AND NEW YORK

First published 2012
by Routledge
2 Park Square, Milton Park, Abingdon, Oxon, OX14 4RN

Simultaneously published in the USA and Canada
by Routledge
711 Third Avenue, New York, NY 10017

Routledge is an imprint of the Taylor & Francis Group, an informa business

© 2012 April Carter

The right of April Carter to be identified as author of this work has been asserted by her in accordance with sections 77 and 78 of the Copyright, Designs and Patents Act 1988.

All rights reserved. No part of this book may be reprinted or reproduced or utilised in any form or by any electronic, mechanical, or other means, now known or hereafter invented, including photocopying and recording, or in any information storage or retrieval system, without permission in writing from the publishers.

Trademark Notice: Product or corporate names may be trademarks or registered trademarks, and are used only for identification and explanation without intent to infringe.

British Library Cataloguing in Publication Data
A catalogue record for this book is available from the British Library

Library of Congress Cataloging-in-Publication Data
Carter, April.
People power and political change : key issues and concepts / April Carter.
p. cm.
Includes bibliographical references and index.
1. Government, Resistance to. 2. Protest movements. 3. Democratization.
4. Regime change. I. Title.
JC328.3.C285 2011
322.4--dc23
2011019667

ISBN: 978-0-415-58048-9 (hbk)
ISBN: 978-0-415-58049-6 (pbk)
ISBN: 978-0-203-18110-2 (ebk)

Typeset in Bembo
by Taylor & Francis Books

Contents

Acknowledgements	vi
Introduction	1

PART I
Resistance and political change — 5

1 People power and nonviolent methods in historical perspective — 7
2 People power and people's war compared — 22
3 People power and changing theories of revolution — 49

PART II
Central concepts and debates — 73

4 Power, violence and unarmed resistance — 75
5 Constructing 'the people': body politic, nation or class? — 91
6 People power and electoral democracy: 'electoral revolutions' and democratization — 116

PART III
Implications of globalization for success of people power — 143

7 Global trends, transnational solidarity and international politics — 145

Conclusion — 174

Appendix: People power movements against political repression since 1975 — 178
Bibliography — 181
Index — 197

Acknowledgements

This book draws on my own interest for over 50 years in popular struggles against repression, and in particular the role nonviolent methods can play in them. It also draws heavily on the experience and writings of activists, researchers and academic analysts, both of particular resistance movements and of broader comparative and theoretical issues.

But very specific thanks are due both to Margaret Canovan and John Gittings for their expert advice on particular chapters, and more general suggestions on argument and presentation. Above all I owe a great debt to Howard Clark, who has given me the benefit of his extensive experience with nonviolent movements in many parts of the world over more than 40 years, and his wide-ranging knowledge of the relevant literature. He has read drafts of every chapter, given me timely encouragement, and made many valuable suggestions both about theoretical and factual issues, as well as providing me with many helpful references. Any errors are my own.

Introduction

The popular uprisings in Tunisia, Egypt and many other countries in the Middle East in early 2011 brought images and accounts of unarmed rebellion onto television screens and front pages over many weeks. The 'Arab Spring' was the latest manifestation of a style of popular resistance that has become increasingly frequent since the late 1970s: overthrowing the Shah of Iran in 1978–9, undermining dictatorships in both Latin America and Asia, precipitating the overthrow of the Soviet bloc in 1989 in Eastern Europe, and in 1988–91 playing a role in the Baltic states in prompting the dissolution of the Soviet Union itself. Since then there have been many major popular protests in Africa, against individual autocracy and one-party rule, and – where multiparty systems have been created – further mobilization against political corruption and blatant rigging of the electoral process. The ousting of President Milosevic in Serbia in 2000 also prompted a wave of 'colour revolutions', as well as so far less-successful protests in former Soviet states.

This book was completed whilst the Arab rebellions were still unfolding and their longer-term success and impact uncertain. Although their importance and special features are noted in a number of chapters, they are not the primary focus of this study. Popular rebellion has a long recorded history, and development of essentially nonviolent methods of resistance (rather less well recorded) can also be traced a long way back. Both Chapters 1 and 3, therefore, include very brief consideration of the longer-term historical context of unarmed resistance and its methods of protest.

In the first half of the twentieth century Mahatma Gandhi was a central figure in dramatizing the potential of nonviolent resistance, and promoting a nonviolent theory and strategy, and his role, ideas and later influence are therefore briefly assessed. Gandhi's precepts and strategy are also one source for developing a comparison, in Chapter 2, between the strategies of unarmed resistance and guerrilla warfare, which have both been adopted in order to achieve national liberation or revolutionary change. The primary emphasis of this book, however, is on the movements of unarmed resistance since the 1970s, which have developed their own strategies, methods, symbols and ideas, and often influenced each other. It is these struggles that have often adopted the concept of 'people power' (first widely used in the Philippines in 1986) and projected it into the media and academic journals.

Several key points need to be clarified early on. The first is that not all unarmed movements are in a strict sense nonviolent movements, abstaining from any form of defensive physical force or physical destruction (for example of symbolically and strategically significant buildings). The second is that unarmed resistance has quite often coexisted with limited forms of guerrilla warfare (notably in the movement to overthrow apartheid in South Africa), or alongside separate guerrilla struggles (as in the Philippines), or developed – temporarily or more permanently – out of an armed struggle. These issues, and particular examples, are explored further in the first two chapters of this book. In addition, unarmed resistance can in particular circumstances degenerate into serious violence and bloodshed, as in Romania in 1989 and in Libya in 2011.

The third important proviso is that, despite the remarkable success of many people power movements in gaining their initial goals, sufficient cohesion and ruthlessness among the key groups in a repressive regime – and relative imperviousness to international pressures – can sometimes suppress major movements of resistance. Obvious examples are Tiananmen Square in 1989; Burma in 1988–90 and 2007; and the Green Movement in Iran in 2009 – although the impact of the 2011 uprisings prompted further protests in Iran.

A survey of the people power movements of recent decades also indicates another important distinction between them. Some have arisen in highly repressive regimes that allow no (or purely token) popular involvement in politics and choice of rulers. The goal of the rebels is then a total change of regime and the nature of politics. How far these movements qualify as 'revolutions', and whether a genuine revolution can be nonviolent, are questions discussed in Chapter 3, with particular reference to 1989, and to the related literature on revolutions.

But a significant number of people power protests have taken place in countries which do hold periodic elections involving opposition parties, but are in reality marked by authoritarian leadership, corruption and violent attacks on opponents, and where usually the election process is rigged. The primary goal of people power, therefore, may be to oust the leader and political party abusing office. These examples of people power often mobilize particularly around elections, and challenge attempts to 'steal' the election from the opposition, both during the electoral process and after announcement of false results. These movements do, however, imply the need not only for institutional reforms, but for a deeper change in political culture – which can be much harder to achieve than forcing a political leader to step down. 'Electoral revolutions' are discussed in Chapter 6.

The purpose of this book is not to provide a primer on the history and theory of nonviolent or unarmed resistance – these issues have been covered in a growing literature (Carter et al., 2006). Nor does it provide a detailed analysis of specific historical cases, which often figure in the literature on nonviolent action, and have also been covered by historians and area specialists, although many movements of unarmed resistance need further research. Instead, this discussion uses summary examples to explore a number of issues arising in politics, sociology and international relations.

People power movements raise central questions about the nature of power and violence and the relationship between them. The effectiveness of many movements seems to vindicate theorists who stress that power 'from above' rests on power generated 'from below', and make a clear distinction between power and violence. But theoretical reflection, and analysis of specific political examples, have suggested to a number of scholars that a more complex interpretation is needed. Moreover, both power and violence are highly contested concepts within a large literature in the social sciences. These issues are addressed in Chapter 4.

People power claims its legitimacy from expressing the rights, needs and wishes (often long suppressed) of 'the people'. But many actual examples of people power also illustrate the ambiguities of defining who 'the people' are. Occasionally the protests do embrace virtually all the people. More often, the protesters represent a clear majority, but there is a minority who are indifferent or still support the regime. Occasionally there may be (especially in times of crisis) at least two ideologically opposed 'peoples', as in the major demonstrations for opposed presidential candidates in Ukraine in December 2004. A people may also be defined by ethnicity, religion or class, and sometimes also divided on these lines. Furthermore, the relationship between those who engage in prolonged and dramatic protest and the more passive members of the population also poses interesting questions about how a 'people' is politically constituted and whether popular uprisings can represent those who do not participate. These issues are discussed in Chapter 5.

People power is closely linked to the idea and goal of democracy. It is most immediately associated with the ideal and experience of participatory democracy. But in recent decades people power has often been associated with a strategy of using electoral mechanisms to achieve either gradual or immediate change. Debates in comparative politics about the processes of democratization, and the role of 'electoral revolutions' indicate a growing interest in the contribution of popular movements using unarmed resistance to promoting more democratic forms of politics. Some of the issues thrown up in this literature, and the implications of people power movements in former Soviet states and sub-Saharan Africa, are considered in Chapter 6.

People power has occurred primarily within 'nation states', but many campaigns have involved resistance to direct or indirect forms of empire, and there is almost always a significant international dimension. Transmission of symbols, methods and strategies of campaigns across frontiers is of growing importance. National movements seek support from outside, and may be the focus of widespread transnational solidarity and action. The increasing role of international governmental organizations in promoting human rights and electoral democracy – for example through systematic provision of election observers – also has some influence on both governments and oppositions. Chapter 7 explores the impact of globalizing trends, including new forms of communication, on people power. It also explores briefly some of the problems of providing substantial support to resistance movements from outside, and the possible validity of claims that governments can use resistance movements to further their own strategic, economic and political ambitions.

The primary focus of people power movements to date has been the achievement of political independence from foreign rule and/or some form of democratic self-government. In the past 40 years in particular, the goal has almost always been to replace dictatorship or one-party rule with a multiparty electoral democracy that respects human rights and constitutional rules, and avoids serious corruption. This has generally been true even where severe economic hardship and sense of social injustice provided a strong motive for rebellion. But, once the formal institutions of national independence and parliamentary democracy are in place, new questions arise about the extent of popular, and indeed governmental, control over economic and environmental forces that shape people's lives. This issue is raised briefly at the end in relation to a number of movements of popular resistance.

PART I
Resistance and political change

1 People power and nonviolent methods in historical perspective

This chapter sketches in the background for interpreting today's people power movements, and has four main aims. The first is to illustrate and discuss the meaning of people power in more detail. The second is to indicate the range of nonviolent methods available: their differing cultural and historical sources in earlier centuries; their role in nineteenth- and twentieth-century social movements; and their importance in the evolution of unarmed national liberation struggles. The third is to consider in particular Mahatma Gandhi's contribution from 1906 to 1947 in developing the ideas and strategy of nonviolent resistance, first in South Africa and then in the movement for Indian independence, and to assess his continuing influence. Finally, the chapter notes very briefly how in the past few decades the strategy, methods and symbols of nonviolent action have been elaborated and transmitted between campaigns.

The meaning of 'people power'

After 29 days of mounting popular demonstrations in Tunisia, the president, who had imposed his dictatorial rule for 23 years, was forced to flee the country on 14 January 2011. The large and rejoicing crowds outside the Interior Ministry pictured on the TV screens that evening waved flags and slogans in Arabic, and one held up a homemade sign, clearly directed to the outside world, that read 'people power'. The unrest, spurred by unemployment and economic hardship, rapidly developed into a popular political uprising against a brutal and corrupt regime; some protesters termed it a 'mafia state'. The police killed scores of demonstrators in those 29 days (and they and other adherents of the old regime killed more in the next few days), but the uprising itself was unarmed and predominantly peaceful. Western media responded by hailing the Tunisian uprising as the first example of apparently successful people power in the Arab world, and some began to label it the 'jasmine revolution'.

The demonstrations began in the town of Sidi Bouzid, where a young man, Mohammed Bouazizi, supporting his mother and the education of his sisters, made a precarious living by selling fruit and vegetables from a small cart and was often harassed by the local authorities. After they seized his cart, and insulted him when he tried to object, in anger and desperation he set himself on fire. Local townspeople took to the streets, and the images spread through Facebook and Twitter to other parts of Tunisia, where increasing numbers joined in the protests. This striking story simplifies a more complex background of economic hardship and protest, and long-term attempts to develop political opposition inside and outside the country. But the extent of the popular response was of revolutionary significance for Tunisia and the Arab world.

The term 'people power' was first widely used by demonstrators in the Philippines in 1986 to describe their peaceful overthrow of President Marcos, and since then has become a common political and journalistic description of the succession of peaceful national uprisings demanding major political change. 'People power' has three major advantages as a shorthand for this now common form of uprising:

- it reflects how those engaged in strikes, demonstrations and occupation of key buildings, and facing down armed security forces, see themselves: the people rising against oppressive rulers;
- it links the idea of resistance to the idea of democracy, which is the goal of these mass protests;
- it suggests the central strategy (conscious or intuitive) behind such primarily peaceful revolts: that rulers can be toppled when the ruled refuse to obey them any longer.

Using 'people power' to define determined large-scale resistance at a national level has two other advantages:

- it is now widely accepted and understood – although the term can be misused either to refer to minority pressure group activity or as a synonym for democracy; and
- it is both more accurate and more illuminating than many earlier terms coined to describe this kind of uprising.

The essentially nonviolent methods adopted either spontaneously or as a strategy in national people power movements have been used and elaborated in different forms of popular protest over many centuries and in very diverse cultural and political contexts (see below). But because resistance movements, and in particular nationwide uprisings against tyrannical governments or foreign oppressors, have historically been identified with violent and armed revolts, finding appropriate descriptions of mass unarmed resistance has proved difficult. By the early twentieth century the term 'passive resistance' had been coined. But activists in liberation struggles have often looked for words that rejected an image of passivity, and that had resonance for their own culture. Therefore Gandhi, in the course of the 1906–14 struggle against systematic legal and political discrimination against Indians settled in South Africa, chose the term *satyagraha* ('truth force' or 'soul force'). After the Second World War, African campaigners for independence from colonialism who adopted unarmed resistance claimed they were taking 'positive action'. The demonstrators in Burma in 1988 dubbed their tactics 'political defiance'. In Latin America, where unarmed resistance became significant from the 1970s in helping to overthrow military dictatorships and authoritarian regimes, *firmeza permanente*, or 'relentless persistence', was the description chosen. Whilst in the Palestinian Occupied Territories, the struggle that began in 1987, when people laid aside their guns and engaged in non-cooperation and boycotts, became known as the 'intifada' or 'shaking off' of Israeli control. Although the 'Second Intifada', that began after the breakdown of peace negotiations in 2000, rapidly became linked to armed resistance and suicide bombers, there has been a parallel and developing strand of unarmed protest.

The references in the same paragraph to campaigns led by Gandhi, the most famous exponent of strict nonviolence, and to the Palestinian First Intifada, in which demonstrators regularly threw stones at Israeli forces, highlight another important aspect of people power: that the term (and the ideas it encapsulates) embraces two distinct approaches to unarmed resistance. One approach is the evolving tradition of specifically nonviolent resistance, which stresses avoidance of all forms of physical force for moral and political as well as strategic reasons. The other is more pragmatic. People adopt street protests, strikes, boycotts, civil disobedience and peaceful occupations and blockades, because these are the methods immediately available to them, and/or the oppressors have overwhelming military might. But their unarmed status gives them the moral high ground – widely recognized in media responses to the 2011 popular protests and emphasis by demonstrators themselves that they were acting peacefully.

Some of the well-known examples of people power since Gandhi have emphasized the importance of avoiding resorting to even minor forms of violence. Whilst this commitment is always difficult to maintain in a movement involving large numbers of people over a period of time, there have been struggles where there are leaders at various levels making a political and moral case for avoiding violence and promoting an ethos of nonviolence. National leaders who become figureheads of nonviolent struggle, for example Aung San Suu Kyi in Burma or Ibrahim Rugova in Kosovo in the 1990s, and prominent intellectuals, such as Adam Michnik and Jacek Kuron in Poland in the 1980s, who stress the need to avoid violence, help to identify the struggle with nonviolence both inside the country and in the international media. Sometimes religious groups demonstrate and reinforce a nonviolent discipline, for example Catholic monks and nuns in the Philippines in 1986, and the Theravada Buddhist monks, committed to nonviolence by their monastic code, central to the mass protests in Burma in 2007. Specific seminars and training in nonviolent action – provided for instance to hundreds of clergy, nuns and lay people in the Philippines – can also lessen the likelihood of the resisters' turning to violence if frustrated or provoked (Zunes, 1999: 142). Ordinary demonstrators have also at times grasped the importance of avoiding provocation to security forces and of maximizing international sympathy: crowds in Central Eastern Europe in 1989 chanted 'no violence'.

But in other cases of popular resistance, for example the mass protests and strikes that ousted both the El Salvador and the Guatemalan dictatorships in 1944, where there is no explicit commitment to avoid forms of violence, the label 'nonviolent' can be misleading. Even struggles that deliberately avoid provocative violence for strategic reasons, as in the East German uprising of June 1953, when building workers abstained from breaking down a door to trade union headquarters, and demonstrators locked up or destroyed any weapons they found, may involve crowd attacks on hated officials and some defensive violence against security forces (Ebert, 1969: 223–5). Moreover, occupation of public buildings, such as parliaments as in Serbia 2000 and Georgia 2003, tends to include degrees of physical force, such as breaking down doors or pushing aside guards. Unarmed movements occasionally involve attacking or burning down key symbolic buildings, as in the burning of the Belgrade TV headquarters, and during the mobilization against the Shah of Iran in 1978 (see Chapter 3). But both these struggles qualify as important examples of 'people power'. An additional difficulty in calling some movements nonviolent is that, although the official strategy and the methods used may be inherently nonviolent, there is quite often a degree of social coercion, or even force, used to ensure communal participation, for example in strikes or boycotts. This was true of the independence movement in Zambia in the early 1960s.

The increasing number of unarmed resistance struggles in recent decades has led to a growing literature discussing the theory, strategy and methods of such resistance and describing individual movements (Carter, 2009). This literature has included a debate about terminology. Gene Sharp's now classic study *The Politics of Nonviolent Action* (Sharp, 1973) helped to establish 'nonviolent' action or resistance as a frequently used term – even though he stressed political and strategic rather than moral arguments for avoiding violence, and has included a very wide range of unarmed struggles under that rubric. More recently Howard Clark (2009a: 4) has suggested 'unarmed resistance' is more accurate in describing many struggles as it is more neutral and more inclusive. Kurt Schock (2005: xvi), who equates people power with 'unarmed insurrections', defines these as 'popular challenges to government authority that depend primarily on nonviolent action'.

A number of theorists of nonviolent action have since the 1960s chosen to use the alternative description 'civil resistance', which conveys that the mode of struggle is unarmed, is undertaken by those who are (or are claiming the status of) citizens, and that it relies on social power (Randle, 1994; Roberts and Garton Ash, 2009). It can also suggest the idea of 'civility', and understanding of the political and possibly moral case for nonviolence in specific protests, without an absolute commitment to nonviolence. I have therefore adopted it where it seems appropriate in this book. Sometimes the term 'civilian resistance' has also been used, but, as Kieran Williams has noted, this would strictly exclude military or police resistance, which can – as in the popular opposition to the 1968 Soviet occupation of Czechoslovakia – be very important (Williams,

2009: 110–11). Civil resistance therefore conveys images similar to those evoked by people power, but is – like its equivalent nonviolent resistance – used also to cover social movements by specific sections of the population, for example the US Civil Rights Movement.

The growing academic literature on social movements has begun to include discussion of people power campaigns. Sidney Tarrow, for example, incorporates a discussion of the Serbian resistance to Milosevic and transnational support for it in his book *The New Transnational Activism* (Tarrow, 2005: 109–13). People power certainly uses many methods developed by earlier social movements, 'forms of contention' influencing 'repertoires' of action – concepts introduced by Charles Tilly in his study *From Mobilization to Resistance* (Tilly, 1978: 143–59). People power demonstrations also adopt new methods introduced recently by peace, feminist and green movements, such as forming human chains – a tactic used in the Baltic republics of the Soviet Union in 1989 to link symbolically Tallinn to Vilnius.

But social movements tend to promote specific social causes, or the demand by sections of the population for recognition of their rights or legitimate interests. People power movements unite large sections of the population in a common effort to achieve greater political freedom and a more democratic government. Moreover, many social movements flourish within representative democracies, whilst people power normally presupposes either semi-authoritarian or wholly dictatorial rule, or foreign occupation.

On the other hand, initially limited social movements can turn into a national, people power struggle. An obvious example especially well documented is the Solidarity Movement, which began as a series of strikes, notably in the Lenin shipyards in Gdansk, which rapidly spread and in due course embraced intellectuals, professional groups, students and the significant social grouping of small farmers, and was actively supported by the Catholic Church. Solidarity sought to reform Communist Party rule rather than overthrow it completely, but was clearly a major challenge to the essential nature of the regime and to Soviet dominance. A national struggle against political repression and rigged elections may also encompass more limited campaigns by particular occupational or social groups. For example, Janet Cherry has analysed how in Zimbabwe significant resistance since 2000 has been mounted by a range of trade unions, such as those representing radical teachers or workers on commercial farms, by urban community associations, organizations representing youth and students and religious bodies. A campaigning group of women, Women of Zimbabwe Arise, has been particularly active in spearheading opposition (Cherry, 2009: 50–63).

The now emblematic example of people power is represented by concentrated popular opposition to a repressive regime, as in East Germany in 1989, when tens of thousands, after attending prayers for peace, demonstrated on the streets of Leipzig on every Monday in October shouting 'we are staying here' (to indicate a more militant strategy than the mass emigration through Hungary earlier in summer of that year), and 'we are the people'. After some clashes on

2 October, about 70,000 demonstrated nonviolently on 9 October, despite thousands of police poised to unleash violent repression. Two weeks later the General Secretary of the East German Communist Party resigned and on 9 November crowds peacefully crossed through the Berlin Wall and began to demolish it (Maier, 2009: 261–63).

Although many recent examples of people power suggest a brief, dramatic confrontation, highly organized mass popular resistance movements, for example those for national liberation, have often lasted for many years, or even decades, and developed through different stages. It is these long-term unarmed struggles that can be most directly compared with the strategy of 'people's war' (see Chapter 2).

Opponents of a regime may attempt to spark mass resistance but only achieve quite limited protests that are easily suppressed. These protests do not in themselves qualify as people power as defined here. Nevertheless, people power is often preceded by years of much smaller-scale organization and resistance, for example the limited dissent of Charter 77 provided Civic Forum leaders in the Czechoslovak Velvet Revolution of 1989. People power may also emerge out of a growing popular mobilization, for example the shipyard strikes in Poland in 1970 and 1976 that led up to Solidarity. Frequently, people power can be seen as the culminating stage of a longer, if often intermittent, build-up of civil resistance.

Background to nonviolent methods

The methods of protest and resistance adopted in different societies often reflect particular historical and cultural precedents, but also draw – at least in recent centuries – on a very wide range of possible methods that have been used by resistance movements throughout the world. These methods may be adopted by individuals or groups as the obvious response to the oppression or injustice they face; they may be promoted and elaborated by wider social movements; and they may be adapted to popular unarmed uprisings against central government or foreign rule. Thus refusal to obey an order deemed to be morally wrong is the basis of a long tradition of individual resistance by members of various Christian churches to military service, open civil disobedience to resist unjust laws or state demands has been adopted by social movements resisting unjust discrimination, and concerted refusal to pay taxes has been a strategy of some national liberation movements.

Drawing on cultural and religious traditions and institutions

Some modes of dissent are embedded in traditional societies. Gandhi himself was able to draw on the Indian practice of fasting as a form of pressure, and the long-standing observance of *hartal*, a day of mourning which involved religious rites and abstention from work (Bondurant, 1958: 118–19). Confucianism has recognized a right of moral remonstrance to unjust rulers; although often this has taken the form of a rebuke by an individual scholar, self-immolation has also been a more extreme form of remonstrance by scholars seeking reform in the Korean Confucian tradition. Korean students engaged in a desperate opposition to military rule adopted this method in 1986 (Kluver, 1998: 219–31).

Adherence to specific religious commitments has also quite often entailed conflict with a state that upholds an authorized set of religious beliefs and practices and demands public observance of them, or prohibits other forms of belief and worship. Christianity has often required its adherents to resist the state, for example by refusing to serve in the army, and in its original evolution within the Roman Empire this resistance usually took the form of hidden worship or open nonviolent defiance, creating martyrs who refused to worship the Emperor. Christian beliefs ceased to be closely associated with commitment to avoid arms after it became the official religion of the Roman Empire, and divisions within Christianity have often been associated with wars and armed rebellions. But the Reformation in Europe revived traditions of hidden religious observance, political disobedience and acceptance of martyrdom, both among Protestants resisting Catholic rule and Catholics defying Protestant monarchs. The Reformation also prompted theologians and philosophers to debate the obligation of subjects to unconditional obedience. Lutherans and Calvinists tended to endorse two extremes. The first allowed a purely individual 'non-resistance', when individuals sometimes had to obey God first to uphold their faith, but had to suffer the penalty passively without any organized opposition. The other extreme was tyrannicide and armed rebellion in defence of their faith; and some Catholic theologians opted for the latter (Skinner, 1978, Vol. 2). The more radical forms of Protestantism, however, generated a renewed commitment to renunciation of armed violence, that sometimes encouraged quietism and communal escape from the wider world where possible (for example the Amish), but also fostered an active Christian nonviolent resistance that has been manifested in organized political opposition to war and slavery (for example the Quakers and Mennonites).

The repertoire of methods of nonviolent protest has been enriched by drawing on various religious beliefs and practices that carry symbolic meaning in a particular society. Forms of worship such as prayer and religious chants or hymns have quite often been a means of protest, or incorporated into demonstrations. During the 1952 Defiance Campaign against the pass laws in South Africa women prayed outside the court where resisters were being tried for their defiance, and prayers were incorporated into the US Civil Rights campaign demonstrations (Sharp, 1973, Part 2: 137–8). Religious services have themselves been used as a means of dissent, or have been the starting point for protesting on the streets, for example the mosque meetings in Iran in 1892 during the struggle against the Shah selling the salt monopoly to a British company, and the services that launched the final major round of demonstrations in December 1978 against the Shah's rule (Abrahamian, 2009: 165, 168). The Protestant Church services in Leipzig in 1989 provided a base for initiating popular resistance and maintaining nonviolence. Churches have also provided spaces for organizing resistance, as in the case of the Catholic Church in Poland during the 1970s and 1980s, or the Mothers of the Plaza de Mayo in Argentina (Garton Ash, 1983: 25–6; Ackerman and Duvall, 2000: 276).

Forms of worship or religious symbols have also been adopted to defy or deter repression of dissent. Thich Nhat Hanh records that Vietnamese Buddhists took their family altars into the streets and practised religious observances to block deployment of troops in Hue and Quantri in 1966 (Sharp, 1973, Part 2: 138). In the Philippines demonstrators facing armed troops in 1986 held up statues of the Madonna in the hope of dissuading devout Catholics among the soldiers from crushing them with tanks (Zunes, 1999: 148–9). The campaign among the Pathans in the North-West Frontier region, part of the Indian independence struggle in the early 1930s, incorporated the crescent into the Indian Congress flag and used the slogan 'Allah Ho Akbar' (God is Great) as one of its slogans. One tactic was for women holding the Koran to lie down in lines in front of the police (Bondurant, 1958: 136). In another context, some of the demonstrators in Thailand in 1992 found that if they sat down in the Buddhist lotus position they were less likely to be attacked by the police than those who tried to run or crawl away (Satha-Anand, 1999: 170).

Finally, modes of action that occur within several religious traditions, for example fasting, vigils, processions and pilgrimages, have become important expressions of nonviolent protest. They are quite often used in campaigns drawing upon a specific religious tradition, where they may have particular resonance. But these forms of action have also been abstracted from their original religious associations and are widely used as general forms of symbolic political protest. They also have their more militant and specifically secular counterparts in hunger strikes, pickets and marches. Funerals for figures significant to the resistance, or of individuals who have been directly martyred for the cause, can provide not only a genuine outlet for mourning and (usually) a relatively safe means of demonstrating political resistance, but also a way of reasserting basic religious or cultural commitments. After security agents murdered three human rights activists in Santiago, Chile, in March 1985 and left their bodies in a ditch, 15,000 people took part in the funeral procession from the cathedral (Ackerman and Duvall, 2000: 290). Placing flowers, candles or crosses at graves or symbolic monuments can also help to maintain low-level resistance or reinforce religious commitment (Johnston, 2005: 124). Sometimes, however, such action can instead serve as a signal to revive wider resistance, for example a group of dissidents including Vaclav Havel were arrested in January 1989 for laying flowers at the spot where the student Jan Palach had set fire to himself twenty years earlier, in defence of the Prague Spring (Urban, 1990: 114). The concept of finding sanctuary from secular repression in holy places can also be adapted to give a degree of protection to protesters, or to make a symbolic claim to the idea of sanctuary.

Historic sources of political resistance

Most methods of nonviolent protest derive, however, from secular resistance by different social classes or groups that have experienced systematic oppression and injustice – although at times resentment at social injustice has also been intertwined with religious dissent, notably during the Reformation in Europe. It is also important to note that, when looking back to the past, essentially nonviolent methods of protest have often been combined with targeted violence against property or people, or with more indiscriminate rioting or armed resistance. So some of the literature on nonviolent resistance draws on episodes or historical movements that may have been presented primarily or solely in terms of rioting or armed rebellion. This is true, for example, of some of the historical illustrations used by Gene Sharp in his analysis of the methods of nonviolent action, such as the American resistance to the Stamp Act in the 1770s (Sharp, 1973, Part 2: 238, 241). Theorists of nonviolent action have seen their task in part as uncovering a hidden history, and this is a continuing commitment.

Peasants

The intermingling of nonviolent and violent modes of resistance has been especially true of the long tradition of peasant unrest and rebellion in many parts of the world. Some peasant uprisings, for example in Russia and China, have indeed primarily taken the form of armed violence (see Chapter 3). But in medieval and early modern Europe resistance was often clearly focused on opposition to unjust feudal dues, tithes or state taxes and was more nuanced. Even major armed peasant uprisings, such as the Flanders revolt of 1323–8 and the 1381 English Peasants' Revolt, began with resistance to unfair taxes, and included forms of non-cooperation and organized obstruction of tax collection (Te Brake, 1993: 52–3; Vallance, 2009: 47–54). The 1525 German Peasants' War was preceded by peasants round Lake Constance refusing to pay tithes and burning tithe grain and by rent strikes in the Upper Rhine and Black Forest areas (Blickle, 1981).

At other times peasant non-cooperation was the primary response. Sharp notes examples of peasants in Norway refusing taxes in the sixteenth, seventeenth and eighteenth centuries (Sharp, 1973, Part 2: 241). George Rude, tracing widespread unrest in France in the seventeenth century (including an insurrection in Calvinist Languedoc), notes that in the Catholic areas of Quercy and Perigord peasants at the end of the century challenged 'the whole existing order by refusing to pay taxes to the King, tithes to the Church, or to perform servile manual labour for the upkeep of the roads' (Rude, 1980: 64). French peasants, responding to high food prices and the increasing pressure of feudal dues, refused in 1789 to perform these dues, seized common land and burned land registers and sometimes manor houses. Thus rural unrest contributed to the political revolution unfolding in the towns and in Paris, but was also somewhat separate from urban concerns.

Hunger for land (and sometimes, as in Latin America, a belief that the land has in the past been stolen from them) has fuelled a major response by peasants to poverty and injustice: land seizures. Peasants subordinated to large landed estates and the rural and (sometimes) urban poor have seized uncultivated land belonging to major landowners, as in southern Italy immediately after the First World War. George Rude argues that in Latin America peasant militancy has most often been expressed by indigenous dispossessed peasants seizing land. In the nineteenth century land seizures, for example in Bolivia and Mexico, were localized and spontaneous and initially nonviolent, but turned to defensive violence if force was used to evict the peasants. Since the early twentieth century, with the formation of peasant unions, land occupations have taken place on a much larger scale, for example in Peru in the 1940s and Colombia in the 1950s (Rude, 1980: 68–71).

Political uprisings take place primarily in towns and cities, and especially the seat of government, so methods of peasant resistance focused on limited opposition to local landowners or money lenders or hunger for land do not transfer directly into expressions of people power. (Where peasant revolts have threatened rulers in the past, they have found urban allies and marched on the main cities.) But the strand of peasant opposition to unjust taxes, which has taken the form of refusal to pay, has often become a significant method of resistance in more prolonged campaigns of people power, for example the independence struggle in Malawi in the 1950s and the Palestinian First Intifada.

Workers

The primary method of worker resistance, the strike, has always potentially had a dual focus: on securing gains for particular groups of workers, and as a political means of challenging or even destabilizing a government. Strikes in Europe have been traced back to at least as early as weavers in small towns in Flanders and France in the mid-thirteenth century and to Italian city states in the fourteenth century (Cohn, 2004: 11). But large-scale industrialization united uprooted strangers in the workplace and enabled them to form a new basis of solidarity and resistance. Agricultural labourers on large estates also adopted the strike weapon and by the twentieth century were often, like their industrial counterparts, organized in trade unions.

The degree to which strikes have generated sabotage, violent retaliation against workers breaking ranks or battles with police has varied with the social context. But in essence strikes are based on economic non-cooperation, and their potential and the variety of forms withdrawing labour could take (the sit-in strike, for example, has often had significant tactical advantages) was increasingly understood. This is one form of civil resistance that has been extensively analysed, in terms of the various kinds of strike, different types of trade unionism and the variety of political contexts in which strikes have occurred. By the early twentieth century the general strike was quite often adopted to gain specific political concessions (such as universal male suffrage, the demand during the 1909 Belgian general strike) or was proposed as a method of preventing war (as envisaged in resolutions of the Second Socialist International). The general strike was also recognized as a potential method of revolution by the leading Marxist activist and theoretician, Rosa Luxemburg, in her 1906 pamphlet *The Mass Strike: The Political Party and the Trade Unions*, as well as being the revolutionary goal of anarchosyndicalists. It has since been central to many recent people power movements.

Soldiers and sailors

When the poor cannot find work they have quite often enlisted in the army and navy. Governments have also conscripted peasants and urban workers to fight their wars, or even seized men off the streets to man their navies, and then subjected them to low pay, poor food and brutal discipline. Conscription has sometimes prompted conscientious objection by individuals, religious groups or political movements. It has probably always prompted indirect forms of evasion and a tendency to desert. Resistance to conscription often has a communal context, for example peasant reluctance to lose the labour of their sons on the land, and has also (as in Britain and the USA in past centuries) sometimes taken a communal form, with potential recruits and other townspeople opposing military recruiters, or demonstrations against the draft (Clark, 2010: 468–9). Less frequently, soldiers (or quite often sailors) have taken the much more radical and political step of joining together to rebel against their conditions of service. Mutiny has sometimes meant men turning guns upon their officers, but other mutinies have been conducted more like industrial disputes, with the men drawing up a list of grievances and demands, and effectively going on strike, as in Spithead and the Nore mutinies by British sailors in 1797 (Guttridge, 1992). Although officers have sometimes sympathized, in general mutinies have been an extension of class conflict to the military sphere.

Mutiny has in addition been a significant form of resistance to particular wars, notably the widespread mutinies in the French armies on the Western Front in 1917. Resistance to war by reluctant conscripts has also fuelled a wider revolutionary movement demanding a change of regime, notably in Russia in both 1905 and 1917. Finally, resistance to orders by members of the armed services is a particularly crucial element in many successful examples of people power and revolutions, because governments ultimately rely on troops to suppress popular unrest, and mutiny means that the regime's ability to use force is crumbling.

Social movements

During the nineteenth century a number of social movements for particular causes emerged and had transnational dimensions, including international congresses and growing awareness of the scope of possible protest and resistance. The most important movements (other than the growing international cooperation between socialist parties and trade unions) were those against the slave trade and the institution of slavery, those opposing war and the upsurge of agitation for the emancipation of women. Action by the slaves themselves usually took the form of armed revolts or, where possible (as in the United States), escape; and much of the campaigning by white opponents of slavery focused on constitutional methods. But sympathizers in the USA also helped escaped slaves and found themselves involved in defying the law after the Fugitive Slave Act was passed in 1857. The women's rights campaigns tended to concentrate on petitions, public meetings and lobbying legislators, but by the early twentieth century campaigners for the vote turned as well to methods such as mass demonstrations and tax refusal, and the more militant began to disrupt political meetings, chain themselves to railings and when imprisoned go on hunger strike. Campaigns for women's rights also included use of nonviolent action for other causes, for example strikes for better pay and defiance of laws that prevented dissemination of information about limiting childbirth and availability of contraception. Feminist ideas and demands spread from the USA and Britain to continental Europe, as well as to Asia and the Middle East, where many women were radicalized by taking part in the developing movements against colonialism, including street demonstrations and forms of unarmed defiance.

National liberation movements

It was indeed some of the nationalist movements of the late nineteenth and twentieth centuries that encouraged the widespread adoption and explicit recognition of the potential of mass popular non-cooperation (transcending class conflict and gender divisions). The failure of armed revolt against the Austrian Empire in 1848–9 led the Hungarian nationalists to adopt a longer-term strategy of systematic peaceful non-cooperation with the political regime (including mass tax refusal) and economic boycotts. This struggle was a significant factor in Hungary gaining autonomy and dual status with Austria within the empire in 1867. The potential of such 'passive resistance' was hailed by the theorist of Irish national independence and founder member of Sinn Fein, Arthur Griffiths, in a 1905 pamphlet *The Resurrection of Hungary: A Parallel for Ireland* (Randle, 1994: 39). The Hungarian example also influenced the Finnish campaign of national resistance to Russian domination of Finland in 1899–1906. But the nationalist struggle most closely associated with unarmed resistance is the Indian independence struggle against British colonialism, which culminated in British withdrawal in 1947, and is closely associated with Gandhi.

Gandhi and his influence

Gandhi began to develop the methods of *satyagraha* during his leadership of the 1906–14 campaign by Indians settled in South Africa against systematic political discrimination, emphasizing the need for strictly nonviolent struggle. His aim was eventual conversion of and reconciliation with the opponent, or at least a mutually acceptable negotiated accommodation.

When Gandhi returned to India in 1914 he brought with him the prestige of having gained significant success in a campaign that had been widely publicized in both India and Britain, and a developed strategy of nonviolent resistance. Important examples of unarmed resistance to the British had occurred in India well before 1914, notably in the widespread 1905–8 Swadeshi (self-reliance) movement, that involved mass rallies and processions, an economic boycott of British cloth and other foreign goods, promotion of economic self-reliance through creation of alternative businesses and institutions, independent arbitration at village level and creating a national system of education. All these were elements in Gandhi's later campaigns (Chandra, 1989: 124–34). Moreover, the movement for independence included both more conventional forms of political lobbying and negotiation at various stages, and the attempt during the Second World War by the Indian National Army led by Subbha Chandra Bhose to win independence by force of arms through alliance with the Japanese. But the organized defiance against new British legislation sanctioning arbitrary detention in 1919 (the Rowlatt Bills), the 1920–2 Non-Cooperation Campaign for independence, the Salt March and mass civil disobedience of 1930–2, and the Quit India campaign in 1940, were all led and conceived by Gandhi and he remains a symbol of the independence struggle.

Widespread international support for an anti-colonial movement, sympathetic reporting of the campaigns and Gandhi's own role as a tireless propagator of his ideas (reflected in 100 volumes of his Collected Works) propelled the practice and theory of *satyagraha* into the political consciousness of many.

Often those taking part in the campaigns did not accept or understand the strict moral requirements of *satyagraha* – indeed Gandhi controversially called off the 1920–2 campaign because his supporters attacked and killed a group of policemen – but the potential effectiveness of mass unarmed resistance was established. A number of movements immediately adopted a consciously nonviolent strategy, notably the struggle for universal democratic rights in South Africa promoted by the African National Congress from 1912 until 1961 (when there was a turn to limited guerrilla warfare as a response to severe government repression), and the developing Civil Rights movement in the USA.

Gandhi's model of nonviolent resistance was taken up, as we have noted, by some African independence movements, but others turned to guerrilla warfare (see Chapter 2). Gandhi's example and his strategic approach have, nevertheless, continued to have considerable influence on many taking part in varied social movements and on activists and leaders in a number of movements of national resistance and people power. Aung San Suu Kyi, for example, has studied Gandhi (Wintle, 2007: 358). Richard Attenborough's 1982 film *Gandhi*, which has been widely shown around the world, came out at a time when there was an upsurge of unarmed resistance, and so helped to revive his influence when otherwise younger generations might have forgotten him. The film has had a documented effect in opening up new possibilities for some activists (for example in Chile), and has been used in China by dissidents (Ackerman and Duvall, 2000: 291; Goldman, 2009: 258).

Transmission of nonviolent methods today

In the last few decades, however, inspiration for most of those taking part in resistance has almost certainly come primarily from other recent examples of people power. In some cases veterans of one campaign offer information and tactical advice directly, and analysis of the range of nonviolent methods available and strategic considerations in planning unarmed resistance has also been disseminated to some movements in recent decades. But the most likely inspiration for many protesters is simply news of the widely reported and photographed examples of people power in different areas of the world, in particular those which have been both dramatic and in an immediate sense successful.

Imaginative kinds of action, and significant symbols used by a varied range of protests, have been copied. A tent city was set up in Kiev, capital of the Ukraine, in December 2004 during the 'Orange Revolution' to shelter the thousands who had come from the provinces and the most committed demonstrators (Krushelnycky, 2006: 293–9). Tents were also pitched in Beirut in March 2005 during the 'Cedar Revolution', which demanded an end to the Syrian military presence, and in Tahrir Square in Cairo and the Pearl Roundabout in Manama, Bahrain, in early 2011. Crowds holding candles in processions and large rallies featured widely during the 1989 winter demonstrations in Central Eastern Europe (Prins, 1990: xx). Tibetans in a large candle-lit vigil illustrate the cover of this book. The vigils by the Mothers of the Plaza de Mayo in the 1970s, calling on the Argentinian Generals to reveal the fate of their 'disappeared' children, have been taken up in China by the 'Mothers of Tiananmen'.

Modes of action can also encapsulate the idea of nonviolent action: for example peaceful crowds sitting in front of armed and helmeted police; people surrounding tanks and talking to the soldiers in them (August 1968 in Prague), or an unarmed young man standing in front of a tank (one of the images from Tiananmen Square). An even more expressive message has been conveyed by young women offering flowers to troops and putting flowers in their gun barrels, a symbol of the 'Revolution of the Carnations' in Portugal in 1974 – though it was soldiers who initiated this revolution and the people then joined in. The Georgian demonstrators in the 'Rose Revolution' in December 2003 consciously adopted the same tactic. TV pictures from Tunisia in January 2011 included images of flowers draped over a tank, and in February 2011 Bahraini demonstrators, after they had been shot at on an earlier demonstration, advanced holding plastic flowers.

Newspaper photographs, TV pictures and, increasingly, pictures taken on mobile phones and transmitted via the Internet circulate these images around the world, together with the reported words of protesters, eyewitness reports and journalists' accounts and analysis. In the past few years, as the Internet age has developed, the role of personal blogs, Facebook and Twitter have become more central. Changing communications media are discussed in Chapter 7, together with the nature and implications of various kinds of official external international support and unofficial transnational solidarity.

2 People power and people's war compared

A clear division between popular unarmed and armed resistance was not – with a few exceptions – clearly perceived until the twentieth century, when two opposed models emerged. Liberation through mass non-cooperation and non-violent defiance was particularly associated with Gandhi and the Indian independence movement. Liberation through guerrilla warfare was epitomized by the thought of Mao Tse-tung and the campaigns he led against the Japanese and the regime of Chiang Kai-shek. Unarmed civilian protest had often been used before (as noted in Chapter 1) and so had guerrilla tactics. Both were, for example, important elements at different stages in the American Revolution against the British crown in the 1770s. What was distinctive about both Gandhi and Mao was that they developed a strategy linked to a political theory, and that they posed and symbolized conscious choice between unarmed or guerrilla struggle for later movements.

This chapter, therefore, starts by clarifying the concept of guerrilla warfare, and outlining very briefly its development through the nineteenth and twentieth centuries. Although guerrilla struggles emphasize armed resistance and overthrow of regimes by force of arms, they differ from earlier peasant rebellions and armed revolts, which were almost always bloodily defeated in battles with the militarily superior forces of kings and aristocracies. Instead guerrillas seek to undermine the regime, mobilize widespread popular support and avoid direct armed confrontation until they have acquired the military strength to seize control of the state, or it disintegrates from within. There are therefore many interesting parallels with long-term movements of unarmed resistance: both try to develop the power of the people. Indeed, guerrilla warfare as a strategy of political liberation is often called 'people's war'.

The literature on civil resistance has tended to emphasize how a nonviolent strategy differs from armed struggle. But Hannah Arendt, the political theorist who comes closest to a sympathetic understanding of the potential of unarmed resistance, quite explicitly sees guerrilla warfare (despite its use of armed violence) as predominantly reliant on the power generated by popular support rather than the 'pure' violence of destructive weaponry (Arendt, 1970: 51).

A few studies have compared the strategies of civil and guerrilla resistance as a means of resisting military occupation (Boserup and Mack, 1974: 68–81;

Alternative Defence Commission, 1983: 186–248). The military historian and strategic thinker Basil Liddell Hart, for example, examined the difficulties posed for occupying German forces in the Second World War by both unarmed and partisan resistance, suggesting the former tended to pose more problems (Liddell Hart, 1969: 239–40). A recent detailed comparative statistical analysis of a wide range of 323 liberation struggles since 1900, by Maria Stephan and Erica Chenoweth, compares the success of civilian nonviolent campaigns with both guerrilla warfare and terrorism. This study suggests a higher rate of success for major nonviolent campaigns, and least success for terrorist campaigns (Stephan and Chenoweth, 2008).

But the main purpose here is not only to note the crucial differences between people power and people's war, but to explore the striking similarities, in order to illuminate the dynamics of these two key strategies of liberation in the twentieth century. Five strategic aims that people power and people's war tend to have in common (especially when a long-term struggle is involved) are:

- winning majority support;
- mobilizing excluded sections of the population;
- encouraging defection of troops and police;
- building alternative institutions from below; and
- promoting solidarity and fearlessness.

A sixth dynamic of struggle, that civil resistance seeks to incorporate into its strategy, is that repressive violence against the resisters often rebounds. This can apply to guerrilla resistance, but with major caveats.

The discussion in this chapter also suggests that 'guerrilla warfare' as a category obscures the variation between guerrilla struggles: how far they have drawn on popular resistance, or how far they have developed a military logic focused on ultimate armed victory. The overlapping between guerrilla and terrorist tactics is considered at the end of the chapter.

In the past many guerrilla struggles began as unarmed civilian protests, but then regime brutality and intransigence led the opposition to conclude that armed resistance was necessary. Emerging resistance in the Portuguese colonies in Africa, for example, challenging an imperial state ruled by a dictatorship, began by using strikes, boycotts and demonstrations. But a dockers' strike in Guinea Bissau in 1959 ended with police killing 50 dockers, and, in the Mueda massacre in June 1960 in Mozambique, Portuguese troops fired on a peaceful demonstration, killing over 500 (Nugent, 2004: 262–3; Meyer, 2012). Movements, or groups within a movement, are always liable, for a variety of political motives, to switch from unarmed resistance to a guerrilla strategy, sometimes because a faction committed to armed methods came to the fore; the latter happened in Kosovo in 1996.

In recent decades, however, several guerrilla movements have made the opposite journey, and turned to unarmed people power, for example in Nepal in 2006 and the Sahwari movement in Western Sahara (see below).

In addition, civilians using nonviolent methods have seized the initiative from guerrilla groups in toppling military or repressive regimes, as in parts of Latin America from the 1980s, the Philippines in the 1980s and East Timor 1988–99. Therefore there now appears to be a historical trend away from people's war towards a greater reliance on unarmed struggle. Kurt Schock argues that in recent decades there has been a decline in successful guerrilla warfare and upsurge of successful unarmed insurrections. He suggests that this may be due in part to a tendency towards the expansion of state power and a developing technology of violence, which has shifted the balance away from guerrillas towards states. On the positive side, the growth in communications technologies, a normative shift at an international level towards emphasis on human rights and expansion of transnational activism have greatly increased potential support for unarmed movements (Schock, 2005: 16–23). The global context is explored in more detail in Chapter 7.

Jonathan Schell has claimed in his stimulating book *The Unconquerable World*, that 'people's war' marked one extreme of the 'total war' that evolved in the twentieth century: 'turning every section of the population, including women and children, into fighters and victims' (Schell, 2004: 98–9). He implies that nonviolent resistance can be seen as a dialectical response to the extremes of both conventional war (now represented by nuclear weapons) and guerrilla warfare.

But the argument adopted here suggests a different historical dialectic. In the light of the undoubtedly increasing prevalence of unarmed popular resistance, but also the development of a new strikingly ruthless 'terrorism', attacking ordinary citizens and co-religionists as well as military and economic symbols of Western 'imperialism', it appears that in the twenty-first century there is a new realignment of forces. Genuine 'people's war' has to a large degree lost its historic moment. The primary choices today are between social movements and people power on the one hand and resorting to terror on the other.

The evolution of guerrilla warfare

Guerrilla warfare has several distinct historical strands:

- as a purely military strategy;
- as popular armed resistance to invasion and occupation; and
- as a means for people to overthrow an imperial or repressive regime.

The first form of irregular warfare is strictly military: the tactics are not to confront the armies of the enemy directly in a 'positional' war, but harry them from the rear, disrupt supply lines and ambush small contingents. Although originating naturally in contexts where the other side has superior weaponry and ability to win in orthodox military battles, irregular warfare has quite often been adopted by regular armies as an extra tactical arm, and has been undertaken both by regular soldiers, but also by separate military units, such as the Cossack bands in Russia. This approach was well understood by military theorists of the eighteenth century as *la petite guerre* or *kleine Krieg* (Best, 1982: 265–72). When Napoleon's triumphal advance on Moscow turned into a disastrous retreat, his main enemies were starvation and the Russian winter, but the retreating forces were systematically ambushed and killed by Russian troops and sometimes by irregular bands and local peasants. This purely military phenomenon is only relevant to this book in indicating the nature of guerrilla tactics.

Guerrilla warfare, as we now usually understand the term, is linked to a popular liberation struggle, for example the popular armed resistance to the occupying Napoleonic troops in Spain 1808–13, which gave its name to this type of warfare. Clausewitz, writing on military strategy in the early nineteenth century, gave the Spanish example only a passing mention, noting that 'the Spaniards by stubborn resistance have shown what the general arming of a nation and insurgent measures on a great scale can effect'. But he cites the Spanish uprising in the context of recognizing the historical significance for modern warfare of mobilizing the mass of the people, commenting, 'what an enormous factor the heart and sentiments of a Nation may be in the product of its political and military strength' (Clausewitz, 1968: 295).

But this type of guerrilla warfare is usually militarily supported by external allied armies. In Spain, British troops under Wellington eventually drove the French out, though aided by the role of the guerrillas in waging a war of attrition. During the First World War, the guerrilla tactics used by Arabs against the Turkish forces were adopted as a war of liberation against the Ottoman Empire, but they were also directly encouraged by the British forces battling the Turks (allies of Germany), and promoted by the flamboyant British officer T.E. Lawrence. During the Second World War, partisans in occupied Europe collaborated directly with the Allied powers to sabotage railways, blow up munitions factories, ambush German military columns and in general prepare the way for the advance of Allied troops after the Normandy landings. Liberation depended upon the course of the wider war, although communist partisans in Italy, France, Greece and – especially – Yugoslavia also envisaged their struggle as the first stage of a political revolution.

Thirdly, guerrilla warfare became a strategy for revolutionary change, either against imperial rule or against an internal repressive regime. This form of guerrilla warfare might draw on some external assistance in the form of weapons and training, diplomatic pressure by other states or transnational solidarity by ideologically sympathetic movements in other countries, but did not presuppose outside military intervention. The ideology prompting this type of guerrilla warfare in the past two centuries has primarily been nationalism. In the nineteenth century nationalism was usually linked to beliefs in democratic self-rule and liberal ideals. In the twentieth century anti-colonial struggles often became associated with various forms of socialist belief – or there might be competing ideological strands within an independence movement. But by the second half of the twentieth century guerrilla warfare was increasingly linked to leftist or communist parties.

The tradition of guerrilla warfare as a strategy for the self-liberation of a 'nation' was promoted in the 1830s by Italian and Polish émigré intellectuals, who envisaged a people's war of national liberation from imperial oppression, and cited not only Spain but the successful 1820s struggle by Greek guerrilla bands to win independence from the Ottoman Turks and examples from their own history (Best, 1982: 267–72). The Polish intellectuals and gentry discovered, however, the importance of genuine popular engagement when inciting armed uprisings in 1846 against the partitioning powers of Russia, Austria and Prussia. Although independent peasants did give some support, unfree peasants in Galicia turned on the rebels and helped the Austrians suppress the uprising (Lukowski and Zawadzki, 2006: 169–70).

Rural or urban warfare?

One distinction, intrinsic to the strategy and the literature, is between rural and urban guerrilla warfare. Guerrilla strategy has primarily been a way of waging war in the countryside. Guerrilla manuals focus on the advantages of various sorts of terrain. Forests, mountains and (before the systematic use of military aircraft) deserts have all harboured guerrilla forces and hindered their military opponents. Modern political movements have sometimes been driven to abandon urban struggle, where their activists and supporters are too vulnerable to savage reprisals, in favour of taking refuge in the countryside and mobilizing the peasantry. This was true of Mao's wing of the communist movement in the 1920s – after Chiang Kai-shek's massacre of communist supporters in Shanghai in 1927, and of the liberation movements in Portuguese African colonies in the 1950s and 1960s. Revolutionary guerrilla movements have sometimes been able to consolidate their political and ideological support by creating autonomous bases in remoter areas of the countryside and (as in China in the 1930s and 1940s) introducing a new kind of political and social order in them (Snow, 1972; Belden, 1973). The Mozambique guerrilla movement, FRELIMO, succeeded for a time in creating liberated zones, where they set up a revolutionary model of administration and schools and medical facilities.

But guerrilla tactics are possible in towns and cities. Sometimes the geography of the city, like the mazes of the casbah in North African cities, makes eluding pursuit easier, and narrow streets can be blocked. Small groups can sabotage key installations and melt away. Railways can be disrupted by sabotage in the marshalling yards as well by explosive laid on lines running across fields or deserts. Therefore, important as terrain has often been, the key to guerrilla success that is stressed in the specialized literature is the ability of the guerrillas to melt into the local population and gain support from that population.

But even well into the twentieth century guerrilla forces have tended to seek a rural base as well as conducting operations in the towns. In Cyprus the Greek guerrillas in EOKA under Georgios Grivas held out for a long period in the Troodos mountains, as well as organizing bombs and assassinations of key military or political figures in urban areas. In Cuba, Fidel Castro and Ernesto

(Che) Guevara embarked on their now legendary expedition from Mexico on the yacht *Granma* with 80 men in November 1956 and, after being surprised by troops on landing, a much reduced group took to the mountains of the Sierra Maestra for the next two years. According to Guevara's manual *Guerrilla Warfare*, urban warfare should concentrate on sabotage (of telephone lines, railways, water mains and sewers) and occasional ambush of small patrols or one or two policemen or soldiers (Guevara, 2009: 43–5). Guevara stresses that urban guerrillas should be totally subservient to a rural central command, perhaps influenced by the failure of an urban uprising planned to coincide with the landing of *Granma* and by the fact that in the late 1950s a rival political group led students in an abortive attack on the presidential palace in Havana (Kapcia, 2008: 21–2).

The tactics adopted by guerrilla forces based in the countryside, but seeking to demonstrate their reach and the extent of their support by action in the cities, have been more varied and less clear-cut than rural guerrilla strategy. The same can be said of primarily urban guerrilla movements. On the one hand, leaders of the armed struggle have sometimes encouraged popular civilian defiance in the form of demonstrations or strikes. On the other hand, the focus for guerrillas in urban areas is usually on sabotage, bomb attacks and assassinations, which have sometimes been clearly targeted against the regime and at others have indiscriminately killed civilians as well as soldiers or security police. Urban guerrilla warfare often has a demonstrative role, capturing headlines and providing dramatic evidence at home and abroad of continued resistance, and so potentially embarrassing the regime. It may harass government security forces, but in itself does not provide a strategy for revolutionary change unless it is linked to a well-organized and well-armed guerrilla force, or unless it promotes a mass upsurge of civil resistance, or both.

Where guerrilla movements are faced with military odds they cannot overcome, but can use large rural areas difficult for the regime to control, and where they also have havens across the border in neighbouring countries and perhaps international support in training and arms, they can pursue an alternative strategy. By maintaining a stalemate they may eventually persuade the opponent that the war cannot be won and is not worth the costs. This essentially became the strategy of the guerrilla movements such as FRELIMO in the Portuguese African colonies.

Differences between guerrilla strategy and civil resistance

Theorists of civil resistance tend to stress that the strategy and impact of unarmed struggle, and especially a disciplined nonviolent resistance, differs radically from guerrilla resistance. Guerrilla warfare can be seen primarily as an armed struggle, which initially often relies on inspiring awe and gaining widespread publicity by spectacular acts of violence, gains strength through capturing arms and recruiting more fighters, aims to set up liberated areas under guerrilla military and political control, and culminates in seizures of the capital city and the institutions of government by a now superior military force. In the last phase guerrilla tactics (in the classic theory enunciated by Mao and developed by the Vietnamese General Giap) give way to creation of a conventional army. So victory depends finally on force of arms – even though military strength cannot be divorced from political, economic and psychological factors.

Guerrilla strategists do not, however, always agree about the relationship between armed action and political activism. For example, Eduardo Mondlane and FRELIMO argued against the idea (promoted by Che Guevara on a tour of Africa) that a small armed unit could act as an inspiration for popular mobilization, and stressed instead the need for political mobilization from the ground up (Meyer, 2012; Mondlane, 1969). However, even if the importance for guerrilla movements of gaining popular support, and the overarching role of political objectives, are recognized, it can be argued that commitment to armed resistance carries the danger that an initial emphasis on the political dimension of struggle can be overtaken by military imperatives in the later stages. Eric Wolf (drawing on research by Douglas Pike) suggests this switch occurred in South Vietnam – though here the increasing military role of the US backing the South Vietnamese regime, and the growing number of North Vietnamese troops, clearly influenced the logic of the National Liberation Front (NLF) strategy (Wolf, 1973: 206–7; Pike, 1966).

Proponents of civil resistance also argue that, however just the cause for which guerrillas fight, their methods are likely to involve significant bloodshed and hardship for the general population, and to encourage (and to some extent legitimize) brutal repression by the regime, which will seek (often with some success) to dismiss the guerrillas as 'terrorists'. By contrast, nonviolent strategy seeks to undermine the regime by mass peaceful non-cooperation and civil disobedience, through its persistence to win sympathy and support from some previous supporters of the regime, and to develop international backing. Maintaining, if possible, strict nonviolence is intended to reduce the reasons for, and the likelihood of, violent repression. But it is also meant to ensure that, if the regime does use excessive violence against nonviolent protesters, some of those perpetrating the violence may begin to question their role or be won over, and at a broader political level they will lose legitimacy both at home and abroad.

Moreover, whereas guerrillas rely on being able to escape and hide until the later stages of open confrontation, and need a strictly controlled underground network if they are to operate throughout the countryside and the cities, unarmed resistance – although it may need a hidden communications network – generally relies on open defiance and willingness to risk, or even court, arrest. Leaders in prison often become a focus of domestic and international support. (This can to some extent also be true of captured guerrilla leaders, but the pivotal role of the jailed Nelson Mandela in South Africa arguably reflected the complex mix of guerrilla and civil resistance tactics in that long struggle.)

Theorists of nonviolent action, therefore, suggest that since the dynamics of guerrilla and civil resistance seem to be so essentially distinct, mixing the two is necessarily detrimental to any sustained attempt at nonviolent strategy. Guerrilla conflict is likely to intensify hatred and a desire for revenge between the opposed sides, manifested in cycles of provocation and repression. Civil resistance, on the other hand, focuses on the goal of a peaceful outcome, even if the initial response by the regime involves repression and bloodshed. Where the goal is the Gandhian ideal of converting the main opponent, resistance seeks to gain support through the willingness of its supporters to suffer for their cause without inflicting violence in return. Even if an unarmed strategy allowing for limited forms of 'violence', and involving significant economic and political coercion, is adopted, the hope is to win over all but the most intransigent and compromised sections of the regime in order to overthrow it and to create a new political order, or enable a negotiated accommodation. A movement which relies primarily on nonviolent methods is also likely to attract much greater external media and diplomatic sympathy – especially within liberal democracies. Therefore, strategic writings on civil resistance urge that if guerrilla resistance does exist alongside a civil resistance movement, as in Burma in the late 1980s, then the best solution is to keep the two forms of struggle as distinct as possible – though there may need to be negotiation and agreement between the leaders of both (Beer, 1999: 178–80).

The problems of mixing guerrilla methods and a strategy based on the theory of nonviolent resistance have been experienced in actual resistance struggles. Analysts of the First Intifada have stressed the problems created when – although it was predominantly an unarmed struggle – some Palestinian guerrillas from outside did engage in occasional armed retaliation (Rigby, 1991; King, 2007). There were several other difficulties in relation to the First Intifada: the background of Palestine Liberation Organization guerrilla tactics such as plane hijackings, Arab hostility to the Israeli state and what Rigby describes as 'the siege mentality of the bulk of the Israeli public' and the intransigent role of the Israeli forces in response to the Intifada. But, as noted in Chapter 1, the intifada was never a strictly nonviolent struggle, as opposed to an unarmed one – young men did not see throwing stones at Israeli forces as a form of 'violence'. Although the intifada roused sympathy and support among Israelis on the left and in peace groups, Mary King notes that the Israeli government and US official and unofficial commentators tended to describe the First Intifada in purely violent terms (King, 2007: 6). Nevertheless, despite the problems of mixed messages and a final breakdown of the unarmed resistance, the First Intifada did create a sense of political potential among Palestinians living in the Occupied Territories and paved the way for serious negotiations in the 1990s about an autonomous Palestinian homeland. (Whether the resultant 1993 Oslo Accords were a good initial outcome for the Palestinians has been hotly debated, but is a separate issue.)

Guerrilla fighters and theorists, by contrast, when they stress the importance of politics, and know that their strategy depends on undermining all the power bases of the regime, often see some role (though usually subordinate to the military strategy) for civilian protests. Guerrilla organizations may also (as in the case of the IRA and Sinn Fein) work with a political front. Even if the guerrilla organization does not directly foment civil unrest, it will tend to benefit from it. In Nicaragua, for example, the struggle against the dictator Anastasio Somoza saw widespread social protests in the 1970s by students, professionals and workers, as well as guerrilla raids. In the final phase of 1977–9 strikes and big demonstrations took place, as well as the relatively sustained military offensive by the Sandinista (FSLN) guerrillas. The Sandinistas had significant civilian political support, notably the Group of Ten drawn from intellectuals, the clergy and radical members of the banking and business elite (Grynspan, 1991: 95–100). Moreover, although Mao envisaged a conventional military victory as the culmination of a guerrilla strategy, Regis Debray (1967: 108), writing about Latin America in the 1960s, suggests that it is 'a general strike or generalized urban insurrection that will give the *coup de grace* to the regime and defeat its final manoeuvres – a last minute *coup d'état*, a new junta, elections – by extending the struggle throughout the country'.

Similarities between civil resistance and guerrilla strategy

Despite the important contrasts between unarmed and armed struggles, when the aim of both is to mobilize 'the people' there are nevertheless significant parallels between them in terms of strategy and the dynamics of struggle. These parallels are explored below, noting relevant caveats.

Winning majority support

Both unarmed and guerrilla movements, whilst recognizing that there will be varying degrees of active support for their struggle, seek to gain the sympathy of the great majority of the population. Sometimes widespread latent opposition to an imperialist power or brutal internal dictatorship already exists; at other times it may be necessarily to build belief in national identity, democracy or social justice. But either way success in the struggle is intrinsically linked to gaining and organizing wide popular support. In the case of unarmed resistance, which relies heavily on non-cooperation, the necessity of mass support for the success of strikes and boycotts, or tax refusal and noncompliance with government orders is obvious. Selected groups can engage in some forms of action intended to challenge the regime, such as vigils or hunger strikes, or spectacular acts of civil disobedience, but hope to trigger a wider protest. For example, four women initiated a hunger strike in Bolivia in December 1977 against the Banzer dictatorship, to be joined eventually by 1,200; and the 1930–1 campaign of civil disobedience for Indian independence was launched by Gandhi, who with members of his ashram (community) marched to the sea to challenge the government monopoly on salt production by symbolically making salt from sea water. In both these cases the initial action did precipitate national resistance: in Bolivia it was led by the militant union of tin miners; in India it was planned and promoted by the Congress Party (Boots, 1991: 48–62; Bondurant, 1958:

88–102). One purpose of civil disobedience is usually to fill the jails, although at times there may be tactical reasons for deliberately limiting numbers. Indeed the democratic credentials of unarmed resistance depend on mass engagement; and effective use of people power to overthrow a regime usually depends on launching a general strike, or on thousands (or even millions) flooding the streets.

The classic theory of guerrilla warfare stresses that the guerrillas rely on the wider population. The most famous image comes from Mao Tse-tung, that guerrillas survive in the rear of enemy troops like 'fish' in the 'water'. The conditions for creating such popular support, according to Mao, are that the political goals of the guerrillas and the people coincide, and that the armed guerrillas are disciplined to respect those on whom they depend. When Edgar Snow managed to visit the communist base at Yenan in 1936, a leading commander Peng Teh-huai – after outlining basic military tactics – noted that the partisans should have not only greater mobility but superior intelligence: 'Ideally, every peasant should be on the partisans' intelligence staff.' He concluded: 'Finally, it is absolutely necessary for the partisans to win the support and participation of the peasant masses' by implanting themselves in people's hearts, responding to their demands and sheltering in their shadow (Snow, 1972: 317, 318). Ernesto (Che) Guevara insists that 'The guerrilla fighter counts on the full support of the local people' and 'the guerrilla fighter takes up arms *as the embodiment* of the angry protests of the people against their oppressors' (Guevara, 2009: 16, 17).

Both unarmed and guerrilla struggles have to overcome obvious socio-economic divisions, between town and country and between the middle and working classes, if they are likely to succeed. Whilst stressing the concerns and winning the loyalty of the Indian peasants, Gandhi supported the rights of industrial workers (for example, he led the 1918 Ahmedabad mill workers strike), and he later gained money and support from prominent businessmen. Mao challenged the previous Marxist orthodoxy by relying on the peasants and the countryside as the main arena for revolution in the Chinese circumstances, but still looked to the urban workers as a potential leading force. Moreover, in his policies before (and, initially, after) coming to power he courted the moderate middle classes. The victory of the Red Army over Chiang Kai-shek in 1949 was assisted by the alienation of many of the urban and professional classes – exemplified by a speech by Professor Chang Hsi-jo in January 1946 to 7,000 students – from a corrupt and authoritarian regime, and by economic chaos (Jaffe, 1947: 312–20).

It is important, however, not to be starry-eyed about the nature of mass support in both civil resistance and guerrilla campaigns. Firstly, certain social divisions, such as ethnic and religious differences, may prove very hard to overcome. Although there was some Muslim engagement in the Indian independence campaigns, the mainstream support came from Hindus, and this divide – despite active efforts by Gandhi at various times to work with Muslim leaders – was a precursor to the eventual creation of a separate Muslim Pakistan, and the dreadful bloodshed of partition. Moreover, even when nonviolent methods are used there may be (as noted in Chapter 1) a good deal of social pressure – extending to social ostracism or physical violence – to ensure participation in resistance. Guerrillas with arms in their hands and fearful for their lives must be tempted to use violent intimidation to secure important information or support where the local people (perhaps from fear of brutal retaliation from security forces) are reluctant to offer aid. They also execute suspected informers (as did the armed wing of the African National Congress, the 'Spear of the Nation').

Secondly, in both unarmed and guerrilla struggles there may well be rival political groupings contending for popular support, so that even if there is a widespread desire to change the regime, the people may be ideologically split. Even in resistance movements where the methods used against the regime are in essence nonviolent, rival political parties may resort to violence and intimidation against each other, as in Zambia in the early 1960s. Guerrilla warfare has since the mid-twentieth century been largely (though not exclusively) promoted by Marxist groups, and therefore – despite stressing popular support – guerrilla organizations have been likely to see themselves acting as a Leninist vanguard, directing popular discontent into the 'correct' channels, and crushing or incorporating rival ideological and political parties. There may even be questions about the link between the organized political wing and the military wing of a revolutionary party. Debray, drawing on the Cuban experience (where Castro and his colleagues only gradually turned to Marxism), and Guevara's deductions from it, stressed the need to combine political and military leadership, which can then act as a political vanguard and unite the countryside and the town in a revolutionary strategy (Debray, 1967: 106–8).

Mobilization of formerly excluded sections of the population

Ethnic and socio-economic groupings in some cultures have suffered discrimination and social exclusion and may therefore be more difficult to draw into a nationalist struggle. As a result in guerrilla campaigns ethnic minorities have sometimes opposed the nationalist resistance (as in South Vietnam in the 1960s). Minority ethnic groups with a territorial base have taken up arms to gain their own independence, whereas the mainstream population opts for civil resistance. This has been the case in Burma, and was also true of the Philippines in the 1980s, complicated there by the fact that a Marxist opposition was also waging guerrilla warfare (Mendoza, 2009: 179–80).

Where the social hierarchy has created a group suffering extreme discrimination, like the Dalits (untouchables) in India, engaging their support and overcoming the prejudices of the majority of the population creates problems for a resistance movement. Gandhi did explicitly espouse the rights of the Dalits, whom he named 'Harijans' – the children of god – against orthodox Hindu discrimination. For example he backed the Vykom Temple *satyagraha* of 1924–5, in which untouchables claimed the right to use a road passing a Hindu temple (Bondurant, 1958: 46–52). He also fasted in prison in 1932 for untouchables to be included in the main electorate, although the untouchable leader Dr B.R. Ambedkar denounced Gandhi and, during the 1931 negotiations with the British, supported the idea of separate political representation for the untouchable community (Brown, 1989: 257, 265–8).

The universal categories of gender and age are, however, the most relevant to the potential active support for both unarmed and guerrilla struggles. Women cannot only join, but can play a major role in unarmed resistance. If the emphasis is on nonviolent confrontation, then women tend to appear less threatening in general; they often play a key role in winning over troops or urging them not to fire. Regime violence against women is also likely to arouse greater repugnance.

Whether women are in reality especially suited to nonviolent resistance or always more likely to maintain a nonviolent discipline is, however, a complex question. Historically women have quite often been prominent in riots or acts of violent revenge. Cultural differences are important: in some parts of Africa the women have traditionally urged their men to fight in battle, and their presence at a demonstration might increase the likelihood of a riot. Moreover, the putative link between nonviolent resistance and feminine attitudes is itself contentions. Some feminists have repudiated a Gandhian strategy that stresses voluntary suffering and a refusal to strike back precisely because it seems to reflect the victimhood of women in many societies.

Nevertheless, in general it is reasonable to assume that women of all ages are more likely to take part in essentially nonviolent modes of protest, whereas young men and boys are more likely to turn to both spontaneous and planned forms of violence. In the First Intifada, for example, the height of the unarmed struggle coincided with large-scale participation by women (King, 2007: 93–9; Dajani, 1994: 33–61). Even in cultural contexts that tend to confine women to the home, they have taken to the streets in mass popular protests, for example in the widespread nationalist civil resistance in Egypt in 1919 against British rule (Daly, 1998: 239–51). The very fact that women have often not been taken seriously as political subjects has at times created a space for resistance. A notable example is provided by the group of mothers of some of the thousands of those who 'disappeared' in the Dirty War waged by the Argentine military government against the opposition. The 'Madres de Plaza de Mayo' challenged the junta by demanding to know what had become of their 'disappeared' children, through a continued public presence that started in 1977 (Fisher, 1989).

Indeed, theorists of civil resistance tend to claim that involvement of women is one of the strengths of this strategy, although how far women have played a truly equal or independent role has varied. In one of the most dramatic episodes of the Indian independence struggle, the 'raid' on the Dharasana salt works in 1931 (memorably described by the United Press correspondent Webb Miller), it was men (including turbaned Sikhs with a warrior tradition) who were assigned to march in waves until clubbed to the ground, and women who had the feminine role of nursing the wounded (Fischer, 1954: 100–2).

Although women were at the forefront of the boycott campaign in the Zambian independence movement, research suggests that they saw themselves as acting on the orders of male leaders. On the other hand, in Zimbabwe, undoubtedly still influenced by patriarchal attitudes, Women of Zimbabwe Arise has played a militant and leading role in opposing the Mugabe regime, whilst stressing nonviolence, and gave rise to a parallel men's movement Men of Zimbabwe Arise (Cherry, 2009: 56–7). The First Intifada gave women in villages and refugee camps an unprecedented opportunity to create committees and take part in the struggle, previously controlled by a male leadership committed to guerrilla tactics – though this phase proved brief.

There have also been women leaders of major nonviolent struggles. Aung San Suu Kyi, who is a Buddhist and does believe in Gandhian nonviolence, symbolizes through the combination of her graceful femininity and unflinching courage and determination the spirit of nonviolent resistance (Wintle, 2007). But her leadership role depends to a considerable degree on being the daughter of Burma's independence leader (thus emphasizing the extent to which several Asian women leaders have become prominent because of their fathers or husbands). Corazon Aquino stepped into a leading role in the 1986 Philippine people power movement because she replaced her assassinated husband as a presidential candidate.

Since guerrilla warfare requires at least basic military skills, often imposes extremes of physical hardship, and encourages glorification of armed warriors and macho values, it might appear to be a form of struggle designed for young men, and naturally excluding rather than incorporating women. But the apparent bias towards young men is not wholly true of all guerrilla struggles. Men have certainly predominated among actual guerrilla fighters, although women did take up arms in a number of the partisan struggles in the Second World War, notably in Yugoslavia where there were up to 100,000 women fighters (Jancar, 1988). A few women also fought in the guerrilla armies of the Chinese communists; in Nicaragua about 30 per cent of the opposition fighters were women during the final overthrow of Somoza in 1979; and in Zimbabwe about 4,000 women fought in the resistance of the 1960s and 1970s (Belden, 1973: 291–93; Harris, 1988; Cock, 1992: 182). FRELIMO as a matter of ideological principle tried to incorporate women as fighters in Mozambique, although there was apparently some resistance from men to this policy (Nugent, 2004: 268).

Women have, however, much more often played auxiliary, though important, roles in guerrilla struggles: in the guerrilla wing of the South African resistance some women trained alongside men, but generally worked in communications, and sometimes in intelligence (Cock, 1992: 163–5); in Yugoslavia women acted as doctors and nurses to the partisans, but also as messengers, and were central as political organizers. Guevara (2009: 106–9) stresses in principle that women can fight as equals; he also suggests that in practice they will be a small minority of combatants, but can give support in traditional domestic roles, and take a major part in conveying messages, providing medical aid and acting as teachers to peasants and guerrilla fighters.

Women's involvement in resistance movements depends not only on whether the mode of struggle is unarmed or armed, but perhaps even more crucially on the extent to which the society taking up resistance has subordinated and sequestered its women. The Algerian guerrilla struggle against the French is interesting in this respect. The mythology of the struggle, at least on the Western left, includes images of women planting and carrying bombs and becoming heroines of resistance. Frantz Fanon wrote a perceptive analysis of women in the resistance 'Algeria Unveiled', which discusses Western attitudes to Muslim women and the veil, attempts by the colonial French to abolish the veil, and within that context the decision to use unveiled, attractive, Western-dressed, Algerian women to carry guns and grenades in their handbags past French police and troops, who would automatically have searched Algerian men, during the campaign of assassinations and blowing up settler cafés. Fanon (1970: 21–52) also discusses the move back towards the veil when the French had captured and tortured Westernized women resisters, and the difficulties of carrying weapons whilst appearing to have free hands. Parallel to the practicalities of struggle he suggests a political and psychological move, first towards an emancipation linked to removing the veil, and then a reversion to the veil as an act of resistance and national opposition to French colonialism. But a feminist activist against discrimination against women in Muslim states, who lived in Algeria when young and experienced the 1950s struggle, has argued that relatively few women took active roles in the resistance, although they did perform a great many traditional feminine roles such as providing food, fuel and medicine to armed groups (sometimes at considerable but unrecognized risk), cooking and laundry, or secretarial services. The central role of women was to symbolize national and religious identity (Helie-Lucas, 1988).

Age need not be a bar to supporting a national movement. Again, this is more obviously true of unarmed struggles: all adults can support consumer boycotts or tax resistances; the old and the very young can also take part in marches and rallies. An interesting example of the old trying to protect young activists occurred during the mass nonviolent resistance to the Milosevic regime in Serbia in 2000, when Ivan Vejvoda records that a 'grandparents support group' emerged to back protesting students, and 'one could on occasions see senior citizens defending young protesters under attack from the police' (Vejvoda, 2009: 308). High-school children have quite often been prominent in civil resistance. It was the children of Soweto, protesting on the streets in 1976 against the compulsory introduction of Afrikaans into their schooling, that revitalized civil resistance in South Africa. High-school pupils, and apprentices, were also prominent in 1978 in the revolt against the Shah of Iran (Abrahamian, 2009: 170–1). So both pensioners and schoolchildren can play front-line roles in civil resistance, although there are moral questions about deliberately endangering under-age children.

Guerrilla campaigns can use old and young as lookouts or sources of intelligence, and they might act as messengers. In exceptional circumstances children engaged in fighting in China – Edgar Snow (1972) wrote, in *Red Star Over*

36 *Resistance and political change*

China, about the 'Little Red Devils' in the communist forces. But guerrilla warfare necessarily tends to assign all those who cannot fight effectively to secondary roles, rather than allowing them into the 'front line' of the struggle.

Persuading troops and police to change sides

Winning over sections of the armed forces and civilian or security police can be crucial in the final stages of a civil resistance movement, or in more sudden eruptions of mass popular protest like those in Tunisia and Egypt in January 2011, when 'people power' confronts the regime. Even if the security forces do not actively support the opposition, they may be sufficiently alienated from the existing government to look towards a new regime, or be unwilling to take part in killing and wounding large numbers of 'their own' people. Where possible repressive regimes often use ethnically distinct forces, a tactic used by the Soviet regime: for example non-Russian troops were brought in to crush a major strike in Novocherkassk in June 1962, after the local garrison apparently refused to shoot (Haynes and Semyonova, 1979: 76–81).

Troops and police can of course withdraw support from the regime at different levels. One scenario is for the rank-and-file soldiers to refuse to fire on demonstrators, and perhaps persuade their immediate commanders to go along with them, often a decisive factor in revolutions (see Chapter 3). In Iran in 1978–9, although troops did fire on crowds, demonstrators appealed to the soldiers with slogans such as 'Brother soldiers, why do you shoot brothers?', and handed out carnations to troops. Towards the end of the uprising soldiers were deserting, handing over their weapons to protesters, or occasionally firing on their own officers. The Shah knew he could no longer rely on the army (Abrahamian, 2009: 170–4). But, in 1989, Chinese students appealed largely in vain to soldiers at a military camp on the outskirts of Beijing, as 'sons and brothers of the people' to refuse to fire on demonstrators (Mok Chiu Yu and Harrison, 1990: 103). Georgian demonstrators in November 2003 pursued a strategy of fraternizing with police, offering them food and putting carnations in their gun barrels; and the police (already alienated by a failure to pay them for three months) failed to fire when the demonstrators later took over the parliament building (Jones, 2009: 332).

Resistance from below in security forces can range from covert disobedience to open mutiny. Middle-level commanders may also baulk at repressing mass popular resistance. A documented (and more recently confirmed) example is Commander Xu Qinxian, of the 38th Army, who did refuse to lead his troops against Tiananmen demonstrators in 1989, and was later sentenced to 18 years in prison. At the time there was speculation that some other sections of the Chinese forces rebelled against shooting protesters, but such speculation is hard to confirm, and it is clear that most of the army obeyed. Deng Xiaoping later thanked officers who had enforced martial law (Lawrance, 2004: 243–4). At the climax of the Indonesian unarmed uprising in May 1998, officers, mostly from the Air Force, Navy and Marines, shielded students who were demonstrating and cautiously backed some of the student demands (Boudreau, 2004: 234). In Ukraine leaders of the opposition began from the end of 2002 to contact, through a network of retired army officers, mid-ranking members of the armed forces to explore possible forms of future support (Binnendijk and Marovic, 2006: 418–19).

Thirdly, some or most of the generals, or key officials in the security police, may refuse to crush demonstrators. President Milosevic did issue an order to shoot at protesters in Belgrade in October 2000, and those in command of the security forces disobeyed the order. A leader of one of the parties who had contested the election, Zoran Djindic, apparently approached the chief of the security police operations unit. Contacts between opposition parties and middle- and higher-ranking police and military officers had begun after protests in 1996–7, and especially after the NATO intervention in the Serbian attack on Kosovo in 1999 and bombing of targets in Serbia (Vejvoda, 2009: 311–12).

If the high command of the armed forces is split, as in the Philippines in 1986, it is not always clear how far they are defending electoral democracy against an authoritarian regime or promoting their own political interests. In a situation of mass unrest there is also scope for trying to bring off a *coup d'état*. The position of General Enrile, who formed the Reform the Armed Forces Movement, which apparently supported Corazon Aquino, the opposition candidate in the presidential elections, and attempted unsuccessfully to overthrow President Marcos, has in particular been much debated. Vincent Boudreau, drawing on expert studies, argues that Enrile planned to create a military junta, but, when besieged by troops loyal to Marcos, had to turn to Aquino and the Catholic church for support (Boudreau, 2004: 184). Enrile's own political ambitions became evident subsequently. But, as events evolved, the split in the armed forces aided the civil resistance, and – in an ironic reversal of roles – unarmed civil resisters massed to protect the military rebels against attack by troops loyal to Marcos (Mendoza, 2009: 182–3; Johnson, 1987).

Where the regime is itself a military junta, as in Burma, or the military and police security forces enjoy privileges based on sustaining the political leadership, and also fear that they will be held to account for their brutalities if the regime does fall, as in Zimbabwe under Mugabe, it can be particularly difficult to get the top commanders to change sides. Where there is extreme poverty, increasingly true in Zimbabwe after 2000, lower-level soldiers and police have immediate material incentives to suppress the political opposition, and may fear popular anger.

Sheer numbers of protesters and a sense that the regime is already divided at the top political levels, or on the verge of being toppled, and possibly confusion over orders, can dissuade ordinary troops and police from firing on unarmed crowds, as happened when the Berlin Wall was dismantled in November 1989. At the earlier October demonstrations in Leipzig, which paved the way for mass resistance in Berlin, it has been suggested that Leipzig political officials decided not to use the large number of security forces deployed in readiness to quell the protests, and incurred the wrath of some members of the Politburo (see Chapter 3).

Officials at the top level of the security forces have sometimes seen the advantages of negotiating a peaceful transition of power with the opposition. The head of the National Intelligence Service in South Africa played, according to evidence now available, a crucial role in promoting secret negotiations between the Afrikaner National Party government and the African National Congress (ANC) (BBC, 2009). The ANC itself was involved in organizing a limited guerrilla struggle, although by the late 1980s widely supported civil resistance was being promoted by unions and in the townships. So the South African struggle combined both unarmed and violent approaches (see below).

In key examples of a guerrilla struggle developing into a 'people's war', winning over regime troops is often one of the objectives. The American journalist Jack Belden describes how, in the last stage of Mao's war against the Kuomintang regime in 1947, when it had turned into a confrontation between conventional forces, the 'Eighth Route Army' would treat captured enemy soldiers well, subject them to political propaganda, and encourage them to enlist with the communists, which many did, significantly swelling numbers of troops. But if prisoners of war wished to leave, they would in due course be allowed to do so. Deserters from Chiang Kai-shek's army would also be welcomed into the ranks (Belden, 1973: 458–9). In Cuba there was not the same emphasis on winning over the forces of the regime, although Guevara in his manual on guerrilla warfare urges that normally captured prisoners should be humanely treated. But the impact of the guerrilla campaign and opposition to Batista did demoralize the regular forces, leading to several attempted mutinies (Kapcia, 2008: 23; Wolf, 1973: 272–3). East Timorese guerrillas adopted a policy of treating captured Indonesian soldiers well and sometimes releasing them. This approach capitalized on the disaffection among some Indonesian troops after the Dili massacre of East Timorese taking part in a funeral procession in November 1991, and reflected a strategy of seeking links to the opposition to the military government inside Indonesia (Stephan and Chenoweth, 2008: 31).

Stephan and Chenoweth measured defections by the security forces and found that 'of the successful violent campaigns ... defections occurred about 32 per cent of the time and of the successful nonviolent ... about 52 per cent of the time', but that such defections were very much more significant for the success of nonviolent struggles. But they note that their data set does not measure sensitively degrees of defection (ibid.: 21–2, 24).

Building alternative institutions

The creation of alternative forms of social, economic, cultural or political action has not always arisen in the case of sudden eruptions of people power – though these have often been preceded by evolution of various kinds of civil society or community-based organizations, creating a basis for later mass resistance. Many long-term civil resistance struggles have, however, involved creating such parallel structures either as auxiliary means of sustaining resistance, or as a central component of their strategy, sometimes creating a new society in embryo. Guerrillas, on the other hand, need to secure a liberated territorial base to develop alternative institutions, where there may in any case be an administrative void. But where they have done so they can create models of the ideal they are fighting to achieve.

Methods of resistance often naturally generate constructive responses. Strikes have created great economic hardship for the striking workers, so prompting unions and local communities to provide food and economic relief.

Prolonged boycotts of consumer goods create a need to provide alternatives: general strikes and mass non-cooperation prompt creation of alternative political organizations, such as the workers' and soldiers' soviets (councils) that came to the fore in the 1905 revolution in Russia. The landless occupying land not only begin to cultivate it but often set up cooperatives and alternative forms of local self-government (in contrast to rancher domination of agricultural workers on large latifundia); and striking or dismissed workers who seize a factory tend to create a form of workers' control opposed to standard capitalist modes of ownership and control of industry.

The Palestinian First Intifada combined mass resistance through tax refusal, strikes, boycotts and resignations from institutions associated with the Israeli occupation, with the development of popular committees to provide an alternative administration, and developed autonomous medical and welfare services and economic self-reliance in response to Israeli sanctions (King, 2007: 228–39; Ackerman and Duvall, 2000: 410–14). Participating in aspects of this alternative structure was then made illegal by the Israeli authorities.

Creating a parallel society has sometimes been a central form of resistance, as in Poland, Czechoslovakia and Hungary in the 1970s and 1980s. Dissident intellectuals not only protested about abuse of human rights (for example Charter 77 in Czechoslovakia), but circulated information and ideas in samizdat journals and books, held unofficial seminars, and attended concerts, performances and exhibitions of music, drama and the arts not authorized by the regime. These 'parallel structures' in the realm of culture were, Vaclav Havel argued, 'inseparable from the phenomenon of "dissent"' (Havel, 1987: 101). In Poland in the late 1970s parallel structures began to flourish openly, for example an independent student union arose in May 1977, journals addressed to young Catholics, workers and farmers were founded, and the publishing house Nowa Huta began to publish previously banned books. Moreover the series of unofficial lectures by well-known scholars developed by January 1978 into the independent 'Flying University', which offered a series of courses to students in politically sensitive subjects such as philosophy, modern history, the social sciences and literature, promoted by regular lectures and a 'flying library' of relevant books (Bromke, 1981: 100–1). Jacek Kuron, active in KOR (Committee for the Defence of Workers' Rights) and remembering workers' attacks on Party Committee headquarters in Poznan in 1956 and Gdansk in 1970, urged in a widely quoted slogan: 'Don't burn down the Party Committee headquarters, build your own.' After the suppression of Solidarity in December 1981, leading figures argued for an emphasis on the decentralized creation of alternative social, economic and cultural institutions (Zielonka, 1986: 101–2).

But the most extensive development of parallel education and political structures took place in the unarmed struggle of the Kosovo Albanians, resisting the policy of political suppression and Serbianization of Albanian education and culture pursued by President Milosevic of Serbia in the 1990s. Primary and secondary schools and university-level courses employing over 20,000 teachers were funded by an alternative 'taxation' system inside and outside Kosovo. As part of the struggle the Albanians also organized in 1991 their own referendum on a declaration of independence for Kosovo (then still legally a province within Serbia, though one which had been granted considerable political rights and relative autonomy under the 1974 Yugoslav constitution) and then in 1992 held parallel elections for their own president and parliament (Clark, 2000: 70–121).

Parallel institutions arising from an unarmed resistance movement, whether tolerated or forced into a precarious and at least semi-underground existence, can help to undermine a regime, but are usually limited in how far they can demonstrate a new polity, economy and society. In guerrilla warfare, by contrast, the flowering of alternative institutions is limited to liberated geographical areas, but may be much more comprehensive in scope within them because they exercise control and may be filling a void. The clearest example comes from China. Thousands of students, intellectuals and artists were increasingly attracted to the communist cause (partly on patriotic grounds during the Japanese occupation) and journeyed to their base at Shensi, where they were caught up in educational and cultural activities under communist ideological direction (Schram, 1966: 206–7; Snow, 1972: 241–73). The communists set up a system of government in the areas under their control, promoting basic education, levying taxes, organizing labour for some collective projects, and trying to maintain rudimentary communications and their own currency and banking system (Belden, 1973: 142–88). Once the Japanese had been defeated, and the civil war had begun (in 1946), more ambitious attempts at land reform to benefit the peasant farmers in the liberated areas was a strategy to attract support from the desperately poor peasants in the rest of China (Belden, 1973: 219–366). FRELIMO, as noted above, also attached great importance to setting up a model administration in the areas it controlled in Mozambique, and providing a vision of a better society which would be embraced by the peasants, although the positive assessments of their accomplishments by ideologically sympathetic Western observers have been queried (Nugent, 2004: 269).

Promoting solidarity, dignity and fearlessness

Both nonviolent and guerrilla strategies aim deliberately to transform those involved in the struggle: to convert apathy or despair into political consciousness, turn a sense of inferiority and worthlessness into pride, overcome private self-protection and pursuit of material goals with a sense of solidarity, and make the fearful courageous. Even unarmed struggles that do not consciously try to change attitudes often do so, because people (at least for a time) become inspired with a sense of their own power to bring about social change and with hopes for a better future.

Gandhi's whole approach was designed to inculcate self-reliance, self-belief, a willingness to resist and fearlessness. His close followers practised austerity, self-discipline and communal living in his ashram. To motivate thousands to adopt the same attitudes he used exhortation, promoted his 'constructive programme' and considered carefully the most appropriate tactics of nonviolent defiance. Starting from a very different cultural and political context, Vaclav Havel (1987) argued in 'The Power of the Powerless' that individuals could 'live in truth', and transform themselves from passive participants in post-totalitarian regimes to active citizens, by acts of individual defiance.

Guerrilla campaigns often deliberately promote the necessary attitudes of pride, a sense of responsibility and unselfishness through basic training and education of their recruits. The Chinese communists did so systematically through propaganda, promoting heroic myths, slogans and songs, and explicitly praising and blaming individuals in public meetings and wall newspapers (Snow, 1972: 323–4). Guerrilla armies tend to develop basic rules of discipline and solidarity during fighting, for example never to leave any weapons behind as stressed by Guevara; and always to carry their wounded with them, as the Yugoslav Partisans did, also stressed by Guevara (2009: 27, 54).

Mao, whilst concerned to avoid needless loss of life in his guerrilla war, underlined the necessity of fearlessness. Stuart Schram quotes a striking passage from Mao's 'Basic Tactics' that begins: 'When we see the enemy we must not be frightened to death … we are all men.' If the fear is of weapons, guerrillas can devise a way to seize these weapons. The real fear is of getting killed: 'But when we undergo the oppression of the enemy to such a point as this, how can anyone still fear death?' (Schram, 1966: 212–13).

However, even where exhortation, the power of example or sustained propaganda seek to transform the attitudes of those resisting, it is the experience of struggle itself that tends to change people. This is true of both guerrilla campaigns and unarmed struggles. It is this psychological liberation of the oppressed that Fanon (1965: 73) celebrates and sees as one of the key arguments for 'violence' that frees the resister from 'his inferiority complex and from his despair and inaction, it makes him fearless and restores his self-respect'. But, as Barbara Deming argued in her critique of Fanon, many of the points he makes about violent struggle apply also to a mass campaign of nonviolent resistance (Deming, 1971).

Souad Dajani writes of the unarmed Palestinian First Intifada that 'the very act of resistance transformed the resisters' and empowered them, although they were also frustrated by Israeli responses (Dajani, 1999: 56). Howard Clark quotes the leader of the unarmed Kosovo Albanian resistance: 'By means of active resistance based on nonviolence and solidarity, we "found" ourselves.' Albanian people for the first time 'feel that they have a power … feel citizens despite the occupation' (Clark, 2009b: 281).

There are examples of people power when many thousands of people suddenly pour into the streets and display amazing confidence, determination and courage, even when faced with guns or tanks. The uprising against the Shah of Iran in 1978–9 is a striking example. Men and women interviewed in Tahrir Square in Egypt by TV and press journalists often said that they had lost their fear: for example, Mona Seif, a postgraduate student who had spread the call on the Internet for the protest on 25 January 2011, commented 'once you're here among the people, you don't feel scared' (Macintyre, 2011b: 9).

But this willingness to confront armed troops or organized violent mobs usually occurs in a situation of potential revolution; and in less propitious contexts unarmed resistance has been crushed by ruthless regimes, as in China in 1989 and in Burma in 2007. Regimes may nevertheless then feel constrained to make at least token concessions or more actively seek popular support, as to some extent happened in China in the 1990s. Even the Burmese (Myanmar) military junta promised a referendum on the constitution in 2008 and an election in 2010 – promises it has since gone through the motions of keeping (Fink, 2009: 366). Sometimes memory of resistance lives on and in due course animates a new upsurge of defiance (for example the 2007 Burmese mass protests harked back to the people power of 1988). But there are no guarantees of either short-term or long-term results.

Violence against the resistance rebounds

Theorists of nonviolent action have argued that one of the key strengths of this mode of struggle is that violent repression cannot be justified, as more plausibly it can be against forms of armed resistance of major rioting. Even those who order or take part in beating or shooting demonstrators can respond to those who maintain brave and disciplined nonviolent protest despite such retaliation. Richard Gregg developed the theory of 'moral jiu-jitsu' to explain the psychological mechanisms involved, when the violence of the oppressors rebounds against them and begins to change their minds (Gregg, 1960: 43–65). Revulsion against taking part in violent repression is one reason why security police, soldiers or officers begin to defect in revolutionary contexts. But it can also occur at earlier stages of struggle.

Moreover, although fear of violent retaliation can undoubtedly be a deterrent to further open protest, brutal overreaction by the regime can mobilize so far inactive sympathizers or bystanders to take to the streets. For example, after riot police and soldiers deliberately killed many students protesting at Rangoon University on 18 March 1988 in the 'Red Bridge' incident, the next day there were further student protests, and the day after over 10,000 people demonstrated in central Rangoon (Fink, 2001: 51–2). The 1919 Amritsar Massacre, when British-led soldiers fired repeatedly on a peaceful crowd gathering to protest against proposed restrictions on civil liberties in the Rowlatt bills, aroused deep distrust of the British and widespread popular anger, and prompted the 1920–2 non-cooperation campaign which mobilized thousands of students to carry out an educational boycott, many prominent lawyers to boycott the law courts and the mass of ordinary people to boycott British cloth and engage in public demonstrations (Chandra, 1989: 184–90).

Well-publicized incidents of violent repression of unarmed demonstrators can have a significant influence on previously uncommitted third parties, and can mobilize international public opinion, leading to forms of diplomatic pressure, exclusions from international bodies or even economic sanctions. For example, the reporting by foreign journalists of the 1991 Dili massacre of East Timorese demonstrators by Indonesian troops led to international condemnation (see Chapter 7).

Gene Sharp (2005: 406–13) has suggested that the multiple potential impacts of violent repression can act as form of 'political jiu-jitsu', changing the overall balance of political forces. Sharp makes clear that not all acts of brutal repression have these effects, and Brian Martin in his theory of 'backfire' has examined the various devices regimes can use to minimize outrage over their repression, for example perpetrating torture, rape and killing in secret when public protests are over, intimidating activists and witnesses, distorting information that does emerge and justifying their reaction by vilifying the protesters, or mitigating widespread outrage by official measures, such as enquiries, that simulate concern to prevent further brutalities (Martin, 2007: 169–204). Sometimes the regime may decide that some loss of legitimacy and international condemnation is worthwhile if ruthlessness is likely to suppress resistance, as in China in 1989 or Burma in 2007. A key factor is how dependent the regime is on wider international support (see Chapter 7).

Some guerrilla campaigns have mobilized considerable support among the wider population or at an international level, because their cause was widely seen as just, but also because their own violence was usually discriminate. This was certainly true in South Africa after 1961. Marxism–Leninism, which has influenced many twentieth-century armed movements, has at a theoretical level opposed 'terrorism' as a tactic, in contrast to mobilization of mass power. Guevara (2009: 28–9) stresses the role of sabotage and condemns indiscriminate terrorism, though he condones selective assassination of a prominent 'leader of the oppressive forces who is known for his cruelty'. Urban guerrilla warfare has, however, quite often included bomb attacks on civilians seen as supporters of the regime, as in Algeria.

But even guerrilla campaigns which target civilians can win wider support if their enemy deploys ruthless repression, because in most contexts the scale of military violence used by the regime so outstrips the level of violence used by the guerrillas, that the moral balance is tipped towards the resistance. Fanon (1965: 70) suggests this when he insists there is no equivalence in the violence: 'for machine-gunning from aeroplanes and bombardments from the fleet go far beyond in horror and magnitude any answer the natives can make'. The disparity in the technology and destructiveness of force used by the regime is likely to be most pronounced if a major imperial power is trying to repress a poor primarily agricultural nation. But it is inherent in the logic of guerrilla warfare that the regime always starts out much better armed. Thus atrocities perpetrated by the regime are always liable to mobilize international sympathy on behalf of the armed resistance.

Guerrilla warfare and scales of destruction

Nevertheless, guerrilla warfare, by its very logic, can easily result in extreme savagery and many thousands of deaths and injuries on both sides. Fanon (1965: 70) suggests that there is an inevitable cycle of 'terror, counter-terror, violence, counter-violence' and a 'circle of hate'. Schell argues that 'people's war' represented one response to the tendency, identified by Clausewitz, for war to run to logical extremes. Whereas the Western development of the ultimately destructive technologies of nuclear weapons promoted political stalemate, poor peasants in Asia and Africa were developing their own methods of guerrilla warfare 'that, in their own way, were scarcely less absolute' and politically a great deal more effective in changing the map of the world (Schell, 2004: 63–4). Schell briefly examines the evolution of guerrilla warfare, from the armed popular resistance in Spain, met by ruthless French reprisals, through nineteenth-century colonial wars, the Chinese communist struggle, and Algeria to Vietnam. He concludes that people's war marked one extreme of violence.

Schell's main focus is on guerrilla resistance by the very poor to the armed might of Western states, in particular Vietnam. The defeat of the French at Dien Bien Phu in 1954 could be seen as vindicating Giap's guerrilla strategy. But the period of active US involvement from the mid-1960s to the early 1970s involved mobilizing half a million American troops, unprecedented use of bombing as well as napalm, herbicides and 'free fire zones', and embraced not only North and South Vietnam but also Laos and Cambodia. Estimates of civilian casualties and deaths among the National Liberation Front fighters due to US military action vary, but run into hundreds of thousands. American, North Vietnamese and South Vietnamese military casualties were also high. In addition the prolonged struggle resulted in savage acts of violence by both the Saigon government and troops, and by the National Liberation Front, which is accused of systematic killing of about 10,000 village elders to make an internal takeover easier (Laqueur, 1978: 104).

It might seem plausible that guerrilla warfare strictly within nation states (as opposed to participation in a wider anti-imperial struggle) can be less cruelly destructive. This is not necessarily true, as the prolonged struggle by the Tamil Tigers in Sri Lanka, which involved ruthless levels of force and intimidation by both sides, and ended only in 2010, illustrates. But in Sri Lanka there has been an intractable conflict between two opposed ethnic communities. The Sandinista struggle in Nicaragua against President Somoza is a better advertisement for a guerrilla strategy and a genuine example of 'people's war'. Despite many early setbacks, and a period of factional internal divisions, between 1977 and 1979 the growing civilian opposition to Somoza was the background for intensified guerrilla attacks that ousted the dictatorship in July 1979. But it is estimated that, even in this relatively small country, guerrilla warfare resulted in at least 30,000 deaths (Grynspan, 1991: 100).

There is a scenario in which guerrilla warfare can minimize levels of violence by both sides: an 'ideal type' of 'people's war', which swings the great majority of the population against an increasingly discredited regime, that begins to crumble from within. The overthrow of Batista in Cuba approximates to this model. The guerrillas in the mountains managed to gain local peasant support, partly by stimulating the local economy and guaranteeing to buy peasant crops, and some of the middle class changed allegiance. The guerrillas were helped (as noted earlier) by an underground movement among the Cuban military against Batista and the urban worker resistance (Wolf, 1973: 270–3). So, although the rebel army has been estimated as at most 2,000 men, the regime disintegrated.

Options for guerrillas who fail: a turn towards unarmed resistance?

Guerrilla groups do, however, quite often fail to attain their objectives. In an anti-imperial struggle maintaining resistance may result eventually in a change of policy or regime in the imperial state – disillusionment with the fighting in the Portuguese colonies encouraged the opposition to internal dictatorship that led to the 1974 'Revolution of the Carnations'. But in other contexts final victory may seem remote or impossible. Guerrilla groups have then a number of options. The most negative is to turn towards organized crime, such as drugs, as has happened in some parts of Latin America. But most have maintained political objectives. Some struggling for political independence for ethnic groups in border regions or islands have continued resistance for decades despite severe repression, as some minority ethnic groups in Burma have done. Other have had to scale down their objectives and the scope of their struggle, as the Naxalites in India have done (see Chapter 7). Most interestingly, a significant number of guerrilla movements have decided either to work with unarmed resistance movements or to experiment at least provisionally with a civil resistance campaign, or to recast their strategy as primarily one of unarmed rather than armed resistance.

The option of combining continued low levels of guerrilla tactics, such as sabotage, with people power was adopted by the African National Congress (ANC) in South Africa. The ANC had failed to move beyond what it aptly labelled 'armed propaganda' (which had been deliberately restricted in its initial stages to sabotage of installations to avoid killing innocent civilians) to genuine 'people's war'. It was, however, able to work with an upsurge of people power in the trade unions and the townships in the 1980s, and did so by attacking the police and targets of the township campaigns, such as rent offices (Lodge, 2009: 229).

The strategic option of abandoning (at least temporarily) armed struggle in a particular area and joining with unarmed political groups engaged in civil resistance was tried in Palestine in the late 1980s. Although the First Intifada initially brought substantial political gains and led to serious negotiations designed to create a Palestinian state, when the Second Intifada broke out in 2001 the proponents of unarmed struggle were sidelined (partly due to the brutal reaction of Israeli security forces to initial protests) and the struggle was violent more or less from the outset. Nevertheless, some forms of civil resistance have continued to take place (see Chapter 7).

In Nepal the turn to people power appears to have worked. Maoist guerrillas, disillusioned with political corruption and a failure to address major economic and social problems of the poor, especially in the countryside, built up their base in rural Nepal during the 1990s. But they decided to combine with the organized unarmed resistance in urban centres in a campaign of strictly civil resistance in 2006 to overthrow the increasingly autocratic monarchy. (There was a precedent for effective people power in the 1990 Movement for the Restoration of Democracy in which workers, housewives and professional people successfully – in the short term – demanded that the king end the ban on political parties and revise the constitution; Schock, 2005: 123–5.) The 2006 people power uprising won and created a new constitution, a peace agreement with the guerrillas was reached, and the guerrilla movement ran in the elections to the new assembly (Vishwakarma, 2006; Vanaik, 2008). However, illustrating the problems of combining unarmed and armed struggle, the issue of disbanding the guerrilla forces has continued to create problems within Nepalese politics up to the time of writing. The strategic switch in the 1990s by the East Timorese movement for independence from Indonesia away from guerrilla tactics to civil resistance also achieved its goal (see Chapter 7).

A less dramatic, but interesting, example was the decision in 2005 by the Sahrawi resisters to the occupation of Western Sahara by Morocco to move away from an externally led guerrilla campaign to civil resistance (Stephan and Mundy, 2006: 1–32; Zunes and Mundy, 2011). A similar process of changing strategy is apparently being attempted in Kashmir, where Muslims turned in 2008 to a campaign of unarmed resistance, documented by Booker Prize winning novelist Arundhati Roy, who was threatened in 2010 with arrest for sedition after challenging the view that Kashmir is an integral part of India (Roy, 2009: 163–77; Chamberlain, 2010: 19). A jailed former freedom fighter declared in 2008, 'we have sacrificed an entire generation ... now there is no option but to fight peacefully' (Jaleel, 2008). Two years later, a continuing 'intifada' in which young boys threw stones at the security forces, who often shoot at them, and women defied the Indian-imposed curfew to protest, was reported by an Indian journalist (Boga, 2010: 46–7).

Disparity in weapons and resources between guerrillas and the regime, and cumulative suffering are key arguments for considering an unarmed strategy. For example, hunter-gatherers in the jungles of West Papua, New Guinea, armed mainly with bows and arrows, spears and a few captured AK 47 rifles, have been holding out for 40 years against the occupying Indonesian army. Human rights sources estimate that up to 200,000 West Papuans have been killed by

Indonesian security forces since 1963 (Groom, 2009: 24–5). Against this background, and experience of localized nonviolent campaigns a movement towards greater use of unarmed resistance is now developing (MacLeod, 2009; 2010).

Terrorism versus people power?

The rapid increase in movements of civil resistance in the decades since the 1980s, quite a few of which have culminated as successful people power, and evidence of some guerrilla groups turning towards an unarmed strategy might appear to signal a trend towards less violent modes of resistance. But that interpretation is contradicted by the rise of a new form of guerrilla terrorism, epitomized by the attack on the Twin Towers in 2001 and the bombings in Madrid and London. Whilst these attacks could be seen as a new form of resistance to Western imperialism, the indiscriminate and savage nature of some Islamic guerrilla attacks within the Islamic states of Iraq and Pakistan suggests a conscious commitment to a Clausewitzian logic of total violence.

The strand of 'terrorism' loosely associated with Al Qaeda, is qualitatively different from the earlier concept of people's war. It is also quite distinct from 'armed propaganda' – targeted attacks designed to demonstrate resistance and raise morale, but avoiding unnecessary loss of life, especially among civilian bystanders. The extremist version of guerrilla tactics suggests willingness to rely on acquiescence through fear and on the technology of destruction, rather than on mobilizing widespread support.

The nature of guerrilla resistance is influenced by the changing global context. Guerrilla warfare against old fashioned colonial regimes that had established political and military rule over the territories they controlled could mobilize the people against clear targets and achieve the withdrawal of both political and military rule. Where imperial policies are based on establishing strategic military reach through alliance with compliant local ruling elites, and on influencing the style of internal government, guerrilla tactics need to adapt.

Nevertheless, a minority of those who resort to guerrilla tactics, influenced by their ideological extremism, are potentially illustrating that guerrilla warfare can be a form of total war – not by the breadth of their active support, but by the scope of the destruction they may be willing to inflict, and their refusal to distinguish between specific opponents and ordinary civilians. Those embracing the concept of guerrilla struggle are therefore faced with two extreme choices: to turn people's war into people power, or to seek maximum destruction. There are still in-between options for national or local struggles with genuine popular support and ways of responding to the new global context – the Zapatistas are an obvious example (see Chapter 7).

However, many global trends are promoting the political effectiveness as well as the moral appeal of unarmed people power. There is certainly evidence that repressive regimes have looked with alarm at the example of the 'colour' revolutions in the former Soviet bloc. The head of the Islamic Revolutionary Guard Corps in Iran has apparently studied how to combat 'velvet revolutions' and commented that preventing such a revolution is the Guards' top priority (Milani, 2009: 11). But the most striking choice between the present forms of extremist Islamic terrorism and changing the political map by unarmed and cooperative movements of people power is being played out in the Middle East in 2011. The unarmed uprisings in Tunisia and Egypt in January 2011, which sparked further movements across the Middle East, demonstrate the amazing appeal and potential of people rising collectively to demand greater democratic control.

3 People power and changing theories of revolution

Since the upsurge in popular protests against rigged elections and corrupt regimes after 2000, it has become common to describe them as 'revolutions', often with a catchy label attached. Some of these uprisings have, however, resulted only in limited political change. New theoretical debates about the meaning of revolution have been provoked in particular by the fall of Soviet-style Communist Party regimes across Eastern Europe in 1989, in the Baltic states of the USSR in 1988–91, and also (less well-known) in the Soviet satellite state Mongolia in 1989–90. These popular uprisings invited comparisons with 1848, but also seemed to demand new categories. The events of 1989 are also of particular importance in demonstrating the potential of people power and promoting the concept of 'nonviolent revolution'. The rebellions sweeping across the Middle East in the 'Arab Spring' of early 2011 are the latest major manifestation of popular unarmed resistance (with the exception of Libya from March 2011), but at the time of writing the immediate outcomes were in many cases unclear, and their long-term revolutionary significance even more so.

Historically revolutions have been seen as the outcome of internal civil war, or pictured as crowds with weapons in their hands storming the central symbols of the regime's domination. Participants in would-be revolutions have assumed that they would need to take up arms or defend the barricades, and intellectuals advocating revolution have disagreed about strategy and end goals, but usually envisaged an eventual violent struggle. Academic theorists of revolution writing before 1989 have also often seen armed force as central. John Dunn surveying twentieth-century 'revolutions' in eight countries argued that mass violence was 'one of the key indicators' of what a revolution is (Dunn, 1989: ix–xi).

The predominantly or totally nonviolent character of the transfer of power in many recent 'revolutions' has led to a number of responses. One response is to accept that changing historical circumstances lead to changes in the nature of revolution, including the role of violence. Reflecting on comparative studies of late twentieth-century revolutions, both armed and unarmed, Ted Gurr and Jack Goldstone conclude that, although the role of violence is central to most definitions, the evidence of their case studies (mostly before 1989) suggests 'that this is a misplaced emphasis'. They argue that these studies indicate that revolutions can occur 'without substantial resort to deadly force' and that even when violence is used it need not be 'of high magnitude' (Gurr and Goldstone, 1991: 338–9).

A starting point for reinterpretation, partially developed in the literature on civil resistance, is to ask whether the centrality of violence in earlier revolutions is a misperception, and to undertake a new 'reading' of some of the 'great revolutions' such as America in the 1770s, France in the 1780s and Russia in 1905 and 1917 (Sharp, 1973; Schell, 2004; Conser et al., 1986). This reinterpretation relates in particular to growing resistance before the overthrow of a regime and the nature of the overthrow. Why the later stages of the revolutionary process have often involved armed conflict and terror raises wider questions about the nature of revolution and about changing historical contexts.

Indeed, a second response to nonviolent revolutions is to ask whether they can truly be revolutions, particularly if an element of negotiation and elite cooperation is involved in the transfer of power. Timothy Garton Ash provisionally coined the term 'refolution' when first considering Poland and Hungary in 1989 – although 20 years later surveying 1989 and its aftermath he suggested a model of 'velvet revolution' opposed to the French and Russian model (Garton Ash, 1989; 2009b). Some of the arguments for and against interpreting 1989 as revolutionary are examined in this chapter.

One model of revolution which 1989 did at least partially exemplify is that propounded by Hannah Arendt, who celebrated the American and French Revolutions of the eighteenth century and also February 1917 in Russia, as embodying within them a brief experience of public political action and capacity for spontaneous organization, although this positive element of revolution was soon overwhelmed by other political and economic forces and almost totally forgotten. Arendt in some of her other writings has also recognized the potential of nonviolent resistance.

Commentators on 1989 have, however, queried whether the nonviolent nature of the revolutions, and disposition to compromise, led to some of the subsequent disappointments, and whether a harsher justice should have been exacted. This approach is often summed up in a memorable phrase coined by Ernest Gellner, 'the price of velvet' (Gellner, 1995).

The French and Russian Revolutions have suggested other key characteristics of 'true' revolutions. One is their degree of utopianism and the role of messianic visions. Utopianism can – though it need not – be expressed through ideologies sanctioning violence to achieve ideal goals. Utopian elements were present in 1989, but were submerged by subsequent political and economic developments. The other key issue is class conflict, which is linked to the socio-economic goals of revolution. Class conflict can explain some of the violence used by revolutionaries and the need for defensive violence against subsequent reaction by the deposed classes within the state and their allies at an international level. This dimension was almost totally absent in 1989.

But the virtually bloodless revolutions of 1989–91 (apart from Romania) provided only one model of the unarmed overthrow of regimes. By contrast the Iranian revolution of 1978–9 involved much greater bloodshed by the regime, and stronger expressions of hatred in the chants and actions of the protesters. The actual process of overthrowing the Shah followed a model of mass popular revolution reminiscent of 1789 in France, but it has raised puzzles for revolutionary theory. Revolution is associated with modernization, but the Islamic fundamentalist style of government created in 1979 can be interpreted as a reaction against the previous elite programme of Western-style modernization – although the new regime did adopt modernizing elements (Parker, 1999: 41). Foucault (1990) was struck by the religious framework of the unfolding drama.

Clarifying terminology: revolution, *coups d'état* and rebellion

The concept of revolution is clearly open to conflicting interpretations. But at a minimum it implies a change of political regime, for example from monarchy or dictatorship to a constitutional parliamentary state, or from imperial control to national self-government, not simply a change of government within a regime. It also implies more than a return to the previous political order. The overthrow of the Marcos dictatorship, for example, can be interpreted as a reversion to elite-style politics. It has been described as: 'almost a "bloodless" revolution ... but it also proved ... to be less a revolution than restoration of the ancient regime' (Kessler, 1991: 212). Revolution also suggests some significant change (or at least aspiration for change) in the social conditions of the people as a whole and their collective values and self-image.

Whether the term revolution is used primarily in terms of the overthrow of a regime, or to encompass longer-term results, influences interpretations. It also influences other choice of terminology. If the focus is on the long-term political and social results of regime change, then even major political revolutions, as in England in the 1640s and France after 1789, were followed by a form of counter-revolution and a return to monarchy, though both had major repercussions upon public attitudes and the evolution of politics over subsequent decades. From a long-term perspective it is even possible since 1991 to query how far October 1917 in Russia was a successful revolution (Parker, 1999: 2).

Moreover, if the emphasis in on political, social and economic developments after the overthrow of a regime, some *coups d'état*, for example the 1952 seizure of power by a group of military officers that created Colonel Nasser's new republican regime in Egypt, do qualify as revolutions. On the other hand, if the focus is on the actual means of achieving a transfer of political power, a *coup d'état* can be seen as the polar opposite of genuine revolution achieved through a mass popular uprising. It is this latter interpretation of coup that is adopted here – though subject to qualifications and ambiguities in relation to particular historical examples.

Many *coups d'état* have been carried out directly by the military: Napoleon Bonaparte dispersing the legislature in 1799, and General Pinochet's coup against the democratically elected Marxist government of President Allende in Chile in 1973, are two of a long list of possible examples. Quite often coups are carried out by groups within the armed forces, and by lower-level officers, for example the coup by the Greek Colonels in 1967. Levels of potential support for a coup within the broader population vary considerably: there had, for example, been significant agitation against Allende between 1970 and 1973. *Coups d'état* do not always involve actual use of military force – the July 1952 coup in Egypt occurred without violence or bloodshed, for example – but they do always invoke the threat of violence if there is resistance. But, if the archetype of a coup is a plot by a small group within the military to seize power by force of arms, it is most clearly brought into relief by examples of successful popular resistance to such attempts: the defeat of the Kapp Putsch in the Weimar Republic in Germany in 1920; the prevention of Algeria-based generals seizing power in mainland France in 1961; and (much more contestably) in deflecting the attempt by groups in the security services and Party from deposing Gorbachev in Russia in 1991 (Roberts, 1975; Gorbachev, 1991; Steele, 1994; Varney and Martin, 2000).

This clear-cut distinction has, however, sometimes been more blurred. Whether October 1917 was really a revolution or a Bolshevik coup is one much debated example, although it is sometimes listed as incontrovertibly a *coup d'état* (Leiden and Schmitt, 1973: 22). A 'coup' that was closer to a mutiny by junior officers, and greeted with immediate mass popular support, was the 'revolution of the carnations' in Portugal in 1974, which can be seen as a version of people power (Maxwell, 2009). Even the now classic example of people power, the overthrow of President Marcos in the Philippines, is beset by debates about the role of the defence minister, General Juan Enrile (see Chapter 2). Some coups have also included encouragement of street demonstrations: a well-known example is the coup against Prime Minister Mossadeq in Iran in 1953, largely engineered by the US and British secret intelligence services (as confirmed by released CIA records) in 'Operation Ajax' (Kinzer, 2003). Even some recent examples of mass protest against rigged elections (the 'colour revolutions' in ex-Soviet states in particular) have been interpreted by some on the left as disguised 'coups' promoted by US governmental manipulation (see Chapter 7).

It is also necessary to distinguish revolution from revolt. A famous distinction arises from the comment on the fall of the Bastille by Louis XVI, 'It is a revolt,' and the response by the Duc de Rochfoucauld-Liancour, 'No, Sire, it is a revolution.' The latter suggests both the difficulty of quelling the popular unrest and the desire for fundamental political and social change involved. For the purposes of this book, revolt or rebellion (the terms can be exchangeable) is taken to signify acts of open defiance challenging the authority of dominant groups and social institutions. There can be individual rebels or small groups who promote a rebellious cause, but in the context of people power it refers to politically significant numbers taking action. Rebellion has in the past sometimes been directed against dominant classes or abuses of government, rather than the government itself, as in some medieval peasant uprisings. But rebellion can also describe attempts to topple a government or regime.

Uprising – although in some historical examples it has tragic connotations, as in the 1916 Easter uprising in Ireland or the uprising in the Warsaw Ghetto – is effectively a synonym for a political revolt. It is also used for unarmed mass resistance, as in the 1953 East German uprising (Ebert 1969). Similarly, insurrection can be used neutrally to denote either armed or unarmed rebellion – although 'insurgency' has overtones of guerrilla warfare, as in 'counter-insurgency' manuals.

These terms can be deliberately used to embody a particular political and philosophical position. For example, Albert Camus, in his exploration of types of rebellion in *L'homme revolté* (The Rebel), distinguishes towards the end of the book between revolution, which claims to represent historical forces and to remake man, and rebellion 'which is the refusal to be treated as an object and to be reduced to simple historical terms' (Camus, 1962: 216). Max Stirner, the egoist anarchist philosopher, also distinguished between revolution and insurrection: the former is a collective political act aiming at new political arrangements, and the latter is an expression of individual freedom (Stirner, 1977: 167). These distinctions can be used to critique past revolutions, but are not pursued here. The specifically Gandhian interpretation of 'nonviolent revolution', which includes building up decentralized communal structures from below – attempted for example by Gandhians in Bihar in the 1970s – raises issues too wide ranging to include in this chapter.

Rebellions often start in response to specific injustices and demands for reforms, but, if reform is not forthcoming, or reform measures are then subverted by privileged groups, the rebels may become radicalized and make revolutionary demands, as in the Flanders rebellion that united peasants and many groups in the main cities in the period 1325–8 (Te Brake, 1993). Some rebellions have embraced radical egalitarian goals and significant regime change from the outset, as in the great peasant uprisings in Russia. The seventeenth-century rising, led by Cossack Stenka Razin, was backed by peasants seeking the overthrow of serfdom and the reclamation of their land, and Pugachev's rebellion of the eighteenth century directly challenged the Tsarist state (Rude, 1980; Wolf, 1973). So some major rebellions can also be seen as failed attempts at revolution. A good example is the Taiping Rebellion of 1850–64, which won widespread support in southern China and captured cities such as Wuhan and Nanjing, which became the capital of the 'Heavenly Kingdom of Great Peace'. The ideology of the rebellion (fostered by a version of evangelical Christianity) rejected both the Manchu emperors and Chinese cultural traditions, and promoted primitive communism, social ownership of land and radically egalitarian views on the role of women (Spence, 1996; Gray, 1990: 52–76). The Chinese communists have unsurprisingly celebrated it as a precursor of their own more modern revolution.

The dominant narrative of revolutionary violence

The dominant narrative has, until recently, linked rebellion and revolution almost indissolubly to violence by the rebels and a military response by their opponents. At least three reasons can be adduced. The first is that there is a significant historical basis for this association. In Western Europe, for example, the aristocracy, as a military class with their own bands of armed retainers, naturally turned to war when defending their own privileges or overthrowing a monarch for dynastic reasons. Peasant revolts tended to follow this model, with peasants coming together to swear a common oath and elect 'a captain of the host', and major revolts often had (a sometimes pseudonymous) rebel general. Prolonged and widely supported revolts that challenged the ruling elite often ended in battles in which the rebels were bloodily suppressed. In the case of the major modern revolutions, the 1640s revolution in England ended in destructive civil war, the revolution in America culminated in a war of independence, the French and Russian (October) Revolutions led to civil and international war, and the Chinese revolution involved prolonged guerrilla warfare against both the Nationalist government and the Japanese invaders and became after 1946 a civil war.

A second reason for associating rebellion and revolution with violence is, however, that the historical record has often been distorted. The violence of peasant rebellions in Western Europe has been greatly exaggerated by hostile aristocratic or clerical chroniclers, shocked by the threat to the existing 'order'. They are, moreover, the main sources. A well-known example is Jean Froissart's alarming chronicle of revolts, especially the 'jacquerie', in fourteenth-century France. A few clerical chroniclers did, however, show more empathy with the rebels (Cohn, 2004: 14). In the modern age, Edmund Burke's *Reflections on the Revolution in France*, and later images of riotous sans-culottes and the guillotine, reflect the alarmed response of the upper classes to the events unfolding in Paris. Popular rebellion in this version of history is associated with irrational and bloodthirsty mobs, and overlooks the degree of political organization, the specific demands formulated, the breadth of social support quite often evinced at the time, and elements of unarmed resistance.

A third reason for linking popular revolt against the ruling authorities with violence stems from the obverse side of the ideological coin, the tendency of radical intellectuals and popular memory to romanticize individuals leading rebellions or going off to fight in wars of liberation (Garibaldi and Byron, for example), and heroic revolutionary confrontations. In the nineteenth century armed students and workers erecting barricades symbolized youthful idealism, the struggle for individual or national freedom and desperate courage – associations which carried over to the unarmed students in Paris, who also created barricades against the riot police in 1968. In this iconography of rebellion and revolution the heroism lies primarily in the willingness of the rebels to die and to face unequal odds – taking up arms demonstrates this commitment. Images associated with the great modern revolutions are also images of violence, for example storming the Bastille or the Winter Palace. Depictions and accounts of the storming of the Bastille were romantically exaggerated in the nineteenth century, whilst the Soviet film *October*, which reconstructed the 'storming' of the Winter Palace in Petrograd, probably resulted in more (accidental) deaths than the real events (Cobban, 1961: 146–7; Schell 2004: 177–8). In some cases, revolutionary regimes have promoted heroic founding myths, for example the presentation of the 'Long March' in China.

Reinterpreting the role of violence in past revolutions

The key issue for this discussion is how far the major modern revolutions, which have been central to revolutionary theory and a standard of comparison for 1989, really depended on armed violence. The alternative thesis here is that in the process of making revolution, as opposed to later stages of consolidation, the 'force' of numbers (people power), often backed by popular organization, has tended to be more important than the extent of physical force or armed violence, which has in some cases been subsequently much exaggerated. (Since China was discussed in the previous chapter it is excluded here.)

Given the immense amount of research and ideological and academic reinterpretation invested in the major revolutions, brief commentary risks serious over-simplification. But there is a solid factual basis for an alternative emphasis on the significant role of people power and unarmed protest. The growing agitation over a number of years that preceded the final confrontation in both England in the seventeenth century and America in the eighteenth provide well-known examples of refusal to pay unconstitutional taxes, civil disobedience and political non-cooperation. In both cases political institutions claiming independence from royal domination promoted resistance and created the basis for a new order: in England, Parliament (especially the Commons) led the struggle against autocracy with some backing from the City of London and the courts; in America, the rebels built on the colonial framework to create their own congresses and governments and in 1774 formed a new independent 'United States'. In both countries political opposition ranged from wealthy merchants to artisans. Therefore in both it can be argued that the political revolution had taken place before the fighting started. Parliamentary demands for a new constitutional understanding were summarized in the Nineteen Articles presented to the King in 1642 – the 'revolution before the revolution' (Vallance, 2009: 139 citing Cressy, 2006: 426). John Adams, writing to Thomas Jefferson on 24 August 1815, observed: 'The revolution was in the minds of the people, and this was effected from 1760 to 1775 ... before a drop of blood was shed at Lexington' (Adams, 1856). Both Schell and Arendt cite Adams's view that the revolution was completed before the war began (Schell: 2004: 160; Arendt, 1973: 118).

Schell claims that the war that broke out in 1775 was a war in defence of the new United States; this is reasonably plausible, though it ignores the elements of civil war also involved. In the case of England, it was indisputably a civil war with a cross-section of social support on both sides, and greatly complicated by the intertwining of religious and political issues within England (where passions had also been heightened in response to a Catholic rebellion in Ireland) and by the Presbyterian revolt in Scotland. Parker classifies the English revolution as the last 'Reformation revolt', rather than (as in Marxist interpretations) the first bourgeois revolution, but sees its revolutionary aspect in the impact 'upon structures of authority and rule (Parker, 1999: 28).

In its early stages the French Revolution, which began as a confrontation between sections of the aristocracy and clergy with the king, but evolved into professional and commercial classes representing the 'third estate' demanding the regime to resolve their grievances, had parallels with the parliamentary rebellion in the English Revolution. But the Estates General, summoned for the first time in over 150 years in 1779, did not have the institutional strength of the English Parliament and early contestation centred on the role of the third estate within it, so constitutional struggle was rapidly overtaken by the momentum of popular agitation. The French Revolution had more obvious links to the American, not only in time and because of mutual military or diplomatic support, but in terms of common ideas such as declarations of rights. Both came to represent republicanism and political equality against royal rule and social hierarchy, although their later political and social trajectory was very different.

But the French Revolution has most often been seen as a template for the Russian Revolutions of 1917, by intellectuals in Russia (most notably Trotsky) and subsequent analysts. Indeed, if we focus initially on the overthrow of the regimes, the French Revolution did contain elements that were to be central to the Russian Revolution of February 1917. Women demanding bread, in a context of economic chaos, precipitated the mass popular march on Versailles in October 1779 and the crowd carrying the king and queen back to Paris as virtual prisoners. Women demanding bread on 23 February 1917 precipitated the outbreak of the revolution in Petrograd. In both, large crowds of ordinary people demonstrating in the streets ignited the revolution and the armed forces, whom the regime needed to use to suppress the growing revolt, were liable to join forces with the people. For example, rebellious French Guards sided with the Parisians surrounding the Bastille and secured five cannons to train on the fortress – though the French members of the garrison of the Bastille, who were in Michelet's words ashamed of killing civilians and 'shedding French blood', and their demoralized commander surrendered before the cannons were used (Michelet, 1847: 142–60).

Mutiny by regiments in Petrograd refusing to put down the demonstrations was much more central in Russia in February 1917, and organized workers in Russia also played a much larger role than the artisans in France (Trotsky, 1959: 119–27). Another crucial difference was in the role of the peasantry. In France the peasants effectively accomplished their own revolution in the countryside in 1789, but there was almost no connection between the peasants and the urban leaders of the opposition either in the elections to the Estates General or in later policy making, and urban and rural agitation were distinct. In Russia the peasants played a crucial role in the cities as well, because the great majority of the army were peasants in uniform.

Developments in 1917 were strongly influenced by the almost year-long 'revolution' of 1905, involving general strikes and mutinies in the navy and army, when workers and peasants had created a network of independent soviets (councils) which became a parallel form of government in a system of 'dual power'. Indeed, a number of analysts of revolution in Russia have argued that 1905 was the beginning of a revolutionary process that culminated in 1917, key differences being the attitudes within the elite to the maintenance of tsarism and the role of the army (Donald, 2001: 41–54). Faced with a largely spontaneous revolution from below, the Duma (parliament) moved swiftly on 27 February 1917 to create a provisional government based largely on the liberal parties, while various socialist groups resurrected the Petrograd soviet. Once a new provisional government had been formed in the capital, revolution spread to the provinces, taking the form of mass demonstrations and the rapid forming of public committees in parallel with soviets of workers and soldiers. The Tsar capitulated quickly once the army command collaborated with the new government. Both in Petrograd and throughout much of the country the revolution involved virtually no violence. Rex Wade notes that in most of the provincial cities and towns almost the whole population seemed to be 'ranged against a handful of impotent old officials' and there was often a 'festive air'. But in some places, such as Tver, there was serious violence against political officials and military officers (Wade, 2008: 50). Schell quotes from the Russian independent radical Social Democrat N.N. Sukhanov, who wrote an eye-witness history of the revolution, a source for all subsequent historians, including Trotsky. Sukhanov marvels that the revolution occurred 'with a fabulous ease' (Schell, 2004: 170).

The literature on nonviolent action has given weight to the 'revolution' of 1905, celebrated within the socialist tradition by Trotsky and Rosa Luxemburg, as predominantly an example of prolonged civil resistance, though it ended in an abortive attempt at an armed uprising (Ackerman and Duvall, 2000: 13–59; Sharp, 2005: 71–89). The significance of 1905 within the tradition of unarmed resistance, apart from its intrinsically impressive scale, duration and revolutionary potential, is its impact on Gandhi (who launched his civilian disobedience campaign in South Africa a year later) and the emphasis given to it by one of the first analysts of civil resistance, Bart de Ligt (1989: 119–20). But, as Schell notes, 27 February is an even more remarkable example of 'people power' sweeping away a regime which had lost the support of virtually all the people.

Demonstrating the relatively bloodless character of the overthrow of some earlier regimes obviously does not mean that consolidating a new order was equally lacking in bloodshed. The linkage between revolutions and extensive violence is often associated with the need to oppose counter-revolution, as well as moves towards more extreme policies and repression within the new regime. Assessing the costs of revolution depends on what subsequent developments are seen as logical extensions of the revolution: Goldstone, for instance, noting that revolutions often lead to civil and international wars, includes not only the French Revolutionary but also the Napoleonic Wars when citing the 1.3 million French deaths out of a population of 26 million (Goldstone, 1991: 477).

The comparative lack of armed force needed to topple the regime, as contrasted with the scale of subsequent death, destruction and terror is particularly marked in the case of the October 1917 Revolution in Russia. The overthrow of the Provisional Government based in Petrograd occurred with relative ease because the Petrograd Soviet already had widespread support in and control over the city and the great majority of the troops – Trotsky specifically appealed to the soldiers at the St Peter and Paul Fortress, and they chose to side with the soviet when the government belatedly tried to clamp down. Despite the confrontations between armed workers, when capturing key points throughout the city, and the few troops remaining loyal to the government, when the Petrograd Soviet formally proclaimed the overthrow of the government on 25 October no serious fighting had taken place. Most of the Provisional Government were still isolated in the Winter Palace, nominally defended by loyal troops, but these began to melt away and the rest were progressively disarmed by Red Guards and supporting soldiers and sailors. Eventually groups of the besieging forces entered the palace and arrested the members of the government (Wade, 2008: 241). The extension of the October Revolution to the rest of Russia occurred gradually, in some cases easily, but in others bitterly contested and involving serious fighting, as in Moscow, where at least several hundred died (Wade, 2008: 253–4). Nevertheless, the major violence associated with the October Revolution took place after the Bolsheviks had seized power.

The October Revolution, the subsequent Bolshevik seizure of control, the outbreak of civil war initiated by sections of the military and the right, the external intervention of governments of major states anxious to contain a potentially international revolutionary movement, and attempts to promote such an international revolution, resembled the descent of the revolution in France into civil war and international military intervention and the Jacobin terror. It is these two scenarios that have strongly influenced subsequent interpretations of the nature of a true revolution.

1989: new revolutionary model?

Can revolution be nonviolent?

Some commentators, especially at the time, seized on parallels between 1989 and earlier revolutions. Jurgen Habermas, for example, did discern clear parallels between 1989 and 1789, not only in terms of dominant ideas and ideals, but in terms of the process of achieving a revolutionary overthrow. He stressed the importance of mass action in both cases and compared the popular anger against the Bastille with the popular revulsion against the security forces of the communist states. Later in the same article he argued that 1989 used the methods from a familiar repertoire of modern revolutions. 'The presence of large masses gathering in squares and mobilizing on the streets managed, astoundingly, to disempower a regime that was armed to the teeth' (Habermas, 1990: 9). He also suggested that the severing of Communist Party monopoly of political control could be compared metaphorically with the beheading of Louis XVI. Others drew comparisons between 1989 and the revolutionary wave of 1848–9. Sakwa, however, has suggested that 'the closest analogy' would be February 1917, citing 'unified and good natured crowds' and the minimal use of force (Sakwa, 2001: 172).

However, the dissolution of communist regimes across Eastern Europe in 1989, which (with the exception of Romania, where the security police soon played a murky but key role) was accomplished without the demonstrators in general using any physical violence (let alone weapons), struck many participants and spectators as either a remarkable innovation in the history of revolutions, or else as proof that these events were not truly revolutionary. Janusz Ziolkowski, for example, argued that 1989–90 heralded a new revolutionary tradition, based on 'respect for nonviolence, the rule of law and even a degree of forgiveness for those who have abused power. It is the tradition of Gandhi, Martin Luther King, Lech Walesa and Vaclav Havel' (Ziolkowski, 1990: 46). He also emphasized that the 1980–1 Polish Solidarity Movement, which mobilized 10 million people and could be seen as prefiguring the events of 1989, was 'that historical contradiction in terms: "peaceful revolution"' (ibid.: 56). The Stasi (secret police) and party officials in East Germany feared by December 1989 they might be murdered by angry crowds, whom they had plundered and repressed, but these fears were based on rumours and the precedent of Hungary in 1956 (Dale, 2006: 166–70).

In 1989 the most dramatic image was of East Germans peacefully breaking through the Berlin Wall into West Berlin on 9 November (an estimated three million crossed in the first few days), and thousands taking axes to that symbol of the ideological and political division of Europe (Partos, 1993: 246). This was reminiscent of the Parisian crowds opening the doors of the Bastille to give the prisoners their freedom and then dismantling the fortress. But it was also significantly different. A real shift in consciousness, expectations and actual practice in relation to the use of violence did occur in 1989, when one of the chants was 'no violence'. The Parisian and Petrograd crowds did urgently seek out weapons and expected to fight military repression; and the commander of the Bastille, who surrendered, was immediately murdered. In 1989 the nonviolent discipline of the demonstrators and the restraint of the police and soldiers of the dying regimes certainly included a precarious uncertainty – especially in East Germany, where key officials were believed to be contemplating the Chinese Politburo's choice of using the army against the protesters (Reich, 1990: 88). But there was a widespread understanding, especially among leading political figures in the opposition, that remaining nonviolent was both the most politically effective and morally desirable option in their circumstances.

The commitment to nonviolence was explicitly embraced by groups such as the Protestant church in East Germany, which had earlier fostered signs of opposition such as independent peace groups, and by New Forum; by the Civic Forum in Prague and its Slovak equivalent 'Public Against Violence'. But this understanding was also reflected in many of the major demonstrations where 'no violence' was one of the slogans. Even in Romania, where later Ceausescu and his wife were executed, the first stages were nonviolent. Open defiance began in Timisoara, where people linked arms round the church of Pastor Laszlo Tokes, who had denounced plans to replace villages with high-rise flats, to prevent his eviction. They also burned pictures of President Ceausescu, assembled in the town square, and shouted anti-regime slogans and 'no violence' (Antal, 1994: 2–10).

The lessons of earlier national movements for change in Eastern Europe, for example 1956 in Poland and Hungary, suggested the need for prudent restraint. Solidarity had embraced a 'self limiting revolution'. The restraint of the opposition and its willingness to compromise are highlighted by Garton Ash (2009b) as typical of 1989, and is another reason why some commentators hesitated to accept the label of revolution, since it indicated a willingness to make some concessions to the regime rather than commitment to overthrow it totally. Mutual restraint applied especially to Poland and Hungary, the two countries which initiated the domino effect, where relatively moderate Communist Parties recognized the strength of organized political opposition and were willing to consider that opposition contesting elections. Saxonberg, in his comparative study *The Fall,* classifies the transfer of power in Poland and Hungary as 'institutional compromise' (Saxonberg, 2005).

Emphasis on compromise is somewhat misleading in relation to the collapse of the regimes in East Germany and Czechoslovakia, classified by Saxonberg as 'nonviolent revolutions', although the German oppositionists who came together to form the New Forum on 9 September 1989, and openly published their Manifesto, were still stressing moderation and legality. But in East Germany a mass popular movement was developing, first of spontaneous emigration (through the newly liberalized Hungary) that undermined the regime, and then of organized protest at home that directly challenged it – a combination categorized by Alfred Hirschmann as 'exit' and 'voice' (Hirschmann, 1993). Although the party Politburo deposed its general secretary, Honecker, on 18 October, the regime remained paralysed, and did not open round-table talks with the opposition to create a caretaker government until several weeks after the breaching of the Berlin wall (Saxonberg, 2005: 316). Plans were then made for multiparty elections in March 1990. Because East Germany was one half of a divided nation, and because of the strength of West Germany, moves to reunify Germany began within weeks after the breach of the wall (taking much of the world including the Soviet Union by surprise) and the date of 3 October 1990 was set for German unification (Partos, 1993: 247–9).

The 'velvet revolution' that erupted within Czechoslovakia within a period of three weeks, whose aims were articulated by the hastily created Civic Forum, swept away the inflexible leadership of the party. President Gustav Husak had tried to recover the situation by appointing a new government on 3 December, including five non-communists, but Civic Forum threatened a further general strike. By 9 December all the Forum's demands had been conceded and Parliament formally abolished the leading role of the Communist Party (Urban, 1990: 121). Vaclav Havel soon became the new president and Alexander Dubcek – symbol of the 1968 Prague Spring – chair of the Federal

Assembly. Nevertheless, Civic Forum, anxious to prevent the whole structure of the state from collapsing, did engage in round-table negotiations with the Communist Party prime minister and agreed to the Communist Party retaining ten of the less crucial ministerial posts in the 21-member new provisional government (Lewis et al., 1994: 156–7).

The crumbling of both the East German and Czechoslovak regimes when challenged by people power might be seen as another reason for doubting whether 1989 constituted a true revolution. It seemed almost too easy. It is also interesting from the standpoint of a theory of nonviolent revolution that during 1989 there was, as Saxonberg has noted, no mass defection by soldiers or police to the other side, simply restraint by security forces on the ground in the final stages of mass protest and a failure by the regime to order armed suppression (which would have tested the loyalty of the troops).

But conditions encouraging dissolution of a regime from within are not incompatible with a revolutionary upsurge from below. In fact, as we have seen, participants in both February and October 1917 often felt the same incredulity, and Alexis de Tocqueville, as an eyewitness in Paris in 1848, commented that the victors 'were as astonished at their victory as were the vanquished' (Arendt, 1973: 260). Moreover, the perception that the 1989 revolutions were easily achieved requires a foreshortening of focus on the events of that year alone: they had been preceded by the revolts of 1953, 1956 and the Prague Spring of 1968. Oppositionists who had risked or endured loss of their jobs, systematic security police harassment, house arrest or years of imprisonment saw 1989 as the liberatory culmination of many long years of struggle. Moreover, the 1989 developments in Poland, which were of central importance in promoting hopes of radical change in other East European countries, were a direct outcome of the Soldiarity movement launched in August 1980.

The ease with which the communist party regimes surrendered to the opposition in negotiations, or to resistance on the streets, was of course decisively influenced by the role of Moscow. Since Soviet rule was imposed on Eastern Europe at the end of the 1940s, the primary block on movements of internal reform was the fear of Soviet military intervention, which occurred in East Germany in 1953, Hungary in 1956 and Czechoslovakia in 1968, and stopped just short of military repression in Poland in 1956. A Soviet invasion to quell Solidarity was also threatened in 1981, forcing the Polish regime to impose martial law in December. By the late 1980s, however, Mikhail Gorbachev had launched an unprecedented movement of political reform (glasnost and perestroika) inside the Soviet Union, and favoured significant relaxation of centralized party rule in the wider bloc. In addition Gorbachev had committed himself to a policy of arms reductions, political cooperation and further economic opening to the West, and taking Soviet military action would have destroyed the new direction of domestic and foreign policy. It has also been suggested that Moscow prevented the East German government from firing on demonstrators in Leipzig on 9 October – but a number of competing interpretations of the attitudes of the East German Politburo and local officials have been adduced to explain this forbearance (Reich, 1990: 81, 99; Saxonberg, 2005: 112).

The revolutions of 1989 in Eastern Europe can therefore be seen as twofold: the overthrow of internal repressive rule, but also as nationalist assertions of independence against a weakened empire. The same was true of Mongolia, where what began as popular pressure to achieve genuine perestroika, led by young intellectuals, developed rapidly into more widespread protests and demands for multiparty democracy – although in Mongolia the Communist Party managed to win the first multiparty election (Ackerman and Duvall, 2000: 439–54; Becker, 1992). Nationalism also combined with desire for regime change in the impressive people power movements in the Baltic States within the Soviet Union: Lithuania, Latvia and Estonia. They responded to the opportunities provided by the policy of perestroika (including freedom to form independent groups to contest elections), as well as to the inspiration of 1989, by effectively creating their own national governments and then nonviolently resisting the rather limited attempts by Moscow to force them to remain within the USSR (Lieven, 1993; Trapans, 1991; Beissinger, 2009: 231–46).

Utopianism, charismatic leadership and class conflict

The conscious nonviolence of the means used to overthrow the old regimes, and willingness to negotiate where necessary, are only the starting point for assessing how 1989 differed from 1789 or 1917. One set of differences relates to the character, ideals and goals of the revolutionaries. Harold Wydra (2008: 35) comments that 'the revolutions of 1989 showed the conspicuous absence of charismatic actors, eschatological recipes, messianism or teleological intentions'. Charles Tilly (1993: 233) notes that, whilst the 1989 revolutions did include popular uprisings, a role for intellectuals and a breakdown of the old social order, they did not include 'vindictive violence', 'charismatic vision' or a faith in politics to transform society totally. Similarly Garton Ash (2009a: 20) suggests that, whereas the French and Russian revolutions were utopian, the model of 1989 was anti-utopian.

Messianism and eschatology often derive from religious fervour of the kind sometimes aroused in the Reformation revolts, for example that of the Anabaptists in the German Peasant Wars; they have in the past also been associated with peasant uprisings, notably the Chinese Taiping Rebellion. An appeal to messianism presupposes a certain kind of religious context; it can, for example, be suggested in relation to Iran in 1978–9 (see below). Political revolutionaries may, however, consciously aim to channel messianism and supplant religion: in France, for example, they inaugurated Festivals of Reason; and Wydra argues that the 'revolutionary messianism' of the Bolshevik Party drew on Orthodox traditions and practices to create a new civil religion and theocracy (Wydra, 2008: 42). Utopianism may draw on an initially more secular culture.

The absence of a utopian commitment to create a new world order as an overriding goal did distinguish the revolutionaries of 1989 from those of 1789 and 1917. It can be argued that this was because they were reclaiming the heritage of 1789. There was not an absence of belief in universal principles, but a reassertion of principles that had been submerged by the experiences of fascism, war and communist party rule. Krishan Kumar (2001: 193, 194) notes that 'the themes of 1989 are the great themes of 1789', and that for many East European intellectuals '"the return to Europe" meant precisely the recovery of the lost revolutionary inheritance'.

One obvious reason for the absence of grand new visions was that the Communist Party regime in the Soviet Union had originally been the embodiment of such utopianism, and a terrible object lesson in the danger of sacrificing people in the here and now to an overarching political vision positioned in the future. The leaders and the participants in 1989 were reacting against the experience of decades of communist rule and ideology. Arato (1993: 613) comments on 'the rejection of grand narratives and the hubris of making history'. Apart from explicit rejection of the ideology of the Bolshevik revolutionary heritage, the more modest aspirations of the revolutionaries of 1989 can be linked in part to their preference for nonviolent methods and sense of a relationship between ends and means. Hence also their willingness to consider compromise, as opposed to enforcing their ideals immediately, and abstention from violent retribution against agents of the former regime.

There was not, however, a total absence of a modest utopianism, and the claim by some commentators that 1989 promoted no new ideas has been challenged by Mary Kaldor and Zdenek Kavan, who point to the dissident debates of the 1970s and 1980s (Kaldor and Kavan, 2001: 239–54). In particular, some opposition intellectuals explored the potential of civil society created from below and its link to a new idea of citizenship, giving new life to the concept (Keane, 1988). Debate among intellectuals who explored alternatives to post-totalitarianism also included some aspiration to create a third way between Soviet-style communism and Western liberal capitalism, especially in East Germany, where rapid moves to German unification aborted this possibility. But this theorizing did not long survive the fall of the communist party regimes. It would be more accurate to argue, therefore, that there were utopian aspects to the developing movements in communist party regimes – these included experimentation in the arts, environmental radicalism and, in a few cases, anti-militarist ideas. But the new regimes rapidly fell into line with the dominant economic and military orthodoxies of the West. The majority of people in Eastern Europe, however, probably wanted Western consumerism as well as Western political freedoms. In many cases, notably in the Baltic states and Poland, the culture and ideology of nationalism, often linked to religion, was an additional major inspiration for resistance.

There is no necessary link between revolution and charismatic leadership, especially in the build-up of a movement and the actual overthrow of a regime. A mass popular movement developing from below often depends on a host of local leaders responding to the moment, though it may also be guided or reinforced by established organizations such as trade unions or churches. No individual leader was responsible for the fall of the Bastille or the upsurge in February 1917. The fall of the Berlin Wall had a similar spontaneous quality.

There is also no clear link between either violent or nonviolent movements and charisma. It is in any case an ambiguous concept, much debated and criticized ever since Weber introduced it. The term 'charismatic' is most easily applied to flamboyant figures able to inspire large crowds by their oratory – true of Danton or Trotsky, and arguably of Lech Walesa. Solidarity itself, however, which stressed its grass-roots democratic ethos, rejected Western media build-up of Walesa's leadership, and the movement's own press and symbols tended to caricature him, though affectionately (Laba, 1991: 140–1). If such leaders play a prominent role in opposition there is a danger that they will be too dominant in the new regime. Charisma might also be attributed to figures with outstanding political wisdom and/or moral authority – Gandhi, Aung San Suu Kyi and Nelson Mandela might qualify. In these three cases the movements deliberately fostered their image. When a movement is suffering setbacks and repression, key figures who symbolize the struggle may play an important role in the morale of their supporters and in relation to the outside world. Indeed, a distinction can be made between administrative and political leaders and public figureheads. But quite often there is popular respect and affection for opposition leaders, based on their past role, which invests them with some authority but not any sense of magical qualities: the crowd chanting in Wenceslas Square in December 1989 'Havel to the Castle' reflected such a mood.

A much more important element of earlier revolutions missing from 1989, as noted by Tilly and others, was class conflict. This meant in Marxist terms that there was no major transfer of political control to a new social class. The major revolutions in England and France represented the political and economic claims of previously partially or totally excluded classes to control government. The mobilization of the 'common people' in the towns and the countryside gave momentum to the pressure for change initiated by the propertied classes.

Class conflict encouraged the promotion of utopian ideas and enthusiasm. There were radical elements in the programmes and rhetoric of the leading figures in the English and more especially the French revolutions. But the most utopian ideas evolved over time out of the rising expectations of the poorer classes: for example, the demands of the Levellers, a movement decisively suppressed by Cromwell, that the 'poorest he in England' should have the vote. In France egalitarian beliefs and claims to rights were more in tune with the times, but the claims and political activism of the urban poor encouraged Jacobinism and revolutionary zeal. On a much smaller scale, the experience of poverty and revolutionary expectations led to what Marx labelled 'utopian' socialist experiments (the Diggers in the 1640s), or to socialist conspiracies (Babeuf in the 1790s) – also rapidly crushed. Socialist beliefs and dreams of a new world came to the forefront of revolution when the workers and the peasants were the classes primarily represented in revolutionary activity in 1917 and communist-led victory in 1949 in China.

Class conflict could, moreover, encourage personalized and institutionalized violent revenge by the poor and despised against their previous masters.

Peasants who have suffered from ruthless landlords have in the past used opportunities to take revenge — although their 'revolutionary justice' may sometimes discriminate between the harshest and more reasonable landlords. The urban poor have also often been prominent in violent riots and attacks on the rich.

But in Eastern Europe in 1989 there was no extreme poverty (except in Romania and Albania) and no major class conflict. Apart from some individuals and groups within the communist party *nomenklatura* (elite officials), no internal social group clearly lost out politically as a result of the overthrow. Moreover the 'ruling class' — the diehard *nomenklatura* — were no longer able to appeal to Moscow to use military force to restore their control. The revolutions had indeed been achieved in many cases by a cross-class coalition. In Poland the gap between the workers and the opposition intellectuals was closed after 1976; whilst the workers launched Solidarity, their cause was soon supported by students, professionals and farmers. Although the regime in Czechoslovakia had tried to promote worker antipathy to the relatively small group of intellectuals grouped round Charter 77, and the 1989 demonstrations were launched by students, the genuinely popular upsurge in 1989 was reflected by the plans for a general strike in support of the mounting protests in Prague — although in the event the central Communist Party leadership resigned before the strike was actually held (Williams, 2009: 115–16). So there were no significant class divisions within the early stages of the 1989 revolutions.

There were, however, signs of specific working-class militancy and radical aspirations in East Germany, especially after the scale of elite corruption and squandering of state resources began to be exposed. Gareth Dale records banners attacking bosses living 'like on Dallas' and notes that, after the fall of the wall, workers began to occupy their factories and call for worker control, and to link their vision of democracy to social justice (Dale, 2006: 139–56). But the move towards party elections and unification ended this movement and relegated this strand of the East German revolution to a largely hidden history.

The case for claiming that 1989 (especially in Central Eastern Europe), despite the absence of features associated with 1789 and 1917, did constitute a series of revolutions is made clearly by Ziolkowski (1990: 40), who argues that the concept of reform could not reflect the true nature of the change involved in three simultaneous radical processes: a political move from repressive party control to representative democracy; an economic move from a state-run economy to a market; and a cultural move away from isolation to integration into Western culture. Leslie Holmes (1997: 131), writing as a Western analyst of Soviet systems, has argued that the end result has been 'a rapid and fundamental change of system', which is the basic meaning of revolution.

1989: fulfilling Arendt's revolutionary model?

The experience of 1989, and other examples of people power (though by no means all), do, however, coincide with the theory of revolution developed by

Hannah Arendt. Indeed, the relative absence of class conflict, in the sense of the pressure exerted by the poorer sections of society, means that in her terms 1989 came closer to being a genuine political revolution, and most comparable to the American Revolution of 1776. Arendt argues that the crucial difference between France and America was that, although many in America, especially in the countryside, were poor, they could earn a living and there was not the extreme misery experienced in the cities of France and demands for urgent action to alleviate it. Arendt claims that the very poor came to dominate the Paris sections of the Commune and it was they who Robespierre came to define as 'the people' (*les malheureux*) (Arendt, 1973: 59–114). As a result America became a relatively stable constitutional republic, whereas France suffered from increasing political extremism and terror. Arendt's claims about America would probably be contested by leftist scholarship, which has explored the extent of poverty, for example a striking increase in poor relief in New York, and growth in agitation by the poor between the 1740s and 1760s, such as land riots and tenant protests, as well as urban riots (Rude, 1980: 96–8). Nevertheless, her central argument about the dangers of economic conflict undermining political gains is persuasive.

Arendt's thesis is that modern revolutions require two key elements to coincide: a sense of creating a new beginning and of taking part in heroic events, and a concept of freedom. Arendt's understanding of freedom, however, is not a liberal concept of freedom from state restrictions (Isaiah Berlin's 'negative liberty'), or even liberation from previous oppression, but the exhilarating experience of engaging in politics with fellow citizens and fashioning new ideas and policies. She quotes John Adams on the discovery during the American Revolution 'that it is action, not rest, that constitutes our pleasure' (Arendt, 1973: 34). It is the sense of new beginnings and participation in the freedom of political activity that distinguishes revolution from a successful insurrection. It is these experiences, 'the treasure of revolutions', that seem invariably to be lost in their aftermath.

One of Arendt's central propositions is that the American, French and Russian revolutions all provided very significant examples of people's potential for spontaneous political action, cooperation, self-organization and collective decision-making inspired by a sense of the public interest. This potential for truly democratic politics is expressed in the organizational forms of these revolutions, starting with assemblies at a very local level and by a process of delegation and confederation creating a nation-wide democratic structure. In America the wards and township meetings, in France the 48 sections of the Paris Commune (Arendt, 1973: 239), and in Russia the local soviets provided the grassroots basis for this kind of political action. What Trotsky termed 'dual power' illustrated not only parallel control over the life of the country, but an alternative model of democratic organization.

But this revolutionary expression of free politics is threatened by two main forces. At a political level the council system is undermined and eventually dominated by political parties controlled from the top by professional politicians, often with specific ideologies, and representative of particular interests (Arendt, 1973: 273). At best, as in the American Revolution, the experience of revolutionary participation gives way to a stable constitution guaranteeing civil rights and liberties and periodic elections between parties posing a degree of political choice. At worst, as in the later stages of the French Revolution and after October 1917, a single repressive party seizes control.

The Central Eastern European revolutions of 1989 did not reflect the more extreme sense of new beginnings epitomized in France by creating a new calendar. But they did reflect the sense of exhilaration and of new possibilities arising from mass collective action. In Poland, Solidarity and the evolution of a 'parallel polis' from below in the 1970s and 1980s had provided an Arendtian revolutionary experience. The New Forum in East Germany and the Czech Civil Forum represented a conscious alternative to a system of political parties: coalitions responsive to the demands of various sectors of society and seeking a path to liberal democracy not identical with the Western model. The Czechs were reluctant to abandon the Forum approach, despite the existence of embryonic parties (maintained in neutered form under Communist Party dominance), but with the potential, as happened in 1968, of rapidly taking on new life. Parties proliferated initially in a chaotic multiplicity in 1990, and often affiliated with Civic Forum and the Slovak Public Against Violence, which both won overwhelming support in elections that year. Arendt's lament that the revolutionary experience tends to be superseded by professionalized representative politics, supported by a largely apathetic population, soon came true in Central Eastern Europe. It happened most rapidly in East Germany, where counterparts to West German political parties were formed prior to reunification. Reich (1990: 92) wrote: 'people seem to have lost that intoxicating spirit and energy of the November Spring in Winter'.

The price of velvet and absence of revolutionary transformation?

One criticism quite often made about 1989 is that the protagonists were too committed to nonviolent values, and too willing to compromise to achieve a peaceful transfer of control over the state. This thesis is summed up in Ernest Gellner's striking phrase 'the price of velvet'. Gellner coined this term in an essay focused specifically on the Czech experience (a review of Havel's book *Summer Meditations* written after he became President), and animated by a distrust of easy moralizing. Gellner also reflected on comparisons between Thomas Masaryk, the first Czechoslovak President, and Vaclav Havel (Gellner, 1995). But the concept has been adapted to suggest (as Gellner also does) that the successful resistance went too far to conciliate and include members of the old regime in future governments, instead of exacting justice for past abuses of power.

One possible response focuses on the immediate political realities in 1989. It was urgent to construct new governments which would work effectively. The

Soviet Union was still dominant in the region, and the East European countries were still embedded in the military Warsaw Pact and the economic alliance of Comecon. The West was exerting diplomatic pressure on Solidarity and other opposition groupings not to try to move too fast and risk destabilizing Gorbachev's position. Moreover, in Czechoslovakia itself some of the most discredited supporters of the previous communist regime – for example some members of Parliament – were rapidly replaced and a 'lustration' system of dismissals based on the archives of the security police initiated. (This process, relying on the accuracy of secret police files, had its own injustices.)

It could be argued that compromise and a degree of conciliation created a better basis for future political stability and civilized politics. Although political bitterness and ideological divisions have influenced post-communist politics in Central Eastern Europe, they have not threatened the system of representative democracy. Greater immediate problems arose from the problems of economic transition from a state-controlled economy, arguably exacerbated by the neoliberal economic dogma dominant in the West since the 1970s.

Retrospectively some Russian and Western analysts have queried how much significant change really occurred, either in Eastern Europe or the former Soviet Union. Kumar suggests that what was accomplished in 1989 might be interpreted as a series of 'palace revolutions' rather than true popular revolutions, and that the ruling elite exercised considerable control over the transition to a new political and economic system, as well as retaining considerable influence afterwards (Kumar, 2001: 195). Certainly, apart from some discredited individuals, members of the *nomenklatura* were often well placed to benefit from the new system and happy to change their officially declared beliefs.

But it is important to distinguish between Central Eastern Europe (and the Baltic states), where there was a decisive change in the nature of the regime, other countries in Eastern Europe, where there was further contestation and popular pressure to promote electoral democracy in the 1990s, and the former Soviet states. Stephen White, in his essay on 'Rethinking the Communist Transition' (citing Kumar), looks in most detail at the early 1990s in Russia and the sceptical views of the sociologist Tatyana Zaslavskaya about claims that a revolution had occurred in Russia (White, 2003: 418–22). But he also notes that outcomes since 1989 have been varied.

Although a number of reasons rooted in history, political culture and economic development can be cited for the varying trajectories of post-communist states in the former Soviet bloc, a key factor was how far they had experienced people power revolution below (which Zaslavskaya argued was missing in Russia). The most blatant examples of members of the security police amassing fortunes in the new economic free-for-all, and the worst examples of political repression and corruption, have occurred in states that did see a straightforward transfer of control to former leading figures in the communist party regimes, as occurred initially in most of the former Soviet republics. This absence of real regime change is one major reason for the series of 'colour revolutions' since 2000 (see Chapter 6).

Where there have been demands for regime change in the former Soviet bloc, the goal has been a Western liberal model of electoral democracy and market-led economic growth. The implications of the toppling of the Shah of Iran in 1979 raise questions about the fundamental link (assumed in Western thought over the past two centuries) between revolution and modernization.

Interpreting the Iranian revolution of 1978-9

The uprising against the Shah's dictatorial regime demonstrated key features of earlier revolutions: a series of mass protests and strikes of increasing size and militancy, mobilization of virtually all sections of the population against the Shah, repression by the armed forces, most of whom over time started siding with the demonstrators, and an eventual crumbling of the regime when the Shah fled the country. Abrahamian makes a direct comparison between the Iranian demonstrations and the crowd in the French Revolution as described by George Rude (Rude, 1959; Abrahamian, 2009: 162). The revolution was also, like many revolutions, totally unexpected. Ryszard Kapuscinski in his reflections on Iran suggests that it is this unexpected and apparently spontaneous quality of events that distinguishes revolution from a revolt or *coup d'état* (Kapuscinski, 2006: 104). David Albert has argued that the Shah controlled major economic resources, notably the oil fields, had an efficient modern bureaucracy, one of the largest armies in the world and a ruthless security apparatus, and was actively supported by the USA, despite some human rights concerns voiced by President Jimmy Carter, which (probably) encouraged modest measures of liberalization. The Shah also laid claim to traditional authority. His regime, therefore, looked the most secure in the region (Albert, 1980, 1985).

The mass uprising was, as so often, preceded in late 1977 by intellectuals protesting against censorship and student campus demonstrations spilling out onto the streets. From January 1978 there were waves of demonstrations, not only in Teheran but in the holy city of Qum and other key cities and towns, resulting in deaths of demonstrators; observing the Shia custom of mourning for 40 days before publicly commemorating the dead, the protests took place in 40-day cycles. In September 1978 the Shah imposed martial law in an attempt to end the unrest (Moshiri, 1991: 128). The crowds included high-school and university students, writers and professionals, workers in factories and shops, shop keepers from the bazaars, peasants from the countryside, young women in jeans and women in full Islamic dress. Strikes spread from universities to factories, bazaars, the oil fields, the media and even government offices. The movement also drew major support from the mosques and many Muslim clerics joined the protests. The final mass demonstration in Teheran on 10 December 1978, which drew from a million to two million people, was coordinated and controlled by the Ayatollahs.

The revolution drew on the long tradition of crowd protest within Iran dating back to the late nineteenth century, and in particular the protests against the tobacco monopoly in 1891-2 and the 1906 'Constitutional Revolution'.

Although crowds attacked and ransacked many of the physical symbols of the regime and its Western supporters, and in November 1978 burned sections of Teheran, they abstained from looting (leaving the cash in the banks for example) and from deliberately harming people. Ayatollah Khomeini, influencing events from his exile, carefully avoided any call to arms, and major organized processions and rallies were highly disciplined. The only armed violence occurred briefly in February 1979, after the Shah had left the country, when popular crowds and guerrilla groups (who had backed the unarmed demonstrations) fought the only unit remaining loyal to the Shah, the Imperial Guard.

Observers, including the British Ambassador, commented on the essentially peaceful nature of the revolution, and exponents of civil resistance have seen Iran as an extremely important example of the power of unarmed resistance. Its significance lies in particular in exemplifying the power of non-cooperation and unarmed defiance to overthrow a strong and ruthless dictatorship. It is also important for the amazing courage of the demonstrators, and showing that unarmed resistance can prevail against brutal repression in some circumstance. In other examples of unarmed resistance initial repression by a regime, which creates martyrs, has roused popular anger and determination to resist (as in Czech student protests in 1989 responding to the police attack on a legal demonstration on 17 November that reportedly led to a death). But, as in Burma in 2007, sustained brutal repression often does suppress the movement (at least for a time) – particularly if the regime is not susceptible to external pressure. In Iran in 1978, however, hundreds of thousands continued to defy the armed forces to shoot, even after the declaration of martial law in Teheran and other cities in September 1978. Even though the tens of thousands of deaths, estimated at the time, has since been scaled down to nearer 3,000, or even fewer, by historians, the protesters knew they faced a real danger (Abrahamian, 2009: 175–6). But periods of commemoration for the dead became a means of promoting, and also providing breathing space between, the waves of protest. Iran is therefore a key example in the literature on civil resistance of unarmed protesters prevailing despite ruthless repression.

Whilst the revolutionary process in Iran had similarities with other revolutions, the spirit animating it was more puzzling to many observers. The Ayatollah Khomeini was an important figure head, the momentum of protest in 1978 was sparked by a seminary student protest against a semi-official newspaper attack on Khomeini, and (as already noted) Muslim clerics came to play a key organizing role. Moreover, the symbolism of the martyrdom of Husain (the grandson of the Prophet) and Shiite religious celebrations of his death merged with resistance to the Shah, and a religious sense of martyrdom inspired some of the protesters. It was not, however, exclusively an uprising influenced by Shia Islamic beliefs. The coalition opposed to the Shah included liberals and socialists, Kurds committed to Sunni beliefs, and even Marxist guerrillas. Nevertheless, a religious spirit and willingness to support Khomeini, as well as a determination to oust the Shah, did appear to provide a unifying element. Claire Briere, in an interview with Foucault about the Iranian revolution, commented on the ambiguity and different attitudes among demonstrators, who nevertheless were all willing to shout pro-Khomeini slogans. Foucault himself suggested that religion provided 'the vocabulary, the ceremonial, the timeless drama into which one could fit the historical drama of a people that pitted its very existence against that of its sovereign' (Foucault, 1990: 214).

The Iranian revolution was clearly an assertion of national pride and repudiation of Western, especially American, control. So Shia Islam symbolized that national identity. In this sense the Iranian revolution could be seen as a modernizing nationalist revolution. There are some similarities with the role of the Polish Pope, and the Catholic Church, in consolidating a Polish sense of nationalism in opposition to anti-religious Soviet ideology and Soviet control, even among secular Poles. The Iranian revolution contained, moreover, two elements analysts suggest were missing from 1989. Religious beliefs, oriented to the future reappearance of the missing Imam, did provide a messianic element for oppressed workers and marginalized social groups (Parker, 1999: 95). Khomeini could also be seen as a 'charismatic' figure.

After the overthrow of the Shah, the Ayatollahs rapidly consolidated a regime that ruthlessly suppressed all those political groupings that had cooperated in the process of revolution. In this sense there are parallels with the role of the Bolsheviks after 1917. The ideology and policies of the new regime were – especially in the early years – committed to a version of Islam seeking to reverse many of the modernizing features of the Shah's 'white revolution', in particular the emancipation of women. This anti-modern and anti-Western bias did not extend to the economic and technological sphere – for example the development of nuclear energy, which has become a source of Western concern in relation to Iran's probable nuclear weapon ambitions. The complex political system that evolved, which allowed parliamentary and presidential elections within a wider context of clerical supervision, enabled moderate Islamists with a more liberal agenda to begin to play a political role.

The Green Movement that erupted in 2009, when the moderate candidate for the presidency was defeated as a result, his supporters believed on good evidence, of a stolen election, followed the model of many recent people power protests. It can also plausibly be interpreted as representing a more 'modern' Westernizing trend within sections of the regime and in the broader society. Despite adopting many of the tactics of 1978–9, and showing great courage, the Green Movement has so far failed. A crucial difference between 2009 and 1978 is that the amazing degree of popular unity observers discerned in 1978 no longer obtained. Religious extremism has been associated with the bazaars and some religious cities, and the bazaars failed to shut down in support of the Green Movement as they had in 1978 (Buchan, 2009: 82) But in general Iran seemed to be suffering from the division between the urban elite and the rural population, which has also been characteristic of major protests in Thailand since 2006 (see Chapter 5).

The Green Movement clearly does not qualify as a 'revolution', not only because it has not yet succeeded, but also because its goals (at least so far) have been reform of the existing political Islamic system, not its overthrow (Majd, 2010: 1–66, 262). Indeed, the focal figure for dissent was a former prime minister and cousin of the Supreme Leader, Ayatollah Khameni, who had been cleared by the clerical Council of Guardians to stand for the presidency in the 2009 elections. But the movement has indicated very significant opposition to the nature of the regime, reflecting an in-built tension which is likely to remain and find new expression. There was in fact an (apparently) brief response to the Arab rebellions of 2011 in Iran.

Postscript on the Arab Uprisings

How far the 2011 Arab uprisings will qualify as revolutions it is too early tell. Some monarchs, as in Morocco and Jordan have tried to pre-empt revolution by promises of reform; others as in Bahrain (backed by the inflexible regime in Saudi-Arabia) have opted for brutal suppression. But in the rapid spread of people power across national borders, the demands for citizen rights and multi-party elections, and the potential to alter the realities of regional and global politics, there are parallels between 2011 and 1989. The Arab uprisings also resemble 1989 in their slogans claiming to represent 'the people' and their original commitment to peaceful protest.

By August 2011 major uprisings had evolved differently. In Tunisia and Egypt, deposed autocrats have been brought to trial, and constitutional change and multi-party elections scheduled before the end of the year. However, the behaviour of interim governments has prompted fears that, whilst individual despotic leaders have been toppled, the old regimes remain. There have, therefore, been major renewed protests (especially in Egypt) against repressive measures and demands for more radical political change. Elsewhere, tribal and regional divisions have encouraged armed conflict, as in Libya and Yemen. In Yemen, however, many peaceful demonstrators were still calling for democracy, and international diplomacy may ease President Ali Abdullah Saleh from office.

The most remarkable uprising has unfolded for five months against the Baath Party regime in Syria, where demonstrations have continued despite 3,000 deaths (estimated by the UN) and thousands of arrests and disappearances. The government claims it is suppressing small armed groups, whilst the protesters, opposition representatives abroad, escaped deserters, and journalists eluding the ban on internal media coverage, have publicized the widespread and essentially peaceful nature of the protests. There are important similarities as well as differences with Iran in 1977-79. The similarities are on the one hand the regional importance and strength of the regimes and their ruthlessness in repression; and on the other, the continued fearlessness of the demonstrators, patterns of protest linked to prayers in mosques and the frequent funerals, and signs of conscript soldiers defecting. Key differences are that Syrian rebels seem to have secular democratic, not Islamist, goals and slogans; and there is no dominant external or internal leader, or national organization. It is a true rebellion from below.

PART II
Central concepts and debates

4 Power, violence and unarmed resistance

The concept of power is clearly central to explaining how states control the people who live within their borders, or impose forms of direct or indirect empire. It is also central to explaining how people can resist unjust political or economic repression. The definition of power has, however, been much disputed in social and political theory. One of the most widely cited studies is the 1974 analysis by Steven Lukes, *Power: A Radical View* (recently updated, revised and extended), that claims power is an 'essentially contested concept', i.e. that it cannot be defined in an ideologically neutral and value-free way (Lukes, 2005). The purpose here is not to attempt an extensive analysis of power, or debate conflicting interpretations in the abstract, but to focus on how power has been understood in the past, and can now be interpreted, in the context of civil resistance and in particular of people power. This chapter concentrates on political resistance to oppressive regimes and direct imperialist rule – although it does note wider structural constraints. This discussion also illustrates how power is indeed 'essentially contested'.

The developing literature on nonviolent action and unarmed resistance has given considerable prominence to the 'consent theory of power', which entails both a psychological component of individual 'consent' to the legitimacy of a regime through obedience, and a view of power relations: that the apparent power of rulers rests on the cooperation of the ruled. Therefore governments can in principle be overthrown if the people, who overwhelmingly outnumber rulers and their direct agents of repression, openly withdraw both their consent and their cooperation. Advocates of resistance have often tried to show that ordinary people are potentially more powerful than apparently impregnable ruling elites backed by 'the sword', or by guns and tanks. Shelley in his 'Mask of Anarchy' responded to the Peterloo massacre of unarmed demonstrators in a field near Manchester in 1819 with the stirring exhortation: 'Rise like lions after slumber, in unvanquishable number! Shake your chains to earth like dew ... Ye are many, they are few'. Gandhi argued in his 1906 pamphlet on Indian home rule, 'The English ... are not in India because of their strength, we keep them ... The sword is entirely useless for holding India' (Sharp, 1979: 46).

Recent analysts have, however, urged the need to go beyond a consent theory of power to explore more complex structuralist theories of power for a full understanding of unarmed resistance and radical political change (Martin, 1989; Summy, 1994). Others have looked to the theories of Foucault, and/or to James Scott's much discussed *Domination and the Arts of Resistance* which explores hidden, everyday, resistance (Scott, 1990; Bleiker, 2000; Atack, 2006).

This chapter begins by briefly examining some current definitions of power and key contributions to an interpretation that emphasizes consent and cooperation from below – Etienne de la Boetie, Hannah Arendt and Vaclav Havel in particular. But the main focus is on limits to an individualist consent theory that relate directly to people power movements. Two of the considerations relate to developing a strategy of resistance:

- how conflict between a ruler and 'the people' is complicated by the power structures of different regimes; and
- contexts where the oppressor does not rely significantly on the actual cooperation of the oppressed.

A second set of issues arise, from theoretical concerns:

- the relevance – or otherwise – of structuralist or post-structuralist concepts of power to understanding both the sources of resistance and the limits to what can be achieved; and
- how Gramsci's concept of civil society, as a means of promoting ideological hegemony and of potentially developing resistance, relates to resistance movements.

The chapter concludes by looking very briefly at various approaches to the concept of violence and returns to Arendt's contrast between violence and power in relation to resisting repression.

Concepts of power and violence and relevance to civil resistance

Power is central to social and political life, and can be studied in contexts ranging from global empires to small communities, so disputes about definition are unsurprising. One fundamental distinction that has been suggested – for example by Peter Morriss – is between power exercised as control over others, and power as a capacity to achieve desired goals, which implies voluntary cooperation based on agreement. Morriss suggests failure to distinguish between 'influence concepts' and 'ability concepts' is one source of theoretical confusion in debates about power (Morriss, 1980). Coercive control from above and voluntary cooperation from below to create a parallel society are two key poles in the discussion of civil resistance. However, the central thesis of the original literature on civil resistance is that coercive control is made possible by extensive compliance and cooperation, not only by agents of rulers, but by the population at large. Moreover widespread and prolonged resistance may (as noted in Chapter 2) encompass varying degrees of social pressure and sometimes intimidation.

Kenneth Boulding starts an essay on 'Nonviolence and Power in the Twentieth Century' by distinguishing between domination, or 'power over', and empowerment, or the 'power to do' (Boulding, 1999). But he then elaborates on three broad types of power, that are often combined in society: the ability to threaten or apply sanctions; economic power which can be used to threaten but is largely based on the evolution of production and exchange; and 'integrative power'. Boulding suggests this is the most important and describes it as 'legitimacy, persuasion, loyalty, community and so on' that tends to reinforce power derived from threats and from economic resources. These basic distinctions are relevant to resistance to repressive dictatorships, which threaten protesters with imprisonment, torture or death, or withdraw access to higher education and employment for dissenters, as the 'post-totalitarian' regimes in the Soviet bloc tended to do. Regimes also try to promote their legitimacy both internally and internationally. Conversely, success for the resistance may depend on how dramatically they can challenge that legitimacy, persuade a majority to support their cause, challenge the administrative and economic underpinnings of the regime, and, through what Boulding calls 'disarming behaviour', dissuade key sections of the security forces from applying force.

Boulding's 'three faces' can be related to the now widely used definition elaborated by Joseph Nye between 'hard power', which covers both military capacity to threaten and economic capacity to induce compliance, and 'soft power' (Nye, 2004). It is the latter that Nye wishes to stress (against a 'realist' interpretation of international politics) as having a key additional role in promoting international influence. Soft power refers to projecting a favourable image, promoting cultural values, being active in humanitarian issues and generally winning hearts and minds. Nye's analysis sprang from an evaluation of American foreign policy, and has been adopted by the Obama Administration. Although associated particularly with how states operate internationally, Nye has argued that it can apply to non-state actors – he cited the anti-land mines campaign in an address to the British Council (Nye, 2008). Interestingly, the Iranian regime has accused the West of trying to orchestrate 'soft coups' through people power.

Civil resistance does draw on a version of 'soft power', by promoting ideas and values which will influence opponents and third parties. But it also often uses forms of economic coercion or attempts to undermine and obstruct the administrative capacity of the state, for example by tax refusal, refusal to obey administrative or legal requirements, or through direct civil disobedience fill the prisons. Whilst such protests are quite often symbolic, in a genuine people power campaign they can obstruct the processes of government. Many methods of civil resistance – most notably the general strike – are therefore coercive, or potentially so, as Adam Roberts (2009: 6) has noted.

Weber's concept of domination (*Herrschaft*), which he argues is an important element of social action and can often comprise economic power, but need not do so, is relevant to the theory of civil resistance. In essence domination denotes a situation where 'the manifested will (*command*) of the rulers [emphasis in original]' is intended to and does influence the conduct of the ruled. Weber (1978: 946) notes that viewed from the other end of the spectrum, 'this situation will be called *obedience* [emphasis in original]'. Weber's summary indicates the significance of a key text for civil resistance, the 'Discourse of Voluntary Servitude' by the young sixteenth-century theorist Etienne de la Boetie, who saw individual rulers deriving their real power from the voluntary obedience of their numerous subjects (Boetie, 1997). This text was known to Thoreau and Tolstoy, and was summarized by the German socialist anarchist Gustav Landauer early in the twentieth century (de Ligt, 1989: 104–6). It does not usually figure in English-language political thought, but does get a mention by Lukes (2005: 110, 157 n.13).

Civil resistance is a good example of the exercise of power as it is conceptualized by Arendt. She rejects what she claims is the dominant motif of Western political thought, that understands power as hierarchical rule over others, and interprets – as Hobbes does, for example, in his *Leviathan* – violence as the ultimate expression of power. Instead she argues for a concept of power that flows from the capacity of individuals to act cooperatively to achieve their ends. Those who are 'in power' depend on the consent and cooperation of those they claim to represent. In its pure form violence, which can be magnified by the technology of destruction, is the opposite of power. 'The extreme form of power is All against One, the extreme form of violence is One against All (Arendt, 1970: 42–4). She comments in the same essay that violence cannot be used if soldiers refuse to obey commands to use it and, referring to recent history, adds, 'The head-on clash between Russian tanks and the entirely nonviolent resistance of the Czechoslovak people is a textbook case for a confrontation between violence and power in their pure states' (ibid.: 52–3). Arendt does not, however, believe that unarmed resistance can always prevail over ruthlessly violent regimes – she argues that terror can destroy the power of combined resistance, although it also erodes the effectiveness of states from within.

Habermas has criticized Arendt for developing her 'communicative' concept of power from extreme historical circumstances, the totalitarian regimes designed to eliminate such power, and the revolutions against them. Habermas concludes that, although Arendt does illuminate important though extreme aspects of the modern world', her approach excludes most forms of political activity and more inclusive structural analyses (Habermas, 1986: 75–93). His own definition of structural violence (which seems equivalent to power) suggests that: 'Structural violence does not manifest itself *as force* [emphasis in original]'. Instead it is manifested in systematic blockages to communications, resulting in the apparently uncoerced acceptance of illusory ideologies (ibid.: 88). Arendt's initial frame of reference is, however, relevant to a study of people power.

The Polish, Czechoslovak and Hungarian intellectuals who elaborated arguments for nonviolent citizen resistance from within the logic of their particular political context in the 1970s and 1980s stressed two key themes: the impact of open non-cooperation in a system of manufactured compliance, and the crucial importance of creating civil bonds from below. Havel's influential 1976 essay 'The Power of the Powerless' argued that an individual or small group who asserted their own sense of morality and social responsibility and refused to endorse public slogans, vote in meaningless 'elections', or publicly asserted their intellectual and cultural independence were directly undermining the regime (Havel, 1987). Demanding that the government observe the human rights it had endorsed in international agreements as Charter 77 did, or going on strike as in Poland, were even more direct challenges. The movement towards creating an independent 'civil society' from below, sometimes seen as a 'parallel polis' (the term echoes Arendt's ideal of the Greek city republic), was important in the evolution of civil resistance in Central Eastern Europe (see Chapter 2).

Non-cooperation and the nation state: anti-one or regime change?

The model inherent in de la Boetie's emphasis on withdrawing obedience is autocracy within the modern state. Indeed his essay is often cited with the alternative title 'Anti-One'. The contrast between the many and the one would have been less persuasive in a medieval context of power divided between monarch, aristocracy and church (Roland Bleiker elaborates on Boetie's essay within its specifically Renaissance context; Bleiker, 2000: 55–65). Social contract theory by the seventeenth century assumed an implicit contract between rulers and ruled, which could either emphasize the obligation to obey (unless the state itself was effectively dissolved), as in Hobbes, or could build in concepts of justice and good government that allowed subjects to rebel if the rulers notably failed to keep their side of the contract, as in Locke.

Many recent people power uprisings, whether spontaneous rebellions or a response to blatantly rigged presidential 'elections', have been remarkably successful in forcing corrupt and ruthless political leaders to flee the country or step down from office. The list begins with President Marcos in the Philippines in 1986 through to Slobodan Milosevic in Serbia in 2000, and culminates (at the time of writing) in Presidents Ben Ali of Tunisia in January 2011 and Mubarak of Egypt in February 2011. Prolonged mass protests by a cross-section of the people removed any claim to legitimacy from these political leaders both at home and abroad, and exerted pressure on them to go before they faced greater humiliation and possible legal sanctions.

The modern nation state, however, is obviously more than a relationship between an individual ruler and his circle of supporters and the ruled. Sixteenth-century autocracies were already beginning to develop a state bureaucracy. Weber's concept of the state in the early twentieth century emphasized the role of bureaucratic institutions, including their hierarchy, routine procedures and rationalized norms, in defining the nature of rule. The role of the armed forces and security police is also central to maintaining repressive rulers. Many states today incorporate degrees of corruption and nepotism and arbitrary violence far from the Weberian model, and some have weak administrative structures, but many rulers have the backing of organized political parties and other institutional (or more informal) underpinning. But, with the possible partial exception of a few traditional monarchs asserting claims to autocracy (as in Nepal in 1990 and 2007) or highly individualistic dictatorships in underdeveloped countries, unarmed resistance today means confronting a complex system of government.

Success in toppling a dictatorial ruler usually requires some members of the governing elite and/or significant sections of the military or security services to withdraw support from the ruler. Sometimes the army may remain neutral initially – as happened in Tunisia and Egypt (where demonstrators saw the security police as their enemy and the armed forces provisionally as their 'friends'). At other times the army may turn on paramilitary groups supporting the ruler, as happened in Malawi, where the army quelled the Malawi Young Pioneers, used by Hastings Banda to intimidate opponents. Quite often there are masked or open splits at various levels (see Chapter 2). Ordinary civil servants are less likely to become involved in overt conflict, though occasionally civil servants are at the forefront of opposition, especially where they have not been paid for some time (as, for example, in Benin in the late 1980s). The early phase of unarmed resistance in Libya led to senior diplomats abroad resigning, which underlined Gaddafi's loss of internal and international legitimacy (before armed conflict began). Prolonged resistance campaigns may call on civil servants to refuse systematically to cooperate with the regime, but this strategy is most promising in a national liberation struggle against imperial rule, or a more temporary military occupation – as in the German government resistance to French occupation of the Ruhr in 1923 (Sternstein, 1969: 137–8). The sector linked to the state most likely to initiate or join open resistance is the legal profession, whose obligations to uphold state laws often clash with their training and a 'higher' concept of law. In recent decades lawyers in Pakistan, for example, have been prominent in opposing arbitrary rule.

Toppling a dictator usually therefore requires cracks in the state and security apparatus. Sometimes the most important state institutions may come to see the ruler as a liability because of the strength of popular opposition on the streets. Whether the exit of an individual ruler necessarily results in a change in the whole nature of the regime – which the demonstrators are usually demanding – is more problematic (see also Chapter 6). This question was still being resolved in Tunisia and Egypt in the early months of 2011, where the popular movements were mobilizing after the fall of Ben Ali and Mubarak, to try to ensure a change not only in the presidency but in the wider political system, and testing their power from below against the ability of the institutions of the old regime to prevent a real transformation.

Limits of consent and alternative theories

The understanding of power developed in the literature on nonviolent action, for example by Tolstoy, Gandhi and later by Sharp, follow de la Boetie in stressing that the power of rulers rests on the cooperation and consent of the ruled and can be undermined by withdrawing that support. More recent analysts of civil resistance have queried the adequacy of this 'consent theory' of power for a number of different reasons.

Consent theory is most directly relevant in explaining why civil resistance can undermine political repression (as opposed to other forms of domination), but even in this context it has some problems both as a theoretical model and a guide to action. One set of questions arises from reflection on the varied aims of rulers. Lipsitz and Kritzer have noted that, if a state occupies territory, it may be concerned to acquire its natural resources or to use the territory to settle some of its own population and may be able to displace the indigenous people or outnumber them (Lipsitz and Kritzer, 1975). More directly relevant to this book, specific case studies of resistance movements have queried whether those imposing control have in fact always relied primarily on the cooperation of the ruled. Two examples where the cooperation of those being repressed has not been central are the First Intifada in the Palestinian Occupied Territories and the Kosovo Albanians' demand for independence from Serbia (Rigby, 1991; Clark, 2000). The key problem for the Intifada was that 'whilst Israel desires the territory of the West Bank and the Gaza strip, it does not want the people – the Palestinians', and was not dependent on their cooperation to maintain military occupation (Rigby, 2010: 55). In Kosovo, President Milosevic aimed to 're-Serbianize' the province. Moreover, in neither case did the resistance have decisive economic leverage. Palestinian labour in Israel could be replaced, and Palestinians needed basic goods from Israel; Milosevic was prepared to shut down Kosovo industries. Other examples where non-cooperation may not be central include Tibet and East Timor (both discussed in Chapter 7).

Addressing this problem, Clark has invoked the theoretical distinction developed by Robert Burrowes (derived from Clausewitz) between undermining power and altering the will of the opponent (Burrowes, 1996). Burrowes suggests the central aim is to alter the will – so in the case of Kosovo the resistance needed to mobilize support within Serbia and also internationally to bring pressure to bear on the Serbian government (Clark, 2000: 130). Clark suggests in addition that the resistance needed to draw on forms of nonviolent action that directly challenged the Serbian government – which the leadership was reluctant to do. Maria Stephan argues that where 'foreign occupiers' do not need full cooperation of the 'occupied population', the resistance movement needs to focus on the other sources of support for the occupying regime: its internal population and its international role. She illustrates this thesis with brief case studies of the East Timorese, Palestinian and Kosovo Albanian self-determination movements, noting the importance of finding allies inside the occupying country, but also among other governments, international organizations and transnational networks, and getting support from diasporas. The basic 'power dynamic' should, therefore, shape resistance strategy, although the role of external pressure varies (Stephan, 2006: 59–60).

Many of the objections to consent theory, however, have derived from a sense that the theory itself is inadequate. The concept of 'consent' suggests conscious and voluntary individual decision, but where populations have failed in the past to resist forms of repression it may well have been due to various forms of socially inculcated belief, or acceptance of some kind of implicit contract between rulers and ruled – suggested by Barrington Moore (1978) in his *Injustice: The Social Bases of Obedience and Revolt* – as well as more obvious reasons, such as having some personal stake in the system, fear or belief resistance is hopeless. The earlier theorists of consent were well aware of the need to explain the complex reasons for people's normal obedience and cooperation. Boetie suggested that originally men submitted to force, but 'men born under the yoke' do not know of any other condition and therefore think it natural. Tolstoy, who stressed the potential of mass non-cooperation, focused in his 'Letter to a Noncommissioned Officer' on the role of the Orthodox Church in upholding belief in Tsarism, especially among the peasantry; and Gandhi noted how the English educational system had inculcated the ideology of British imperialism (Tolstoy, 1966: 162–3; Sharp, 1979: 48–9). Sharp gives a range of psychological and cultural reasons for habitual obedience (Sharp, 1973, Part 1: 16–24). But later commentators have wanted to go further.

The academic debate about power has been both enriched and complicated by a range of theoretical contributions in the past 30 years. Lukes incorporates many of these into his updated survey of power. His original distinction between 'three dimensions' of power was based on interpreting studies of society and politics within the USA. The first dimension is derived from analysis based on observing which individuals get their way in political decision-making; the second dimension involves a more institutionally based analysis of control of the political agenda. Lukes (2005: 111) summarizes the third dimension as 'the power to decide what is decided'. In the second edition of his book he makes clear that this third dimension does not encompass all forms of power, but the issue of 'domination': 'how do the powerful secure the compliance of those they dominate?' (ibid.: 109–10). His exploration includes reflections on feminist theorizing about the complexities of women's submission to men and Scott's work on 'everyday resistance' (ibid.: 124–44).

The recent literature on civil resistance has also invoked contemporary theories of power as potentially providing a more conceptually adequate frame of reference. A feminist critique of consent theory has been voiced by Kate McGuinness, who suggests that Sharp's concept of consent is not relevant to understanding the nature of women's subordination under patriarchal structures (McGuinness, 1993). Foucault's writings on domination and consent, which reject exclusive focus on the state or class domination based on control of economic resources, and explore how power relations are diffused throughout the social fabric and cross state and class boundaries, promise possible insights into chan,ging attitudes or forms of 'micro-resistance' (Atack, 2006; Bleiker, 2000; Foucault, 1991a).

Feminist theory can suggest why women often lose out after regime change. 'Feminist' or 'micro-resistance' perspectives can also provide an interesting framework for examining some social movements or forms of dissent – including the background to national political uprisings – but they are not so obviously relevant to explaining the rise and nature of people power movements. Bleiker does illustrate his Foucauldian approach to understanding global politics through 'transversal' dissent with reference to the East German movement of 1989, but his emphasis on factors that transcend national boundaries is common to most analyses. His more unusual exploration of the role of young East German poets practising linguistic 'transgressions' is avowedly a move 'away from great revolutionary acts towards ... less spectacular but equally effective daily practices of resistance' (Bleiker, 2000: 270).

A study inspired by Foucault which does encompass a people power movement is Janet Roitman's *Fiscal Disobedience*, which, drawing on the concept of 'governmentality', focuses on 'regimes' of population and fiscal control in Cameroon and the Chad basin in the 1990s. She starts with the resistance to taxation as part of the struggle to unseat an autocratic government in 1990–2 (see Chapter 6), and notes how the struggle generated alternative services not subject to government revenue control, so an ethic of illegality, especially where agents of the state were also bending the rules, could be seen as both reasonable and justified (Roitman, 2004: 23–47). Her main focus, however, is on the smugglers and highwaymen who operated illegally across national and fiscal borders. This approach raises wider questions about links between various levels of 'criminality' and political resistance that are too wide ranging to address here.

Forms of petty theft and sabotage are included in Scott's discussion of 'everyday resistance', deployed often by peasants, but occurring also in other social settings (Scott, 1985). His theoretical focus is on the role of disguised forms of resistance and 'hidden transcripts' that provide 'a critique of power spoken behind the back of the dominant' (Scott, 1990: xii). Scott briefly attempts to address the question how masked and hidden resistance can be transformed into open revolt. He suggests the concept of 'hidden transcripts' can give us insight into those electric moments when 'the hidden transcript is spoken directly and publicly in the teeth of power' (Scott, 1990: xiii). His two main examples are the crowd booing President Ceausescu in December 1989, and the open challenge by economist and opposition politician Ricardo Lagos on TV in June 1988, when he reminded General Pinochet that he had promised not to seek re-election as president of Chile (Scott, 1990: 204–7). Lagos claimed to speak for '15 years of silence' and his speech did have a major public impact, whilst the booing crowd in Bucharest disrupted what had been a legitimating ritual of public appearances by Ceausescu. But both examples are in some ways misleading. A significant political resistance to Pinochet had been building since 1983 (see Chapter 6), and the Lagos speech was part of this already open opposition. The booing of Ceausescu occurred after the days of open unarmed protest in Timisoara (see Chapter 3), when a crowd assembled in the central square, including children, was attacked by tanks, armoured patrol cars and helicopters. This extreme regime brutality was the main trigger for booing Ceausescu – the crowd also shouted 'Timisoara' and 'murderer' (Antal, 1994: 6–9).

Scott's other explanation was to draw an analogy with water pressure against a dam, a pent-up reserve of frustration that is released by an act of defiance, which is then imitated, making the defiance seem safer. In Romania most people had lived in severe poverty under an increasingly bizarre regime, marked by a personality cult and extreme repression, where an individual could be imprisoned for telling a political joke. So the dam metaphor – though not necessarily linked to 'everyday resistance' – is quite persuasive. It might also apply to the unexpected upsurge of open popular protest in Tunisia in January 2011, which rapidly spread to Egypt and to other countries in the Middle East.

Structural openings and constraints

Analysis of diffuse forms of social power could indicate the limits of political change that can be achieved by people power. Atack quotes Foucault's own view that it is perfectly possible to change a government or regime, but to 'leave essentially untouched the power relations which form the basis for the functioning of the state in its conventional format' (Atack, 2006: 99–100; Foucault, 1991b: 64). Limitations on the extent of revolutionary change can also be adduced from structuralist approaches that focus on types of dominance and hegemony within the international political system or on the global capitalist economy. Structural analysis does not, however, only underline limitations, it may also indicate how particular political regimes and economic systems may be undermined by global forces (see also Chapter 7).

Structural power can be interpreted differently depending on both the ideological slant and the academic discipline involved. Structural analysis often derives from Marx, but his work can provide a basis for varied interpretations, some stressing the interlocking logic of a complex economic, technological and ideological system such as global capitalism, and others identifying the role of specific major institutions (such as multinational corporations and banks), making identifiable collective decisions, as well as more amorphous financial markets, and giving greater emphasis to the role of governments of states. Lukes discusses this issue in terms of a debate between Ralph Miliband and Nicos Poulantzas over the role of the state within capitalism (Lukes, 2005: 54–7). A closely related issue, considered by Lukes, is how far a structuralist interpretation is wholly determinist and how far it allows for conscious individual and collective agency, even if within structurally determined limits. He also addresses some philosophical problems of structural analyses – for example the difficulty of justifying the Marxist concept of 'false consciousness' (Lukes, 2005: 144–51).

A structuralist interpretation of popular revolutionary uprisings has been developed by both internal analysts and Western academics looking back on 1989–91 in Eastern Europe and the Soviet Union. This approach suggests that the political and economic state socialist system of the Soviet bloc was unsustainable because of conceptual flaws and inbuilt institutional weaknesses and inability in the long run to deliver efficient economic growth or compete with global capitalism. Bartolomiej Kaminski (1991), for example, argued that state socialism was inherently defective in its conception and that political attempts to find new economic mechanisms undermined the state itself.

Extreme versions of structuralism, which deny any causative role for individual and collective agency, both by hundreds of thousands of citizens engaging in resistance and by individuals within government, are politically unconvincing and theoretically unsatisfactory. But broadly structuralist explanations can illuminate both the limits and possibilities for resistance movements, and can also suggest the constraints imposed even on 'successful' movements. The eventual overthrow of apartheid in South Africa is a good example. The evolving struggle highlighted the problem of ideological conditioning inherent in racism. Leo Kuper, in his *Passive Resistance in South Africa* studying the 1950s campaigns of peaceful non-cooperation and defiance of the pass laws, noted the psychological distance felt by the majority of the white population towards the Africans they were oppressing, and a denial that they shared the same basic humanity. As a result, he argued, the persuasive aspects of nonviolent resistance were ineffective (Kuper, 1956). Johan Galtung has, however, suggested (in the context of the Palestinian–Israeli conflict) that a possible solution to such 'social distance' is to create a chain of influence that will lead to groups who can have an effect on the oppressors (Galtung, 1989).

The relationship between apartheid and forms of institutional and structural economic power is also important. For a long period the major mining companies and corporations operated profitably within the apartheid regime and benefited from apartheid in their labour practices. Demand for gold and diamonds and South Africa's relatively developed economy enabled it to prosper within the wider global economy. But by the 1980s economic constraints began to favour the resistance; South Africa, despite its gold reserves, was becoming much weaker and had high levels of indebtedness. Heavy expenditure on the military (engaged in fighting in Mozambique and Angola as well suppressing internal rebellion) made an end to apartheid look more attractive to the government and business leaders (Lodge, 2009: 224–5). Widespread international sanctions, including in culture and sport, contributed to isolating the regime, as did the increasing international salience of human rights (see also Chapter 7 on the changing international context). But no political analysis can ignore the role of the internal opposition in challenging and highlighting the brutalities of apartheid, and in particular the mounting communal agitation in the townships and the trade union militancy that developed in the 1980s. This popular resistance fell short of directly threatening government stability, but influenced business leaders and some political insiders to consider a negotiated accord.

South African dependence on the global capitalist economy therefore aided the movement against apartheid. But the role of business interests and global constraints on the viability of a future government, as well as the need to compromise with the existing political regime, imposed strong pressures on the ANC to limit its egalitarian economic agenda. Gillian Slovo notes the bitter criticism her Communist Party father, Joe Slovo, had to face from his comrades for concessions made during the negotiating process leading to a majority government (Slovo, 2009: 175). Since the 1994 elections and the initial presidency of Nelson Mandela, many poor black Africans have become bitterly disillusioned (see Chapter 7).

Ideological hegemony and Gramsci on civil society

Since the 1980s intellectuals involved in resistance struggles in contexts as diverse as Latin America, South Africa, Poland and Palestine have sometimes turned to the version of Marxism developed by Antonio Gramsci, who died in an Italian fascist prison in the 1930s and was therefore himself a symbol of resistance. At a theoretical level he provided a more complex approach to explaining ideological hegemony than earlier Marxist theorists had provided. Gramsci, drawing on Machiavelli's image of the half-animal and half-human figure of the centaur to represent political life, argued that there were two levels of 'force and consent, authority and hegemony, violence and civilization' (Showstack Sasson, 1987: 112). Gramsci argued that there were two 'superstructural levels' (above Marx's economic 'base'). One was 'civil society, that is the ensemble of organisms commonly called "private", and the other the "state"' (ibid.: 113). He explored the notion of 'consent', one that was voluntary in the sense that it involved active acceptance of the values and beliefs of the dominant social order, but was also determined by the nature of that order (Merrington, 1977: 151). Gramsci's analysis suggested the difficulty of changing consciousness and promoting withdrawal of consent where hegemony was largely exercised through civil society, but also suggested that civil society was the arena in which a struggle for a new world view and social order could be most effectively fostered. Moreover, he argued that where the state was not buttressed by a complex civil society – as in Russia before the Revolution – it was more vulnerable to economic crises and popular resistance.

Quite a number of civil resistance movements have developed where political rule was not well-insulated by civil society – obviously true of occupation regimes, and of some countries under openly military rule. Where a regime creates social organizations as an explicit means of control, as in the case of official fascist-style trade unions in Spain under General Franco, the opposition strategy is usually to create alternative (sometimes underground) bodies, as initially happened in Spain. But, as opposition mounted in the 1970s, workers' committees created to organize wild cat strikes began to infiltrate the official trade unions (Preston, 1986; Balfour, 1989). In the communist regimes of Eastern Europe, civil resistance in the 1970s and 1980s generally involved creating alternative institutions, But in the 1956 reform movements in Poland and Hungary, and in Czechoslovakia in 1967–8, when the resistance did not wholly repudiate official Marxist ideology but sought to give it a 'human face', official cultural, student and trade union bodies, or officially authorized groups such as the 'Petofi Circle' (a debating circle sponsored by the Federation of Comunist Youth) could become arenas for dissent and later key vehicles for resistance (Vali, 1961: 227–32; Golan, 1971).

Since Gramsci was primarily addressing the nature of ideological hegemony within capitalism his approach can be used not only to study the relationship between civil society and the state, but also the differing class and ideological interests promoted by civil society bodies, The conflict between liberal, middle-class priorities and the aims of the poor and socialist political factions can be played out within a people power movement. Eva-Lotte Hedman has adopted a Gramscian framework to explore this thesis in relation to the Philippines (Hedman, 2006). Gramsci's interpretation of civil society is therefore more double-edged than the positive understanding of popular initiative and cooperation implied by Tocqueville's celebration of civil society in the new democracy of America in the 1830s, where he saw it as a bulwark against the state rather than a promoter of state control. Tocqueville's view was more often cited by some of the Eastern European intellectuals in the 1970s and 1980s, for example by Ferencz Feher, the exiled Hungarian dissident, in his essay 'The Evergreen de Tocqueville' (Feher, 1995), who explored how democracy could be created from below.

Gramsci's focus is on the more subtle forms of manufacturing 'consent', but, as his references to Machiavelli and the centaur indicate, and from personal experience, he was well aware of the role of violence in upholding some regimes. It is to this issue we now turn.

Power and violence

Violence, like power, is an essentially contested concept. It can be interpreted structurally to designate a whole system of domination, and to emphasize the more indirect forms of 'violence' to human dignity that can be inflicted by extreme poverty, systematic discrimination and denial of individual and political freedoms. Sometimes it has clear rhetorical intent, as in Slavoj Zizek's polemic against capitalist entrepreneurs (such as George Soros or Bill Gates) who claim to promote democracy and tolerance, but are 'the very agents of the structural violence that creates the conditions for the explosion of subject violence', such as terrorism (Zizek, 2009: 31). Often appeal to structural violence is used as a justification for armed resistance, but when adopted by a peace researcher like John Galtung it endorses active nonviolent resistance to economic and psychological, as well as political domination (Galtung, 1996). A concept of structural violence is relevant to civil resistance because open nonviolent challenge to the rules of the system often brings onto the television screens overt violent repression, revealing the physical brutality that is practised routinely, in more hidden ways. The Civil Rights Movement achieved this effect in the racist Deep South of the USA.

It is also possible to use Scott's distinction between hidden and public transcripts. He suggests that, like the ruled, rulers usually have a public transcript which expresses concern for the welfare of the ruled, and a private language much more cynical about the realities of maintaining domination. Use of physical violence and exploitation of fear may be used secretly or indirectly – for example imprisoning protesters discreetly over a period of time, or using semi-official groups to make assaults on individuals look like criminal acts. Rulers do, however, often use violence very publicly to maximize the terror and awe of the population – Machiavelli gives some striking examples in *The Prince*, arguing that it is better for a ruler to be feared than loved (Machiavelli, 1988: 58–66). When challenged by dissent and resistance rulers often adopt a mixture of both open attack and arrest and more hidden forms of gradual arrests and apparently anonymous assaults.

It is the instrumental use of violence to uphold repression, and both its potential to deter or destroy popular resistance and its limits when confronted by cooperative power created by popular protest and rebellion, that is of particular interest in the context of people power. In this context Arendt's categories are (as Habermas concedes) illuminating. As Arendt (1970: 49) notes, it is when there is a dramatic challenge and the regime begins to crumble that the 'power behind the violence' – the obedience 'to laws, to rulers, to institutions' – is revealed as crucial. The issue for resisters (and theorists of civil resistance) is how to move from social paralysis and passivity to mobilizing the power of the people to challenge the regime. Key aims are to encourage fearlessness and to strengthen social bonds from below which will both create solidarity in resistance and cooperation to articulate and achieve political goals.

The spectacle of unarmed demonstrators confronting not only tear gas and rubber bullets, but live ammunition and tanks, suggests that fearlessness is the most crucial response to the threat and use of pure violence. Indeed, the amazing courage of many resisters, recently demonstrated in Tunisia, Egypt, Bahrain, Yemen, Syria and elsewhere, does suggest that individual refusal to obey the regime any longer, and willingness to die for the cause, is indeed pivotal. Systematic repression can deter individuals from taking risks and create a sense of paralysis or apathy, so casting off fear is indeed a vital step as leaders and theorists of unarmed resistance have stressed (see Chapter 2). Ryszard Kapuscinski, reflecting on the Iranian revolution, comments on the pervasiveness of fear under dictatorship, and how its grip is unexpectedly broken, when individuals in a crowd stop obeying the police. He suggests that books on revolution should start by considering how a terrified man suddenly stops being afraid (Kapuscinski, 2006: 109–11).

But most individuals gain courage from acting in concert with others and when they dare to hope for political change. A cooperative theory of power rightly suggests that a sense of solidarity and organizational linkages are even more fundamental. Efficiently repressive regimes try to ensure social isolation, through fear of informers and distrust of others. Arendt explores the most extreme forms of social isolation and individual atomization in her characterization of totalitarianism, drawing on Nazi and Stalinist policies (Arendt, 1958). In less extreme, or less efficiently repressive, regimes the official social institutions can, as we have seen, be subverted through what Hank Johnston (drawing on examples from both Spain under Franco and the Soviet Union) has termed 'duplicitous organization' (Johnston, 2005: 117–18). Or civil society can be developed from below with varying degrees of openness or secrecy, sometimes fostered and partially sheltered by churches, mosques or temples, university campuses, professional institutions or relatively autonomous trade unions.

The recent Arab revolts have focused attention on how widespread popular resistance can be launched without support from a well-developed civil society infrastructure or highly organized opposition – although apparent spontaneity often hides degrees of prior dissent and coordination. Media accounts have, however, stressed the importance of mobile phones and the Internet in spreading news and ensuring rapid communication between protesters and drawing in a wider constituency. The most central role of the new technologies has been in helping to organize protest, and in creating a new form of solidarity and trust, based not on neighbourhood or workplace, but on cyberspace 'communities'. This linkage would be fragile, however, and open to misinformation, without the direct sense of solidarity and cooperation engendered once people get together on the streets and create their own communal geographically based spaces – such as Tahrir Square in Cairo, or the Pearl roundabout in Manama, Bahrain. These become vibrant centres of 'civil society' when not under attack by the regime: Tahrir Square saw religious observance (by Coptic Christians as well as Muslims) and a mass civic initiative to clean up and renovate the square; the Pearl roundabout, according to the BBC (2011c), hosted an art exhibition featuring the struggle and a formal lecture by a lawyer on constitutional monarchy. Both were sites of animated political debate.

The recent events have demonstrated how repressive governments, as in both Tunisia and Egypt, in a rearguard action can try to sow distrust and destroy popular solidarity through releasing criminals, encouraging unofficial violence and looting, and diverting popular energies to safeguarding their own homes and neighbourhoods. By associating the protesters with antisocial violence the regimes also seek to discredit them and justify repressive violence. There is a long history of regimes using agents provocateurs to try to turn orderly political protest into an indiscriminately destructive riot. In Indonesia, the role of Suharto's son-in-law, General Probowo Subianto, is particularly infamous. After some leading members of the armed forces began to sympathize with the opposition, troops under Probowo's command organized and took part in pre-planned looting and burning of businesses, mass rape of women, and indiscriminate killing in the Chinese quarter of Jakarta on 13–14 May 1998 (Boudreau, 2004: 233). Such tactics indicate that repressive regimes, when they deploy vastly superior means of force to any that the resisters might muster, far from fearing that the people will turn to violence, often hope to promote a violence they can crush with some degree of legitimacy. If the protesters appear to be rioting rather than conducting a political campaign, then it is also less likely that large sections of the military or security services will defect to the opposition.

If the resistance fails to undermine the loyalty and obedience of important sections of the ruler's armed and security service, or to promote disintegration of the regime, then there is a danger that sustained violent repression will eventually prevail and violence destroy power. Alternatively, if the previous armed forces only partially split and there is a political standoff, then one possibility (as in Libya by March 2011) must be serious armed conflict. The interplay between violence and power is therefore complex in actual rebellions – as the discussion in the previous chapter on revolutions indicated.

5 Constructing 'the people': body politic, nation or class?

Use of the term 'the people' in political debate nearly always carries a value-laden connotation. For example Aung San Suu Kyi, commenting in September 1988 on the role of agents provocateurs in promoting disorder, stated, 'the people are trying to preserve order and unity while a faction of the government does its utmost to promote anarchy' (Wintle, 2007: 265).

Over time and in varying political contexts 'the people' has had many different meanings, often – though not always – positive. Whilst references to 'people' may be used vaguely to mean some or many individuals, or may primarily refer to individuals pursuing their own specific interests, in its political usage 'the people' always implies some kind of definite collectivity. Within political or legal theory and ritual 'the people' has quite often been conceptualized as a 'body', signalling the continuity through time of a political entity. Political usage of 'the people' also often denotes those who have certain recognized political rights, as in references to the 'will' or 'mandate' of the people in elections. Conversely, where recognized political rights have been usurped, for example by military coup or dictatorship, 'the people' have often tried to reassert these rights. Where these rights have never been properly recognized (or not at all) a popular rebellion in today's world will stake a claim to them.

In a political context the concept of 'the people' also implies a consciousness of unity and a potential for political action. The Greek word, *demos*, is in constant use today in many languages in references to democracy (the rule of the people). Greek usage, however, alerts us to a built-in ambiguity in conceptualizing the people: it often signifies a political collectivity as a whole in which all those who qualify as citizens have some role in government; on the other hand it has also very often been understood to mean 'the many' as opposed to the privileged or superior 'few'. This ambiguity emerges in Aristotle's discussion of democracy in *The Politics*: he suggests that in democratic states the 'demos' is sovereign, but when comparing constitutions he classifies democracy as the rule of the many, as opposed to rule of one or the few (Aristotle, 1948: 128, 131). The distinction between the many and the 'one' or 'the few' is embedded in the theory of 'people power' (see Chapter 4) and the rhetoric accompanying many movements.

This distinction, elaborated further below, is made explicit in Roman political thought. The Roman republic evolved first from monarchy to constitutional aristocracy, and then in response to popular protest to institutional recognition of the political role of the *populus* alongside the primarily patrician Senate: the election of tribunes of the common people was designed to protect their rights. So the republic became SPQR (the Senate and the People of Rome). But the Roman republic, embracing citizens of all political classes, was also often described as the *populus Romanus*, for example by orators such as Cicero (Canovan, 2005: 11–13). This dual legacy still resonates in the idea of 'the people' today.

Appeals to 'the people' tend to be used widely when men and women take to the streets, defy unjust orders and demand a new form of government. The people as a body (but opposed to their current ruler and governing circle) is therefore a concept at the heart of revolutionary consciousness and rhetoric. This view is developed strongly by Jules Michelet in his *History of the French Revolution*, in which he argues that it is a mistake to focus on individuals who appeared to act as leaders; in reality they expressed the sentiments of the masses and often lagged behind the popular momentum: 'The chief actor is the people' (Michelet, 1847: 10).

There is often an overlap between the concept of 'the people' and the concept of 'the nation'. Sometimes the term nation is used as a synonym for the people as a political body. This usage was common in eighteenth-century England and France, as is clear from reading Burke's (1973) *Reflections on the Revolution in France* and from the famous slogan coined by the Abbé Sieyes before the revolution: 'What is the third estate? The third estate is the nation.' This usage reflects the fact that England and France were two of the earliest centralized states that brought together regions with differing local languages and histories into a unified whole and encouraged a sense of common loyalty. By the nineteenth century, however, with the rise of nationalism as an ideology of political movements, the equivalence between the people and the nation has suggested a greater emphasis on the attributes allocated to nationhood, such as common language, culture, religion, ethnicity or shared history. The complexities of interpreting nationalism are briefly considered later in the chapter.

The coalescence of the people and the nation, defined in nationalist terms, has often been reflected in struggles for independence against imperial rule. This usage can be both inclusive and exclusive. A sense of nationhood can reinforce belief in a common identity and adherence to a collective political body. But strong nationalist sentiments tend, in an established 'nation state', to exclude foreigners; and can in an independence movement lead to fragmentation, with ethnic minorities seeking their own political autonomy or independence. The aftermath of these nationalist conflicts can lead to guerrilla warfare or unarmed resistance by ethnic and/or religious minorities in newly created states – as in Burma, the Philippines and Indonesia. When examining recent people power movements it is interesting to see whether and how far the people are defining themselves in nationalist terms and the significance of that dimension of culture, religion, historical experience and, sometimes, historical myth in particular struggles.

'The people' always seems to imply a large and significant political grouping. But in contexts in the past where there was slavery, or a large class of the poor lacking property qualifications for citizenship, or subordinated ethnic or racial groups, those recognized as 'the people' might in practice be a relatively exclusive category. Even in the comparatively democratic ethos prevailing during the American Revolution, black slaves and Native Americans were excluded from the new political settlement, and, in the individual states, which always determined who could vote, property qualifications remained the norm until the 1820s, when there was a shift towards full suffrage for white men (Boorstin, 1969: 273). Women have not counted politically as part of the people in formal constitutions and voting arrangements until (at the earliest) the end of nineteenth century, although they have in practice asserted their political identity by active involvement in popular protest and revolutionary movements for centuries. But 'the people' has always implied the importance of a grouping beyond a very narrow social, economic and political elites.

Indeed, quite often 'the people', sometimes qualified by adjectives such as 'common' or 'little', has been defined in opposition to the aristocracy, the rich or the governing elite, and has implied degrees of class conflict. For example in the Florentine republic in the renaissance, the *popolo minuto* could be contrasted with a rich oligarchy (Strathern, 2005: 51). Struggles for democracy are linked to claims by the poorer and/or less privileged sections of society to have a political voice. The rhetoric of 'the people' therefore has very frequently been invoked to stake a claim to political and other rights for those so far excluded, and. it may in addition be used specifically to promote the interests of the poor over the rights of the propertied rich. In socialist rhetoric the people are often identified with the workers and peasants: the 'Internationale' specifies the 'people's flag'. Emphasis on class is relevant to a few recent examples of people power (although successful movements usually involve temporary transcendence of class interests). A particularly difficult divide may be not only between the poor and the middle classes, but between rural and urban interests and attitudes, which can sometimes undermine the effectiveness of resistance.

This chapter explores, using examples of different campaigns, how these three main concepts of the people – as a body holding political rights, as historically and ethnically defined nations, and as the excluded majority claiming rights – feed into the rhetoric and the practice of people power. It also examines how one interpretation of 'the people' may change into another, and how differently self-defined 'peoples' can come into conflict in relation to particular struggles. This last phenomenon suggests that, whilst some people power movements can temporarily unite diverse social groups, others create tensions that can threaten to intensify political conflicts or even to break up established political units. To stress the divisive impact is, however, misleading. This chapter concludes by reflecting very briefly on how far a unified 'people' can be constituted through struggle.

Despite its centrality to political analysis, debate and campaigning rhetoric, and to the theory of democracy itself, the meaning of 'the people' has received surprisingly little extended academic analysis. An important exception is Margaret Canovan's (2005) book *The People*, which has helped to inform the distinctions made here.

The people as body politic: participatory and representative resistance

Attributing a collective identity to a collection of persons is a complex and much debated issue in social and political theory. Liberal individualists have long expressed suspicion of philosophers or social theorists who posit social wholes or metaphysical entities (Rousseau, Hegel and advocates of nationalism are frequently cited), an enterprise which they argue promotes a politics that subordinates individuals, and therefore their rights and freedoms, to the collectivity (Popper, 1962; Berlin, 1969). We need not reprise these earlier debates here. It is clear that even those theorists who analyse society and government from the starting point of self-interested individuals, as in liberal social contract theory, end up postulating a 'commonwealth', 'republic' or 'state' that does have a legal and political existence independent of the individuals who compose it at any moment in time (unless it has broken down into civil war or total lawlessness, when older social units such as clans come to the fore). The metaphor of the 'body' to denote a people bound by political ties and loyalties and (at least some) shared beliefs and goals has a long history.

When kingship was central to the idea and reality of a political realm, the symbolic, traditional and legal conception of 'the king' transcended the individuals who filled the role with very varying degrees of true royalty, and in due course died. It was essential to replace the individual as soon as possible: 'The King is dead, Long Live the King.' One mode of expressing this duality was to distinguish between the actual and symbolic 'body' of the king (Kantorowicz, 1957). When the king's subjects played an increasingly recognized political role, or deposed the king altogether, the metaphor of the 'body' could incorporate them, or be transferred to them. Hobbes composed his *Leviathan* to demonstrate how 'the multitude' is through a hypothetical social contract 'united in one person' by conferring authority to govern upon a sovereign individual or group, to whom everyone owes obedience (Hobbes, 1985: 227) The engraved title page of the first 1651 edition of *Leviathan* shows a giant king, whose body is composed of a mass of small individuals, surveying his domains. Hobbes himself was primarily a theorist of autocracy, but the logic of the contract was soon used – by Locke and his successors – to defend the rights of citizens to rebel against unjust or overweening rule. The concept of 'the body' is not always used explicitly – but it exists in a more shadowy or abstract sense of a collective entity. Just over a century after *Leviathan* was published, the newly independent Americans declared (through their representatives) that 'We, the people' had, 'in order to form a more perfect union', endorsed the legal contract of the new Constitution of the United States.

Political language has in recent centuries found it hard, even in individualistic market societies, to dispense with the idea of 'the will of the people', though this concept is still often viewed with considerable mistrust. Rousseau's attempt in *The Social Contract* to show how a public interest might be expressed through a popular acceptance of a formulation of this 'general will' has been interpreted as encouraging ruthless extremists to suppress and destroy flesh and blood individuals in the name of an ideal 'will of the people' – as in the Jacobin terror (Talmon, 1952). Claude Lefort, starting from a Marxist perspective and repudiating a focus on Jacobinism, has argued that the image of the body politic, or 'the people as one', underlies twentieth-century totalitarianism, and that this unified people has then been identified with the party and the party with the leadership (Lefort, 1986: 292–306). By contrast, Lefort argues that in normal liberal democracies there is 'no power linked to a body. Power appears as an empty place' (ibid.: 303).

Indeed, in more mundane political contexts political activity through pressure groups or parties is linked to partisan interests, factional squabbles or divisive ideological beliefs, and appeals to the popular will can often be seen as forms of party propaganda, deliberate obfuscation or simple muddle headedness. But there are times of crisis, as in war, or when old regimes fall and new ones are created, when there is a real sense that a 'people' is acting collectively on the public stage and expressing something like a collective popular will. Canovan, citing Lefort, contrasts the nature of day-to-day politics in contemporary liberal democracies, including ordinary elections, with those 'rare, electrifying occasions when the myth of the people is convincingly enacted before our eyes' (courtesy of the television cameras) and the people appear to assert 'their sovereign authority' (Canovan, 2005: 129). She specifically identifies these occasions with 'people power', choosing East Germany in 1989 to illustrate the point. This line of thought is pursued below. I argue, however, that the idea of the 'people' manifesting their presence and authority is not confined to revolutionary upsurges, but can also occur in defence of existing constitutional principles, for example against *coups d'état* or government subversion of constitutional limits (see Chapter 6). Moreover, large numbers of the people do quite often attempt to exert a collective will through the electoral process, as the intertwining of people power resistance and contesting elections illustrates in contexts where the results are liked to be influenced by regime rigging and intimidation. There have been many examples in the past few decades.

The categories developed by Rousseau (1968) provide an illuminating means of exploring the relationship between people power and interpretation of 'the people'. Firstly, Rousseau frames his discussion in terms of a hypothetical and abstract 'original contract'. In the real world this suggests that the people involved understand themselves to be a political body based on adherence to certain political principles, such as the right to exist independently as a state, commitment to reinstate a past constitution and popular rights, defend an existing constitution, or to create an appropriate constitution in the future.

Secondly, Rousseau's distinction between the 'general will', relating to a common purpose and collective good, and the 'will of all', which is the sum of conflicting individual interests and wishes, is also relevant. The validity of people power movements as an expression of a common purpose requires appeal to political principles, such as an overarching rule of law or political rights, as elements in a collective good.

Thirdly, the 'general will' suggests unanimity. Total and lasting unanimity – even in a social contexts where major religious, ethnic or class divisions are absent – cannot be achieved in real-life politics. (Any attempt to manufacture it requires force and fraud.) But there are situations in which, for a brief period, almost all the population seem to unite to achieve a common goal; and this sense of solidarity and common purpose is heightened by participating in open resistance, shared risk and shared slogans and symbolism.

In assessing whether particular manifestations of people power really do approximate to an expression of a virtually united will there are several obvious criteria:

- the sheer numbers taking part in demonstrations or other forms of resistance, such as strikes;
- the closely related issue of how far usually diverse sections of society are involved;
- the persistence of the resisters; and
- the degree and vitality of the organization(s) created to promote resistance.

In practice near-unanimity tends to imply resistance to alien rule or more extreme forms of autocratic or tyrannical government, and therefore to be associated with a desire for revolutionary change.

The general will expressed in action?

It is very rare for most of the population literally to take part in demonstrations, even in quite convincing manifestations of people power. But it can sometimes happen. The Iranian Revolution of 1978–9, against the repressive regime of the Shah, discussed in Chapter 3, was marked by extremely impressive numbers on demonstrations. The mass rally on 10–11 December 1978, which combined political demands with commemoration of the death of the Prophet's grandson Husain on the plain of Karbala, was estimated at one to two million in Teheran (and there were rallies in most cities and towns throughout Iran). Pierre Blanchet, in a discussion about the Iranian Revolution with Foucault, commented on these events: 'What struck me was the uprising of a whole population.' He noted that – after subtracting the very young and old, the disabled and some women who did not leave their home – 'the whole of Teheran was in the streets' with the exception of those totally parasitic on the regime (Foucault, 1990: 214). Foucault's own response was that previously he had regarded the concept of the 'collective will' as a 'political myth' or 'theoretical tool', but that 'we met in Teheran and throughout Iran, the collective will of a people'. He added: 'Well, you have to salute it.' The effectiveness of this will sprang from its clear focus on one goal: ousting the Shah (ibid.: 215).

The second key criterion for deciding whether a people power movement does reflect a mobilization of the body politic is the extent of support across class, religious, ideological and other distinctions which often divide society. This is linked to the issue of numbers, but is not identical, since minorities within the population can potentially promote huge demonstrations and, even when a majority is behind a movement, significant minorities may abstain or be opposed. By contrast, the most impressive people power movements bridge such divides, as in Iran (see Chapter 3) and in Poland in 1980.

People power also often draws in sections of the population normally excluded by law, tradition or their own attitudes from active citizenship. Many movements in traditionalist societies mobilize surprisingly large numbers of women, and schoolchildren below voting age have quite often been courageously prominent in some protests (see Chapter 2).

A third consideration in assessing whether protests reflect a genuine popular will is the persistence of active opposition: a week of widespread protest denotes large-scale unrest, but not necessarily a settled determination by most of the people to achieve a fundamental change of regime or government.

Even relatively brief successful movements, as in East Germany and Czechoslovakia in 1989, last months or weeks. The movements for independence in the Baltic states gathered momentum from 1987 until achieving their aims in 1991. Persistence may be related to adoption of a variety of tactics, which can maximize the opportunity for all sections of society to take part, and allow for symbolic or less confrontational forms of action to maintain the movement in between more dramatic challenges. The First Intifada, for example, promoted several ways of refusing political cooperation with the Israeli administration, including selective economic boycotts and strikes. Even if the regime responds with serious violence against demonstrators and starts to imprison or execute its more prominent leaders, a committed resistance (as in Burma in both 1988 and 2007) is likely to pursue, at least briefly, a test of strength in the hope of winning over some of the police and troops, or of bringing effective external influence to bear on the regime. Where repression is slightly less extreme and/or the movement remains strong, it may continue to promote forms of resistance, as Solidarity did after December 1981 – boycotts of local council elections in 1984 and elections to the parliament in 1985, and refusal to cooperate with the official trade unions proved to be effective tactics (Zielonka, 1986: 106).

If brutal repression does close down open resistance, it could be argued that the popular will has been temporarily suppressed, but may re-emerge. But in that case some open minority dissent might be expected. In Burma there were some small open demonstrations in the 1990s and other indications of dissent. A major challenge was posed in 1998 when Suu Kyi's party, the National League for Democracy, decided to create its own parallel parliament based on the 1990 elections results, a move met by mass arrests of party officials. Significant opposition began to emerge again in 2006, when a few political activists from 1988 were released from prison and organized a petition of half a million signatures for the release of other political prisoners. They then called for candle-lit vigils by worshippers at Buddhist temples, and at churches and mosques, to pray for a peaceful solution to the political impasse, release of political prisoners and aid for victims of recent natural disasters. Tens of thousands responded (Moser–Puangsuwan, 2009: 42–6).

It is reasonable to expect continuation of cautious minority dissent, for example in the form of open letters or appeals, alongside organized underground resistance such as production of samizdat. Dissent has been expressed through symbolic protest – for example through wearing badges, and by occasional relatively safe expressions of the public mood on a larger scale, such as using official celebrations to manifest disguised dissent, or large-scale attendance at funerals or commemorations for significant opposition figures (as in Greece under the Colonels). After martial law was declared in Poland at the end of 1981, increasing numbers began to show their contempt for the official TV news by unplugging their sets and promenading with them in prams at the time of the main news bulletin. In Burma, after the suppression of the 2007 uprising, some showed contempt for the generals by tying pictures of the military leaders to the necks of stray dogs (Crawshaw and Jackson, 2010: 5–6, 22–3). In Latin America local communities banging pots and pans (*cacerolazos*) at set times has since the 1970s signified defiance. But evidence that there is a latent popular will can only be proved ultimately by a resumption of mass open resistance through strikes and demonstrations, or open refusal to endorse the regime's legitimacy when required to vote 'Yes', as in Chile in 1988 (see Chapter 6).

Movements embodying a genuine popular will tend (as noted earlier) to throw up their own autonomous organizations to conduct the struggle and create the basis of a new society. Sometimes the variety and vibrancy of these organizations is an indicator of the strength of a popular movement. Where organizations are formalized it may also be possible to count the membership. Over three million workers from 3,500 factories had joined, or declared their desire to join, Polish Solidarity by 17 September 1980 – by March 1981 membership stood at around 9.5 million (Garton Ash, 1983: 75, 135) Apart from those formally belonging to Solidarity as a trade union, it was the effective political representative of numerous other independent bodies and the wider social movement among the Polish people. Garton Ash (1983: 78) quotes the Provincial Governor of Gdansk, who observed that Lech Walesa was 'most certainly a tribune of the people'. If the popular movement is temporarily crushed, as Solidarity was in December 1981, the organization may – as Solidarity did – continue an underground existence. Alternatively the organizational forms of popular rebellion may be dissolved, but resurrected when a new people power movement emerges, as the memory of the 1905 soviets in Russia inspired the revolutionaries of 1917.

People power as an expression of the majority will

Claims by those protesting against a regime that they are asserting the will of the people suggest a united people with a common will. But many widely accepted examples of genuine people power are more likely to have majority support, as opposed to virtually unanimous backing. Even Rousseau conceded that (after the original contract creating a society) it is reasonable to accept the convention that the majority view should legitimately prevail, and this is the bedrock assumption of parliamentary democracy. But, whereas majorities can be counted in elections (if the count is fair), how to assess majority support in people power protests is less clear cut. Three key criteria indicating virtual unanimity within a resistance – numbers involved, bridging social divides and persistence of protest – can, however, still be applied. Whereas near unanimity may sometimes characterize people power in revolutionary contexts, when a regime is repressive and corrupt but not wholly tyrannical, it may enjoy not only some elite support but be able to satisfy segments of the population.

A semi-repressive regime is likely to deploy the formal mechanisms of representative democracy, but then use force and fraud to subvert them. So it is not surprising that examples of genuine majority resistance may come from the wave of recent movements against rigged elections. In these cases there are likely to be statistics from elections that can help to indicate whether the opposition really is in the majority. One of the more persuasive examples is the overthrow of Ferdinand Marcos in the Philippines in 1986.

The Philippines achieved independence from US imperial rule in 1946 with a US-style constitution. After being re-elected as president in 1969, President Ferdinand Marcos declared martial law in 1971, which was not lifted until 1981, and in the 1970s remodelled the constitution. Even after the end of martial law, and despite some later concessions to US President Jimmy Carter's international human rights agenda, the Marcos regime remained repressive and corrupt. It was faced by armed resistance from a secessionist Islamic movement in the island of Mindanao and a more pervasive communist guerrilla campaign, first launched in 1969, that became a greater threat to the regime in the 1980s. The people power movement was triggered by the assassination of the previously imprisoned senator and opposition leader, Benigno Aquino, in September 1983, when he returned to the country from exile (Kessler, 1991: 194–206). This act violated the tacit norms of what was politically acceptable, and mobilized business and middle-class opposition to the regime. It also intensified the longer-term resistance that had been developing among workers and peasants, and among students, professionals, women's organization and human rights groups. The movement to oust Marcos grew from 1983 to the presidential election on 7 February 1986. The tactics included regular marches and 'people's strikes', which closed down not only factories and offices, but shops and public transport, blocked roads to private vehicles, and organized sit-ins at strategic economic and political sites (Schock, 2005: 74–6; Zunes, 1999: 132–4). After Marcos had attempted to steal the election through obvious fraud and intimidation, Aquino's widow, Corazon Aquino, launched the Civil Disobedience movement on 16 February 1986, calling for a general strike to start on 26 February, and urging a boycott of banks, firms and newspapers that supported Marcos; about two million people assembled to hear her (Mendoza, 2009: 190). Divisions within the military, created by the rebellion led by General Ramos, not only further weakened Marcos, but led to the final act in this drama of people power, when about a million nonviolent protesters protected the military rebels against troops still loyal to the regime (ibid.: 186). Marcos fled the country on 25 February.

By 1986, therefore, the coalition opposed to Marcos had built on growing protest in the provinces in the 1980s and embraced many sections of society. Walden Bello describes Aquino's movement as genuinely 'populist', with a base in the urban middle class, but mobilizing the lower middle class, shanty town dwellers and unemployed workers (Bello, 1986). But, as the Aquino forces provisionally allied with the left, the resistance as a whole spanned ideological divides, from the political wing of the Communist Party and the National Democratic Front (NDF), to the Catholic Church, although there was distrust and disagreements over tactics between the NDF and the centrist forces. The Catholic Church establishment had initially offered 'critical collaboration' to Marcos, but sections of the Church opposed him from the outset, some even backing the guerrilla struggle, others engaged in political action in local rural communities in support of poor peasants. As early as 1974, Cardinal Jaime Sin, Archbishop of Manila, who opposed martial law, held a vigil, backed by 5,000 people, to protest against the military forcibly arresting members of a seminary. By 1984 significant numbers of clergy were taking part in training sessions on nonviolent resistance initiated by the International Fellowship of Reconciliation (Schock, 2005: 71–2; and Zunes, 1999: 138–9). The less influential Protestant churches were also part of the anti-Marcos campaign. Cardinal Sin made a key broadcast on 23 February 1986, calling for the people to come to the help of General Fidel Ramos.

The popular unarmed resistance to Marcos, though marked by political conflict for ultimate control over events and the composition of the new government, could therefore claim impressive support in terms of numbers, persistence and backing from large swathes of society. It could also claim to be asserting democratic principles against dictatorial rule. But Marcos, although he relied heavily on manipulating electoral processes through the electoral commission, intimidation and control of television and most of the radio stations and newspapers, did retain a significant support base. He had recreated a traditional political organization based on villages and neighbourhoods from 1972, ran his own political party and still had backing from a section of the elite. He had secured victory in parliamentary elections in 1978 and felt confident enough to put forward the date of the presidential election to February 1986. The state electoral commission (COMELEC) declared he had won more than 53 per cent of the votes. Clear evidence of fraud, including 30 members of COMELEC resigning in protest, convinced internal and international opinion that he had really lost the election, and the anti-Marcos election watch organization, NAMFREI, declared Aquino had won 52 per cent of the votes. Liberals, Social Democrats and Democratic Socialists all backed Aquino, as did some members of the NDP, despite their official boycott policy (Boudreau, 2004: 184).

The anti-Marcos vote would presumably have been much larger, had not the radical New Nationalist Alliance ('Bayan') based on trade unions and militant farmers, decided to boycott the elections, in part because it distrusted the reformist middle-class coalition represented by UNIDO. After the results were declared, however, Bayan did back Aquino's call for a general strike (Schock, 2005: 76–7). So the final stage of people power promised a renewal of determined majority anti-Marcos resistance if it had been necessary. It also indicated, however, that opposition to Marcos depended on a temporary coalition – the break-up of that coalition, and the role of forms of opposed people power in the later evolution of politics in the Philippines, is discussed in Chapter 6.

The second example of impressive majority opposition considered here is not related to an election, but did occur in the context of a continuing struggle to establish a constitutional framework for government. It was the May 1992 resistance to military dominance in Thai politics. The victory of people power encouraged commentators on Thai politics for the next 12 years to look to 1992 as a turn towards more stable and democratic politics. Ever since 1932, when absolute monarchical rule ended, the military had played a central role, sometimes in the background, but quite often openly seizing control through *coups d'état*. Student resistance in 1973 had succeeded in bring down military rule, but not in a real ending of military dominance or the pattern of coups. May 1992 was an important demonstration of people power that, due to Buddhist influence, stressed the principle of nonviolence. It is relevant to examine this movement here, because towards the end of the chapter we examine much more divisive mass protests in Thailand which indicate how relative unity can become fragmented and how opposed elites can mobilize popular support.

The context of the 1992 protests was another military coup in 1991, headed by General Suchinda Kraprayoon, subsequent attempts by the military to impose an illiberal constitution enshrining military influence, and the appointment of Suchinda as prime minister, contrary to his earlier promise not to hold that position. The resultant movement for democracy gradually gained momentum, beginning in early April with a hunger strike by a veteran but little-known activist who attracted support from crowds who gathered periodically, many coming after work. The major movement of resistance was triggered by a former governor of Bangkok, Major General Chamlong Srimuang, announcing on 4 May that he would fast until Suchinda resigned. Large crowds flocked to support him, but were persuaded to disperse when the speaker of parliament promised to prevail upon the parliamentary parties to amend the constitution. When this failed to happen, the crowds returned to the centre of Bangkok in much greater strength (Satha Anand, 2000: 158–9).

Numbers rose from around 100,000 on 4 May to 500,000 demonstrators on 17 May. There were also protests in the largest provincial cities, but Bangkok was the main focus of resistance. The government tried to quell the protests by arresting thousands; troops fired on and killed and injured hundreds of demonstrators between 17 and 20 May. But the demonstrators kept returning, and the king intervened. Suchinda was forced to resign, and after a period of continuing resistance, which included withdrawing deposits from the Thai Military Bank and promoting boycotts of businesses linked to the military, new elections in September led to a government with a civilian leader (Schock, 2005: 128–30).

The movement mobilized a broad range of support, bringing in the business community that had initially tolerated the coup. Interpretations of May 1992 have sometimes overlooked the role of working-class power in the opposition, but Andrew Brown has argued that this was due to an oversimplified model of 'united' working-class action (Brown, 1997). Trade unions and the urban poor were part of a coalition which embraced students and university teachers, women's rights organizations and campaigners for human rights, development and the environment.

Can more limited protests 'represent' a popular will?

Rousseau declared that the general will of the people cannot be represented, thus denying the democratic validity of electing parliaments to enact the will of the people. It might well be urged that the same applies to people power, which depends both for its effectiveness and its legitimacy on the claim to articulate an approximation to the general will, or a very clear majority will, on mass support from all, or almost all, sections of society.

But one circumstance in which it might be valid to identify a representative form of people power is that of a highly repressive regime, especially if a group endowed with special cultural and moral authority defies the government. The obvious example here is the leading role of Buddhist monks and nuns in Burma in 2007 who articulated popular despair over the rise in the price of fuel and food (Callahan, 2009: 51–4, 63). Their demands soon extended to the release of all political prisoners and concessions to the democracy movement. Initially the monks (joined a little later by separate processions of nuns) went onto the streets in their distinctive robes, with begging bowls and chanting Buddhist verses. They were applauded by bystanders. When other Burmese citizens, such as students and long-term democracy activists, wished to join in, they were initially encouraged to forms a human chain surrounding the marching monks, but later took part in the centre of processions. Other sections of the population, including entertainers and medical personnel, gave support in various capacities (Fink, 2009: 355–8).

The Burmese example might suggest how relatively small-scale protests can in some circumstances rapidly draw in much larger sections of the population. The initial protests against the price rises (caused by removal of a fuel subsidy) were launched by former 1988 activists who had been political prisoners.

When their protest was crushed, hundreds of monks in a town known as a centre for Buddhist education took up the cause. Their demonstration was met by soldiers who assaulted them, creating widespread outrage at this treatment of monks, the forming of the All Burma Monks' Alliance, demonstrations in many other cities including Rangoon and spreading public support. So representation can lead to participation and a form of people power.

Representation of a collective or clear majority would usually be judged by the criteria suggested earlier: collaboration across class and occupational differences, transcendence of different religious allegiances and involvement of women as well as men and of almost all ages. Representative protest claiming to symbolize the will of the people is also most likely to occur in the capital city (even if resistance began elsewhere). The demonstrators who set up their tents in Tahrir Square in Cairo, or kept returning to swell the numbers, played this symbolic and representative role in the overthrow of Hosni Mubarak in February 2011, although there were major demonstrations and later strikes in other cities that were crucial to the total resistance. But the square was the focus for early confrontation with the regime, and later for celebration of a new Egypt.

The people as nation

Many examples of people power that have mobilized significant sections of the populace and achieved their immediate political goal have been movements for national independence from foreign rule. Therefore the resistance has often been able to draw on a sense of national pride and identity, and a narrative of injustice and suffering under alien rule to promote a sense of unity.

At this point brief reflection on the concept of nationalism seems clearly appropriate, but the scope of the literature and diversity of interpretations, as well as the varied associations of the concept in different historical and cultural settings, mean that no neat definition is readily available. Nor would a single definition of nationalism do justice to the variety of national self-understandings displayed by various people power movements. But the literature does raise issues relevant to this discussion. One initial distinction of importance here is between nationalism as a political ideology and/or a political movement, and 'nationhood' (a sense of historically based national identity) that quite often underpins political institutions and creates an automatic association with belonging to 'the people' as a political body. This latter type of civic nationalism can intersect with more insistent claims to national identity as a basis for political rights and self-determination.

Whether shared ethnicity, language, culture or religious beliefs are essential to a sense of national identity can all be debated, with counter-examples – Weber's reflections on the problems of defining nationalism sets out many of the issues (Weber, 1978, Vol. 1: 395–8). National identity is clearly, as Weber concluded, a political phenomenon. It can be seen as a public narrative promoted either by governments from above to enhance their subjects' loyalty and strengthen their control over those living in a particular geographical area, or from below by dissenting intellectuals and political movements claiming a separate national identity and a corresponding right to a sovereign 'national' state. Such claims to national independence have been central to struggles against empires in the nineteenth century and the anti-colonial struggles in Asia and Africa in the twentieth.

Nationalism in the past has sometimes been elitist – a sentiment of Polish aristocrats, but not peasants, for example. But its strength in the twentieth century was linked to its genuinely popular appeal in resistance to imperialism. In recent decades claims to independence have also often been demands by linguistically, religiously or ethnically distinct 'peoples' within a nation state to break away and form their own state. Both nationalist tendencies have been manifest in popular resistance in Eastern Europe and the former Soviet Union (which could be seen as an empire dominated by Russia) since 1989. Both have been present in varying degrees in anti-colonial struggles in Asia and Africa, with the separatist tendencies creating some of the continuing sources of conflict in the post-colonial era.

Despite the nationalist ideological element in claims to political independence, the link between national identity and what is conventionally labelled the 'nation state' (as opposed to other political units such as empire or province) is complex. Some theorists have responded by arguing, as Weber does, that the nation state is primarily defined by effective political control and administration within recognized territorial boundaries. Others have pointed to the gap between markers of national identity and the boundaries of sovereign states, for example Walker O'Connor (1978) stressed that in 1971 only 12 states out of 132 were clearly based on shared ethnic origin. Separatist tendencies and proliferation in the number of states since then has somewhat increased the 'fit' between state boundaries and a shared ethnic and linguistic identity – but also created new minorities, or potentially exacerbated longer-term tensions with minorities within their borders. Some important examples of people power are a response to repression of their minority rights – as in the movement by ethnic Albanians in Kosovo in the 1990s.

Many sociologists and anthropologists have argued that nationalism (although it often evokes a romanticized past) is essentially a modern phenomenon, promoted by modern forms of consciousness and communication, and perhaps necessitated by urbanization and industrialization uprooting earlier communities. Nationalist sentiment has, however, often drawn upon religious beliefs and traditions that have for centuries been a source of identification and loyalty – especially if religion and its institutions are under threat. This overlapping of religious commitments and desire for political freedoms is reflected (in varying ways) in a number of the movements culminating in the revolutions of 1989–91. An interesting case of religious identity providing the core of a political independence movement is provided by Tibet (see Chapter 7).

Some of the best known definitions of nationalism are based on dualistic contrasts, in which one form of moderate and modern nationalism is seen as positive and the other as irrational and dangerous. Hans Kohn made a well-known distinction between Western nationalism, developed out of the Renaissance and the Reformation and based on secular rationalism and social and political realities, and Central and Eastern European nationalisms that drew on myths, concepts of national soul and mission, and a need to assert a separate identity (Kohn, 1945). Writing much more recently in the context of the collapse of the Soviet Union and the ethnic wars in the former Yugoslavia, Michael Ignatieff has contrasted 'civic nationalism' and 'ethnic nationalism', the former based on an inclusive sense of mutual political obligation within a 'nation', and the latter seeking to make inclusion dependent on blood kinship, and creating out of extreme insecurity a sense of identity based often on minor differences (Ignatieff, 1993: 3–9; 1999: 58–9). Anthony Smith, in a survey more impartial in tone, distinguishes between 'territorial nationalism' and 'ethnic nationalism' – subdivided into pre-independence and post-independence movements (Smith, 1991: 82–3). Smith sees the first civic and territorial version as characteristic of anti-colonial independence movements, which tend to be integrative, and the second as productive of secession movements before independence and irredentist or pan movements afterwards.

This dichotomous interpretation does indicate distinct tendencies within the framing of national identity and potential dangers of more extreme 'ethnic' understandings. But many people power movements represent a double reaction against externally imposed rule: an aspiration to political freedoms and democratic self-government, and also the full freedom to practise their religion and to express and develop their national culture. 'Civic' elements are therefore very important, but may combine in varying degrees, and possibly with shifting emphases, with a form of ethnic nationalism within the resistance movement. (The implications of the ethnic nationalist element for the politics of a new regime are beyond the scope of this book.)

Combining civic and ethnic nationalisms

Soviet occupation and consolidation of control after 1945 through direct rule (the Baltic states) or indirect political rule via highly organized communist parties (Eastern Europe) sought to override nationalist allegiances with a new communist class-based ideology. Resistance movements often drew on a highly developed sense of nationalism – though in many cases ethnic minorities with potentially conflicting aspirations and loyalties had resulted from the drawing of frontiers by the great powers in the first half of the twentieth century. On the other hand it would be very misleading to see these movements as exclusively nationalist. As argued in Chapter 3, the Central Eastern European states in particular were shedding over 40 years of communist party domination and ideology in favour of 'European' values and both political and economic liberalism. In the growth of dissent prior to fully fledged people power movements, issues of human rights, intellectual and artistic freedom, and, in several cases – notably in Lithuania and Bulgaria – growing concern over the dire environmental impact of communist party approaches to industrial growth were important issues (Miniotaite, 2002: 28; Randle, 1991: 36–7). (There was in Lithuania a nationalist element in concern for the local environment polluted by Soviet decisions, but these groups were also responding to the transnational green movement.) Environmental protesters added to the upsurge of popular resistance in Lithuania in 1988, and in Bulgaria acted as a catalyst. The Bulgarian Eco-glasnost group responded to a CSCE environmental conference in the capital, Sofia, in October–November 1989 to demand a voice at the conference and to organize a demonstration. Overreaction by the security forces, in the presence of many international observers, protests by other groups and the resignation of Bulgaria's foreign minister created the political crisis that ousted the Bulgarian party leader.

The greatest emphasis on national history, culture and symbols occurred in the movements in the three Baltic states of Estonia, Latvia and Lithuania, which had been independent between the two world wars, suffered extremely brutal occupation first by Soviet and then by German troops during the Second World War, and been incorporated forcibly into the Soviet Union at the end of the war. As a result there had been substantial Russian settlement in all three states. After some initial attempts at armed resistance, many adjusted to the new political realities, but there were intermittent episodes of dissent. Religious and nationalist issues overlapped in the sustained struggle for greater religious freedom by the Lithuanian Catholic Church, which began in the late 1960s with open protests by priests against restrictions on the church, as well as underground training of seminarians. The arrest of two priests in 1971 sparked wider resistance (Reddaway, 1978: 137) The samizdat Chronicle of the Lithuanian Catholic Church was published in the period 1972–88, despite KGB attempts to suppress it and the arrests of priests and nuns who published it. There was also a remarkable degree of defiance from ordinary Catholics, with over 17,000 signing an open protest to the UN about religious persecution in 1972; the KGB arrested those collecting signatures and destroyed the documents (Jancar, 1975: 222–3; Miniotaite, 2002: 18–21).

As Gorbachev's perestroika, and in particular the June 1988 Nineteenth Party Conference of the CPSU, promoted political reform and sanctioned a greater freedom of association and expression, protest rallies in Lithuania began in 1988 to sing the forbidden national anthem and display banned national flags (Miniotaite, 2002: 26–9). Estonian opposition was triggered by the coincidence of the annual Tallinn song festival with protests about the failure to include adequate representation from the newly formed Estonian Popular Front in the official party delegation to the Nineteenth Conference – the festival became a focus for asserting national identity and launched the 'Singing Revolution'. When in September a new Estonian party leadership agreed that Estonian should become the official language of the state, a third of the population turned out to celebrate (Beissinger, 2009: 234–5).

The intensity of nationalist sentiment in the Baltic states resulted in an amazing display of popular unity and commitment when on 23 August 1989, the fiftieth anniversary of the Molotov–Ribbentrop Pact that incorporated these states into the Soviet Union, an estimated two million, representing almost all the able-bodied adult population of the three states, formed a human chain from Tallinn to Vilnius. The size of the demonstration was encouraged by the three Communist Party governments within these states, who were by now committed to much greater independence from Moscow. The substantial Russian-speaking minorities were clearly excluded from the nationalist euphoria and more divided in their loyalties, though some did see economic and political advantages in independence. Beissinger (2009, 236–7, 244) argues that they did not pose a substantial block to the Baltic nationalist movements because many were old-age pensioners and no longer politically active.

Although a sense of national history and culture, and desire for national independence, influenced the Eastern European revolutions of 1989, the significance of specifically nationalist sentiment, as opposed to commitment to human rights and democratic choice, varied. Nationalist sentiment was probably strongest in Poland, which had a history of nationalist resistance to imperial rule stretching back into the nineteenth century (when Poland was divided between Russia, Prussia and Austria). Solidarity activists often encouraged demonstrators to sing the Polish national anthem. But in the 1980s the central symbol of Polish nationalism was the Catholic Church, which had close links with Solidarity and a significant influence on the acceptance of nonviolent methods of struggle (Smolar, 2009: 129–31). The election of Karol Woytyla, archbishop of Krakow, as pope in 1978, and his visit to Poland in June 1979, are usually seen as extremely significant in the evolution of a national sense of renewed identity and commitment to oppose the Communist Party regime.

The most specific example of demonstrators moving from a sense that they represented the suppressed and legitimate demands of the people, as a political body, towards adoption of a specifically nationalist identity, occurred in East Germany. During the October 1989 Leipzig demonstrations (see Chapter 3), the protesters chanted *Wir sind das Volk* ('We are the people'). But after the fall of the Berlin Wall, the chants turned to *Wir sind ein Volk* ('We are one nation') (Garton Ash, 2009d: 379–80). The latter sentiment suggested close identification with fellow Germans in West Germany and, perhaps, a willingness to accept the rapid process of reunification promoted by the West German government. In this instance, however, nationalist sentiment rather than underpinning understandings of the people as a political body, as in Poland, undermined the possibility of the East Germans asserting an autonomous political constitution. Instead the 'Ossies' became the often despised poor relations within the triumphant and affluent West German state. The short-term impact on East Germans is humorously but sharply evoked by the 2003 film *Goodbye Lenin* by the East German director Wolfgang Becker. At a more ideological level, the activists in the civic movement and intellectuals such as Barbel Bohley and Jens Reich in New Forum, who aspired to an independent East Germany pursuing a third way between communism and capitalism, saw the triumph of German nationalism as a disaster. But most East

Germans seem to have embraced the nationalist element in their revolt (Thompson, 2004: 55–6, 58).

It is possible to argue that a sense of national identity can underpin a liberal politics – as that arch liberal John Stuart Mill suggested in the nineteenth century in his *Considerations on Representative Government*. It is also possible to construct a sense of national identity interlinked with liberal beliefs and experience – in the Central Eastern European context Czechs prided themselves on the legacy of religious independence and free thought especially associated with Jan Hus at the time of the Reformation and later struggles for religious and political freedom, and on Czechoslovakia's record of representative government between the two world wars. (Contrasting historical and cultural backgrounds, however, meant that there was some tension between Czechs and Slovaks, which contributed to the breakaway of Slovakia soon after the dissolution of the Soviet bloc.)

But nationalist pride and sense of community can be opposed to at least two key civic principles: tolerance of diversity and respect for minority rights. Therefore people power based on strong nationalist sentiment may be exclusive during the phase of resistance (and have negative effects on subsequent politics). In the strongly nationalist uprisings in the Baltic states against rule from Moscow, the Russian minorities were effectively excluded. In other contexts, however, nationalist minorities may be part of a general resistance movement which is defined primarily by a dominant majority, and may even act as triggers for resistance. This was true in Romania in December 1989, where a protest in Timisoara in the Hungarian minority area started the national uprising (see Chapter 3), although the focus was opposition to Ceausescu's country-wide policies. In Bulgaria, protests by the Turkish minority in May 1989, demanding the right to speak Turkish, to be known by Turkish names and to worship freely as Muslims, preceded wider resistance (Randle, 1991: 35). So different cultural, religious and ethnic groups can also be united, or act in tandem, against a repressive regime.

Religion might potentially be an even stronger binding force than nationalism, and provides a sense of community, a strong framework of moral belief and commitment and precedents for martyrdom. In the recent examples of people power, however, it is the mix of religion and cultural and political nationalism that has proved potent – as in Poland and Lithuania. Moreover, religious institutions and symbols have provided a useful focus for many resisters who did not necessarily adhere to strong religious beliefs, as in East Germany (where Protestant churches played a key role), Poland and Iran. Therefore the specifically political opposition to arbitrary and repressive rule is a key element in the consciousness that it is created by a people power movement. This consciousness may, however, receive strong emotional impetus from a sense that both religious beliefs and national culture have been repressed, and turn people power from a unifying to a divisive experience.

Ethnic minorities, distinguished by a separate language and quite often religion, may suffer especial discrimination within a dictatorial or authoritarian regime, and feel an especially strong sense of national community and identity. Both these factors influenced the development of the Kosovo Albanian independence struggle in the 1990s (see Chapters 2 and 4) against the re-imposition of Serbian domination. This movement has, however, exacerbated tensions with the Serb minority remaining inside Kosovo, whose Orthodox churches symbolize the long historical links between Serbia and this region: these tensions have remained unresolved since Kosovo gained after 1999 an independence recognized by the West, though contested by Serbia and its ally Russia, but formally resolved by the international legal endorsement of Kosovo's independence given by an International Court of Justice ruling in July 2010.

The common people

The people defined by class

In past revolutions against autocratic monarchy and aristocratic elites, appeal to the vast majority constituting 'the people' was plausible. Michelet (1847), defending in the mid-nineteenth century the legacy of the Revolution against revived monarchy, deployed, as we have seen, the rhetoric of *le peuple*. But during the nineteenth and twentieth centuries 'the people' was being widely interpreted in the context of growing socialist movement as the workers and the poor as opposed to the capitalist and landed classes. Radical histories of 'the people' in the twentieth century, for example G.D.H. Cole and Raymond Postgate, *The Common People: 1746–1946*, and Howard Zinn, *A People's History of the United States*, tend to follow that interpretation. 'Common' in this context suggests the great majority against the privileged minority, and may also suggest the hard working, as opposed to the leisured or idle rich (Cole and Postgate, 1949; Zinn, 1980).

In the twenty-first century, despite huge disparities in wealth, political fault lines are often linked primarily to ethnic, cultural or religious identity. Sometimes, however, they overlap, most notably in Latin America, where the poor farmers and workers who have risen in protest against neoliberal economic policies imposed by Washington and rich local elites are also the indigenous peoples dispossessed in past centuries by the Spanish and other colonial empires.

Indeed, some of the most convincing recent episodes of people power that primarily (though not necessarily exclusively) depended on the poor are Latin American examples of resistance to neoliberal economic polices imposed through the Free Trade Agreement of the Americas (FTAA). A particularly striking example was the overthrow in October 2003 of the President of Bolivia, who had privatized energy supplies and symbolized American neoliberal policies. When he planned to export gas to California by a corporately owned pipeline, and threatened to stop the growing of coca (an indigenous crop), a coalition of indigenous farmers, the coca-workers union, trade unions, students and neighbourhood groups launched a campaign that began with 2,000 indigenous leaders going on hunger strike, blockading of cities, declaration of a general strike and

30,000 farmers and tin miners converging on La Paz. The government sent in troops, the demonstrators dynamited bridges to halt tanks, over 80 people were killed and, when several ministers resigned in protest about the bloodshed, the governing coalition collapsed (Crabtree, 2005: 93, 98–103).

Class divisions can, however, result in quite complex coalitions of interests when political parties and politicians are competing to control government. Where people power protests operate within the constitutional and electoral process, rather than as a means of seeking revolutionary political and social change, political leaders of the poor may emerge out of factional quarrels within the political elite and woo support from richer sections of society as well as from poor farmers or workers. These factors apply to the major protests in Mexico after the 2006 presidential elections, which demanded a recount of the votes. The candidate claiming the elections had been rigged was Lopez Obrador, of the centre-left Democratic Revolution Party (PRD), who stood on a platform of tax exemption and government financial support for all those earning the equivalent of US$800 or less a month (about half the population), and had associated himself with support for indigenous rights and opposition to environmental pollution by oil companies, resistance to energy privatization and campaigns against banking corruption. But his associates reassured major business and banking interests that a PRD government would maintain economic stability. Although PRD mobilized half a million supporters in Mexico City on 8 July 2006, brought up to two million onto the streets at the end of July, and produced convincing evidence of electoral manipulation (especially against a background of electoral malpractice in the past), it did not force a recount and refrained from using further forms of civil resistance (Giordano, 2006; Rubio and Davidow, 2006). A more radical confrontation between the state governor and a coalition of trade union, professional and social movements erupted during 2006 in the state of Oaxaca, partly inspired by a fraudulent election for governor, but also reflecting the depth of social divisions in Mexico.

A form of class conflict, the divide between the majority of urban dwellers and the generally poorer and less-educated rural population, is a significant political factor in many countries. It may reflect opposition between Western-oriented modernization and traditionalism, but can also be a product of regime policies which promote the economic interests and social welfare of rural peasant farmers. Most commentators suggest that this divide between rural and urban underlies the failure of the Green Movement in Iran to gain sufficiently wide social support in 2009–10. In Iran the support of the rural population has been used to bolster the regime. But if both the urban and rural population feel strongly enough to engage in prolonged protests the result may be serious political instability. The most obvious example is provided by Thailand since 2005.

The people divided?

The 1992 mass protests in Thailand, described earlier in this chapter, could be seen as a genuine example of the majority of the people opposing the military government. By contrast, the major demonstrations and strikes that broke out in Bangkok in 2006, and have been resumed several times since, resulting during June 2010 in violent and armed clashes, reflect deep social and political divisions in Thailand. Since 2006 opposed manifestations of 'people power' have in effect been a form of unarmed civil war, which threatened in 2010 to become armed civil war. The country has been held together partly by the major political role of the king of Thailand, who still commands a deep respect and a key constitutional role, but the king's failing health by the time of the 2010 crisis created another source of uncertainty.

The conflict in Thailand has revolved around the colourful Thaksin Shinawatra, a telecom billionaire, who was elected prime minister in 2001, and re-elected in February 2005 on a landslide of 19 million votes. Thaksin had won widespread support among the rural poor for his policies of providing medical care and low interest loans, but was also popular for promoting prosperity and financial stability, and his prompt, high-profile, response to the devastating tsunami on Boxing Day 2004. But his style of government, generally described as that of a corporate chief executive impatient of political restraints, a major financial scandal and charges of cronyism prompted the evolution of a major opposition movement in early 2006. Thaksin was accused of major human rights abuses in his 'war on drugs' and in the suppression of a violent insurrection in the three Muslim provinces in the south. The opposition coalition launched in September 2005, the People's Alliance for Democracy (PAD), which took to the streets in February and March 2006 to demand Thaksin's resignation, included a millionaire media owner, Sondhi Limthongkul, former general Chamlong Srimuang (now linked to an ascetic Buddhist sect) who had initiated the 1992 people power movement and stressed the need to remain nonviolent, and representatives of NGOs, university intellectuals and organized labour. It received broad support from the urban middle class (Kasian, 2006; McGirk, 2006). Thaksin responded by calling a snap referendum-style election in April 2006 to bolster his authority, and won 11 million votes – but the opposition had decided to boycott the election, and it was annulled. However, after a period of political uncertainty during which Thaksin briefly stood down, the army stepped in to depose Thaksin whilst he was out of the country in September 2006.

The emergence of two opposed movements claiming widespread popular support and demonstrating on the streets dates from early 2006. The pro-Thaksin rallies and counter-demonstrations were organized by his close associates, but the two columns of villagers who marched on Bangkok and set up camp as the 'Caravan of the Poor and Democracy-Loving Village People' did truly represent thousands of rural poor (Kasian, 2006: 8). In exile Thaksin, despite being found guilty of corruption, continued to play an active role in Thai politics, and retained considerable support in parliament and in the country. A pro-Thaksin government headed by the People Power Party won the elections in December 2007, but was soon opposed by thousands of PAD protesters, clad in yellow, who demanded the resignation of the new prime minister, besieged parliament in October 2008, and forced a final crisis by blockading the Bangkok airport in November and December 2008. The Constitutional Court ended this crisis by ruling the December 2007 election had been fraudulent and banning the prime minister from office. As a result the PAD was able to install its own (unelected) candidate as the head of government. But the pro-Thaksin red-shirted demonstrators soon called for new elections, and underlined the fragility of the government when they disrupted a summit meeting of the Association of South-East Asian Nations by occupying a conference centre in April 2009 (Casey, 2009). Red-shirt protests reached a new intensity in April 2010 when tens of thousands descended on Bangkok, and new levels of violence were reached, on both sides, with the army beginning to use live ammunition against demonstrators, and some protestors taking up arms. In order to prevent a massacre of those in the fortified protest camp, after the government issued an ultimatum on 17 May, leaders of the pro-Thaksin movement then urged protesters to leave the capital, and many complied.

The social and political divisions in Thailand can be presented as a confrontation between the rural and urban poor backing Thaksin, and the PAD with strong links to the courts, the army and business, backed by the middle class. But the Thaksin camp is itself closely bound up with corporate wealth. Moreover, both sides have at various points gained support from students, intellectuals and activists resisting corrupt politics and demanding respect for electoral democracy. In 2010 the red shirts included urban intellectuals opposed to the degree of military influence in Thai politics. The Thai protests are not therefore a straightforward example of two opposed 'peoples' contesting for control in the streets. But neither side can claim convincingly to represent 'the people' as a whole, or to have upheld democratic principles or respect for the law when in office.

The conflicting protest mobilizations in Thailand relate to internal politics. A very different but important example of 'people power' revealing social and political divisions, the 'Cedar Revolution' in Lebanon in 2005, reflects not only internal cleavages, but the impact of regional conflicts (including a large settlement of Palestinian refugees) and extensive external intervention by other states in the region. Lebanon is divided by religion, not only between Muslims and Christians, but between different groupings within each overarching religion: primarily between Sunni and Shi'a Muslims; and a wide array of Orthodox and Catholic churches, Maronites and others. Class divisions also influence politics. One of the major political forces is Hizbollah representing the Shi'a, who are generally the poorer members of Lebanese society and constitute about 40 per cent of Lebanon's four million inhabitants. Hizbollah is backed by both Iran and Syria. The latter had intervened militarily during the 1975–90 civil war and Syrian troops remained afterwards. Israel, which has often engaged in military operations and had a military presence in Lebanon, Saudi Arabia and the USA support anti-Hizbollah parties.

The Cedar Revolution was triggered by the assassination in February 2005 of a former prime minister, Rafik Hariri, a Sunni Muslim who had held office for

12 years. His funeral turned into a demonstration of unity between many Christians, Sunni Muslims and Druze, as hundreds of thousands followed his coffin. Syria was blamed for the assassination and thousands subsequently rallied and set up a tent city in Martyr's Square, Beirut, demanding punishment for Hariri's killers and an end to the Syrian military presence. (Shehadi, 2005; MacAskill, 2005) They succeeded in forcing the resignation of the pro-Syrian prime minister, and with the help of US and French government pressure, and invoking an earlier UN resolution, also subsequently achieved their goal of Syria withdrawing its troops. So the Cedar Revolution has been viewed as a victory for people power, though strong critics of US foreign policy and Israel often interpret it more cynically. But, in March 2005, Hizbollah mustered a huge counter demonstration of at least half a million to proclaim support for Syria (Whitaker, 2005).

Political divisions were underlined again in December 2006, when a new tent city was established calling for the resignation of the government and demanding a greater say for the Christian community (although some Muslims also took part), to be followed by a violent Hizbollah-led strike in January 2007 (Chassay, 2006; Fisk, 2007). Subsequently, further violent incidents, including bombs in Christian neighbourhoods and assassination of anti-Syrian journalists, undermined stability. So, although participation in people power could, temporarily at least, transcend some social divides, it tended to accentuate the most fundamental division between Hizbollah and other parties and religious communities.

Can a 'people' be constituted through resistance?

This discussion so far has focused on the link between popular struggle and differing definitions of the people within contexts where some sense of political and/or national identity already exists – although there may also be important cleavages. But there are contexts in which mobilizing a movement is the primary means of creating a sense of belonging to a unified political body. Movements against European colonial rule in Africa had to operate within often arbitrarily imposed frontiers, comprising a variety of ethnic groups, traditions and languages. Often the common language was that of the colonial rulers. Indeed, one source of identity was being part of a wider African anti-colonial struggle. Although some movements could point to an earlier heritage, for example the civilizations denoted by the Zimbabwe ruins or the Benin bronze sculptures, the emphasis was on a new modern economic and political future. Michael Bratton and Nicolas van de Walle argue that 'although the scope of the "demos" is problematic on a continent where the boundaries of the modern state rarely coincide with a sense of nationhood felt by various peoples', nevertheless, both the 1950s anti-colonial movements and the 1990s movements for democracy 'articulated a view of "the people" that was consistent with state citizenship' (Bratton and van de Walle, 1997: 11).

African independence movements adopted different means of struggle, both unarmed and armed (see Chapter 2), and some gained independence much more easily than others. Whether people power movements were most likely to promote a long-term sense of unity and citizenship is too large a question to address here. But one possible example of the creation of a people through an extremely long, arduous and (despite the role of 'armed propaganda' from the 1960s) predominantly unarmed struggle is today's South Africa. This is a particularly interesting example because of the divisions between races, and historically based political divisions between the Afrikaans-speaking Boers and English-speaking whites. Moreover, apartheid policies after 1948 systematically entrenched divisions through varying forms of discrimination, setting apart Indians, Coloureds and Africans, and encouraging differences between Africans (through setting up Bantustans).

The African National Congress (ANC), formed in 1912, tried to bring together the three distinct African nations (Xhosa, Swazi and Zulu) in a campaign for African rights, which it took to the Versailles Peace Conference of 1919. When the ANC led the resistance to apartheid in the 1950s it worked with organizations representing Indians and Coloureds and with the Communist Party. Jewish immigrants from Eastern Europe were prominent in resistance, but some English-speaking liberals, such as many women in the Black Sash campaign, also took part. The regime repression of the 1960s and 1970s led to the Black Consciousness movement, symbolized by Steve Biko. But when the black townships and trade unions developed mass unarmed resistance in the 1980s, the newly created United Democratic Front (UDF) had a multi-racial leadership and worked with Indian and Coloured communities (Lodge, 2009: 215–16). Despite differences of emphasis, the new resistance maintained reasonable political unity and acknowledged the directing role of the exiled ANC. The only major split was with the Inkatha movement in the KwaZulu homeland in Natal, which persisted damagingly into the 1990s.

Whites were drawn into the movement, partly through resisting or evading conscription into the South African Defence Force, which was both fighting two newly independent African governments in Angola and Mozambique and trying to crush rebellion in the townships. Churches, intellectuals and students engaged in opposition, social attitudes among the young became more critical of racism and business leaders increasingly recognized the need for change. When the National Party government freed Mandela in 1990 it reflected a willingness among many whites, including Afrikaners, to think in multiracial terms.

The four years of formal negotiations (behind the scenes talks had started earlier – see Chapter 3) were part of the process of creating a new people. The negotiations did not mean an end to all protest, as people power was also used as part of the bargaining. As negotiations progressed they were threatened by serious violence between Inkatha and ANC activists (some members of the security services were accused of orchestrating brutal attacks on black members of the public), and by threats of violent resistance from the neo-Nazi Afrikaner

Resistance Movement. But after the ANC and National Party had negotiated an agreement that led to a free election in 1994, open to all races and parties, the pre-election violence ceased.

The 1994 election was the culminating political and symbolic event that helped to consolidate the creation of a new people. Long lines of men and women queued patiently; for many it was the first time they had ever voted. Mandela notes: 'old women saying that they felt like human beings for the first time in their lives; white men and women saying that they were proud to live in a free country at last ... as though we were a nation reborn' (Mandela, 1995: 743). About 85 per cent of the new electorate voted: the ANC received 62.6 per cent of the vote, the Nationalist Party 20 per cent (signalling it had achieved some backing from non-whites) and the Inkatha Party 10 per cent (Benson, 1994: 132). Mandela himself came to represent the new 'rainbow nation', and the Truth and Reconciliation Commission attempted to achieve a degree of justice, through recognition of past crimes, but also to foster a sense of forgiveness and reconciliation.

One important lesson from South Africa is that people power understood as crowds demonstrating on the streets is not necessarily the antithesis of politics through elections, as the earlier contrast between the absence of a 'people' in normal elections and the assertion of a collective will in revolutionary situations might suggest. When people are mobilized to demand their political rights they have often in recent decades played a central role in contesting rigged elections in authoritarian or semi-authoritarian regimes. It is to the interrelationship between the electoral process and many people power campaigns that we turn in the next chapter.

6 People power and electoral democracy: 'electoral revolutions' and democratization

The practice of people power is inextricably linked to a broad concept of democracy, and popular movements that topple dictatorial or authoritarian regimes open up possibilities for democratic government. So far this book has not directly discussed what role people power has played in the processes of democratization, nor linked it to the scholarly literature on this topic.

The striking rise in instances of popular unarmed resistance since the 1970s has coincided with what Samuel Huntington (1991) dubbed the 'third wave' of democratization: the notable increase in the number of states moving away from direct or de facto military rule, one-party domination or personalized dictatorship towards multiparty electoral systems. Many of the moves away from military, dictatorial and one-party rule have indeed been associated with popular resistance. There has been considerable scholarly debate about the nature of transitions, with many initially tending to stress the role of elites. Analysts have also debated which type of transition promotes stable democracy in the longer term.

It is not only the increase in the number of people power campaigns since the 1970s that has been striking. There has also been a significant link between people power and engagement in elections – highlighted by the ousting of President Marcos in 1986. Electoral engagement by the opposition has occurred in several different political contexts. Some movements in highly repressive regimes in Latin America have managed to make use of what were intended to be totally controlled referenda or 'elections', designed to confer spurious legitimacy on the regime. In other cases, in Asia, cautious relaxation of control by dictatorships has created greater openings for an opposition movement to complement popular agitation with finding an official political voice through party politics. A third scenario, typical of sub-Saharan Africa in the early 1990s, is for significant popular protest to force autocratic rulers to accept constitutional revision and multiparty elections, in which the governing party participates, but the opposition have a real chance to compete for office. Strategies combining people power with electoral politics in these three contexts are considered in this chapter.

Since the early 1990s, however, a large category of states has emerged where the regimes, although effectively dominated by an individual autocrat and/or a single party, formally permit multiple parties and hold regular elections, but then rig the outcome. Comparative politics scholars have invented labels for these 'hybrid' regimes, including 'semi authoritarianism' and 'electoral authoritarianism', but the most frequently used is probably 'competitive authoritarian regimes' (Levitsky and Way, 2002). 'Electoral revolutions', in which the opposition has managed to win the election and mobilize people power protests to contest the regime's attempt to hold onto office, have engaged the interest of analysts of comparative politics and of democratization. There has been a particular focus on states in the former Soviet bloc – including the colour revolutions in ex-Soviet states. But some analyses also make comparisons with sub-Saharan Africa. Issues arising in both regions are briefly discussed below.

Combining people power and electoral strategies suggests a commitment to the principles of multiparty electoral democracy. This chapter therefore explores, with reference to particular campaigns, how resistance movements can provide checks against fraud at all stages of the election and strengthen the electoral process for the future. It also examines the case for taking part in rigged elections in order to increase voter competence.

Emphasis on electoral procedure has been the reverse side of large-scale and if necessary prolonged popular protest to demand democratic rights. There are, however, dangers in establishing a habit of people taking to the streets, which might sometimes undermine the respect for constitutional principles and electoral outcomes necessary to create a stable democracy. Justifiable campaigns of people power can potentially encourage in the future more questionable resort by political leaders to calling out their supporters to demonstrate en masse. The two opposed 'people power' campaigns in the Philippines in 2001 provide an interesting reference point for this debate. Nevertheless, ultimately a politically aware population, willing to resist challenges to the constitution, can be seen as a key safeguard. A few examples of such resistance conclude these reflections on people power and electoral democracy.

The third wave: political culture, elite transition and people power

Samuel Huntington (1991) coined the since widely accepted phrase 'the third wave of democratization' in his attempt to explain why and how 35 countries in Asia, Latin America and Europe changed in the 1970s and 1980s from undemocratic regimes to multiparty representative forms of government. Since then commentators have queried details in defining this wave – for example should it be dated from the 1970s or the 1980s. Michael McFaul has posited a 'fourth wave' of attempted democratization in post-communist states (McFaul, 2002). Huntington's work remains, however, a useful common starting point.

Debates about democratization have often focused on class structure and educational levels, and have also raised questions about the positive or negative influence of culture and religion. By the 1990s the third wave of democratization focused attention on regions which had so far been left out, in particular countries in Asia which had seen rapid and dramatic economic development (widely accepted as a significant, or even necessary, condition for democratic government) but had remained dictatorial or authoritarian. One major explanation appeared to be the impact of religion on political culture, and some scholars, notably Lipset and Huntington, tended to posit that Confucianism was an obstacle to democratic change (Lipset, 1993; Huntington, 1993b). Authoritarian Asian governments, happy to stress that there was a separate 'Asian model', reinforced this perception. An apparent exception was South Korea, where there had been student-led surges of popular protest against dictatorship and military rule, often brutally repressed, in 1960 and 1979–80. An effective worker, rural and student unarmed resistance in 1986–7 dissuaded General Chun Doo Hwan from standing for a second term in office, and led to competitive elections in 1988 and gradual democratization (D. Clark, 1987; Shorrock, 1986). But exponents of the Confucian cultural thesis argued that this liberalization was always controlled by the military (Nagle and Mahr, 1999: 261–2).

Social determinist interpretations also embraced the Muslim world, which Westerners tended to see as particularly impervious to democratic forces – although Huntington did concede culture might not be all-determining, his separate thesis on the 'Clash of Civilizations' gave widespread publicity to a more pessimistic view of Islam (Huntington, 1993a; 1993b). The upsurge of people power in Tunisia, Egypt and elsewhere since January 2011 now provides convincing refutation of broad claims about popular attitudes in Islamic countries – though it might be argued that the educated middle classes communicating via the Internet often played a crucial initial role in articulating demands.

Changing regimes must involve an important role of political action. The democratization literature has, therefore, paid considerable attention to the nature and types of democratic transitions. Huntington (1991) proposed a three-fold classification of internal transitions:

- 'transformations', where elites take the initiative;
- 'replacements', where oppositions take the initiative; and
- 'transplacements', where joint initiatives by government and opposition were involved.

(He also had a fourth category of external military intervention to impose a new regime, which is excluded here). Categorizing specific countries under such schemes of classification tends to invite dissent. For example, was the Czechoslovak velvet revolution really a 'transplacement'? A more important and general criticism is that focus on elite transformation from above (which Huntington, like others, sees in Spain and Brazil) can overlook the significant level of popular dissent and resistance building over many years.

An academic tendency to give more weight to the role of elites, and to stress the disruptive rather than positive impact of popular intervention, is reflected in the prevalence of the model of 'pacted transitions'. Using Spain and some Latin

American examples, this approach suggested that the ideal model of transition required careful negotiations, between a moderate faction within the regime and a moderate leadership of the opposition, to agree on future institutions and other key issues, and initially engage in a form of power sharing (O'Donnell and Schmitter, 1986). The important role of moderates in government (for example the king in Spain), and the importance of the processes of negotiation, in achieving some transitions, is indisputable. The South African negotiations in the period 1990–4, for example, which succeeded in overcoming deep social and political divisions and violent challenges, can be viewed as a pacted transition (Sisk, 1995). But a wider question is how the opposition leaders involved gain their bargaining power. When negotiations stalled in 1992, the ANC initiated a campaign of 'rolling mass action' of demonstrations, boycotts and strikes in June, culminating in a general strike in August (Mandela, 1995: 722–5). Moreover, the emergence of a moderate regime faction, though it may be partly a response to wider trends or reflect personal attitudes, may also be shaped by growing popular opposition.

A challenge both to the determinism of theories emphasizing economic development and political culture, and to an emphasis on the primacy of elite controlled transitions, has been posed by analysts emphasizing the key role of sustained popular protest. An ambitious attempt to make comparative and empirically verifiable claims for the importance of 'broad-based nonviolent civil resistance' movements in promoting effective democratization is the 2005 study by Adrian Karatnycky and Peter Ackerman, *How Freedom is Won: From Civic Resistance to Durable Democracy*. The authors argued that, of the 67 transitions from authoritarianism since 1972, 50 involved a significant role for civil resistance. A strong and cohesive civil society coalition is, they argue, critical. Using criteria devised by Freedom House in the 1970s (and widely accepted by many Western analysts) the authors found that, of the 35 states that were in 2005 classified as 'free', 24 had strong civic coalitions before the transition and eight had moderately strong coalitions. The study also claimed that 'the prospects for freedom are significantly enhanced when there was no (or almost no) opposition violence' – this applied to 31 states classified as free in 2005 (Karatnycky and Ackerman, 2005: 8). Testing for regime violence as well as opposition violence the authors argue the key factor was the strategy of the opposition. (They excluded the colour revolutions in Georgia (2003) and Ukraine (2004–5) because these transitions were so recent.) The authors also conclude that the two key elements – a predominantly nonviolent transition and a strong civic coalition – reinforce each other in leading to a democratic government afterwards.

Doh Chull Shin and Rollin Tusalem reanalysed the Freedom House data used by Karatnycky and Ackerman, and generally confirmed both the importance of nonviolent civic activism in promoting relatively stable liberal democracies and the significance of 'strong civic coalitions' (Shin and Tusalem, 2007: 12). Their article explores in addition the regional spread of democracies, which strongly suggests the importance of longer-term structural factors and examines the role of political culture from various perspectives. They also recognize that linking civil resistance to civil society coalitions may effectively import structural analysis and the role of political culture into the equation both before and after transition. But their overall conclusion stresses the importance of 'citizenries' both in transition and in support for subsequent democratic institutions – though they claim understanding of and attachment to democracy is influenced by political culture.

Valerie Bunce and Sharon Wolchik, who have written extensively on democratic transitions, argue that there has been increasing recognition of the value of mass mobilization – citing inter alia the Karatnycky and Ackerman study, and the work of Ackerman and Duvall, and of Schock on nonviolent action (Bunce and Wolchik, 2011). They criticize the concept of 'pacted transitions' for its failure to recognize the role of popular resistance. The elitist implications of 'pacted transitions' are strongly challenged as well by Mark Thompson (2004: 10) in his study of 'democratic revolutions'.

People power and electoral strategy in dictatorial and one-party regimes

Popular uprisings against regimes that allow no significant opportunities for autonomous political action or institutional means to change the governing elite typically take the form of mass demonstrations and strikes. If some of the security forces begin to side with the protesters, or if the ruling elite effectively capitulates, then the result is a successful popular rebellion. But there are other routes to regime change which involve widespread civil resistance. A significant number of people power movements have seized the opportunities provided by regime-initiated and stage-managed referenda or 'elections' to promote genuine opposition, or even oust the ruling elite, through these officially endorsed channels. The different ways in which this intermingling of resistance and electoral strategy has led to regime change are briefly charted below, comparing movements in Chile and Uruguay and in Indonesia and Taiwan.

But resistance movements have adopted differing strategies when a regime decides to stage a referendum or 'election' as a legitimating device, on the assumption that it can control the process and the outcome. Sometimes the opposition may campaign for a popular boycott, because the whole process underpins fundamentally unacceptable policies, as in racially segregated elections promoted by the apartheid regime in South Africa. A boycott may also be chosen if it seems clear that there is no possibility of promoting genuine opposition. This was the view taken by the National Democratic Party, led by Aung San Suu Kyi, in the Burmese 'elections' of November 2010, the first since 1990, when the junta refused to recognize the party's sweeping electoral victory. The boycott was influenced by Aung San Suu Kyi's continued house arrest, over 2,100 other political prisoners and obvious devices to ensure continued military control, noted by *The Economist* (2010), such as prohibitive electoral deposits for individual candidates and reservation of 25 per cent of the seats in national and local parliaments for military nominees. But some members of the NDP joined a breakaway party that did contest the elections, as did a number of other opposition groups. After claiming overwhelming victory in the sham election, the generals decided to release Suu Kyi.

Regime exercises in 'popular consultation' can, however, provide a strategic opportunity to opposition forces, as they may allow slightly more leeway to organize and articulate their views, and there tends to be an unusual degree of international interest and scrutiny. Moreover, if the opposition does manage to demonstrate serious support for its cause, using such constitutional means adds to its own legitimacy and credibility, both internally and internationally.

Latin America in the 1980s

A good example of the opposition using the ballot comes from Chile in 1988, when General Pinochet called a plebiscite to endorse his decision to remain in office as president for another eight years. The resistance decided, despite rejecting the plebiscite in principle, to mobilize around a call for a 'No' vote. Their strategy included an intensive effort to register eligible voters, organizing opinion polls, canvassing voters and – in the run-up to the actual plebiscite – holding large demonstrations (Ackerman and Duvall, 2000: 296–9). The 'No' vote won by 54.7 per cent, against 43 per cent, which was a clear demonstration of majority opposition to Pinochet. Moreover, as Carlos Huneeus observes, the decision to use institutional channels and work within Pinochet's own 1980 constitution maximized the chances of the outcome being accepted by the armed forces. Indeed, members of the military junta – not only from the air force and navy, who were less loyal to Pinochet personally, but also from the army – refused to support him when he tried to ignore the outcome and stay in office. Chile's earlier political tradition of respect for the electoral process aided peaceful transition (Huneeus, 2009: 211–12).

A second example of oppositionists capitalizing on the opportunity to cast a vote is provided by the Uruguayan resistance. Like Chile, Uruguay had earlier experience of constitutional government, but was subjected to military rule in 1973. The regime announced in 1980 a referendum on a new constitution, enshrining the principle of a single-candidate presidential election. Despite martial law, 7,000 political prisoners, new arrests of those campaigning for a 'No' vote, and propaganda identifying a 'No' vote with support for terrorism, 57 per cent (of the 85 per cent of the electorate who took part) voted 'No'. John Keane, who interviewed a number of those involved in the campaign, notes that at the close of voting many occupied polling booths to demand that there should be no destruction of ballot boxes. Deterred from publicly celebrating their victory at the polls, the opposition dressed in yellow and followed the advice of a private radio station to promote a 'smile revolution'. Keane (2009: 659) calls November 1980 in Uruguay 'a remarkable demonstration of people power'.

But whereas in Chile defeating a government plebiscite was the culmination of a campaign, in Uruguay it was the beginning. There was mounting public opposition in 1983–4, including the symbolic protest of banging pots and pans, agitation for human rights, fasts, marches and a rally of 250,000 people on the last Sunday of November 1983 (the traditional day for elections), culminating in general strikes in January and June 1984. Genuine elections were held in November 1984 (Finch, 1985; Roberts, 1991; Weinstein, 1988). Democratic change in Uruguay included an element of negotiation between elites: Julio Maria Sanguinetti, who was president in the period 1985–90, has stressed the importance of dialogue and negotiations between civilian opposition leaders and the military between 1980 and 1984 (Sanguinetti, 1993). But people power, originating in the contested referendum, exerted significant pressure.

Asia: 1970s to 1990s

Using elections as a focus for opposition was an important strand in the rising resistance to General Suharto's 'New Order' in Indonesia from the 1970s to the 1990s. The New Order was launched after the 1965 military coup (against claimed attempts at a communist takeover), when the military eliminated their rivals for dominance under the Sukarno regime, the Indonesian Communist Party, murdering half a million alleged communists, and cracking down on any underground communist organization. Military control was wholly entrenched in March 1967, when Suharto replaced Sukarno as acting president. The military dictatorship imposed stringent restrictions on any organized dissent, banning all independent political organizations and putting in their place state-controlled unions, farmers' associations and 'opposition parties'. Students, who had demonstrated in support of the anti-communist campaign in 1965–6, were initially allowed a slightly more privileged position, but became in their turn a target for repression when they began to demand a restoration of democracy. But the regime did not actually ban the student organizations, and they were at the forefront of campaigns against corruption and popular agitation for political change from the 1970s.

The authorized 'opposition' parties, which from 1973 were the Muslim-based United Development Party (PPP) and the broad-based Indonesian Democratic Party (PDI), were able to take part in elections. Electioneering did create possibilities for protesting and voicing policy demands, even though victory of the ruling Golkar party was ensured by intimidation and by rigging the later stages of the vote counting process. Vincent Boudreau argues that the combination of gradual liberalization, which allowed better organized and sustained resistance to be expressed not only by students and intellectuals, but also by workers, farmers, trades people and other social groups, and the 'shorter cycles of mobilization and protest associated with elections' coincided in 1997 (Boudreau, 2004: 221). The electoral façade had already been disrupted in December 1993, when Megawati Sukarnoputri, a daughter of Sukarno, became leader of the PDI and a figurehead for demands for real democracy, and both the PDI and PPP began to articulate greater opposition to the New Order. The regime's attempts to oust Megawati, and popular agitation to bolster her position, culminated in a confrontation between the regime and opposition groups in July 1996 at the PDI headquarters, followed by arrests of political leaders. Megawati, who headed a breakaway PDI faction, was excluded from those eligible to stand in the May 1997 elections, and her parliamentary immunity was withdrawn. Despite widespread demonstrations before and after the poll, the opposition parties accepted Golkar's official victory.

However, the Asian economic crisis and its repercussions on the Indonesian currency in 1997 became a new focus for widespread, if initially disparate, protest against economic hardship, which gained momentum in early 1998. The students, interpreting a regime statement as authorization to organize protests on their campuses, began from February 1998 to orchestrate a major campaign across Indonesia. Their right to protest on campus was protected by university authorities, and, although they were liable to beatings, arrest and torture if they went onto the streets, they began to forge links with members of the armed forces. By May there was a national movement both inside and outside the campuses attacking corruption and economic mismanagement, and demanding political change. Leading political figures, including the parliamentary speaker, began to call for Suharto's resignation, and many of his military colleagues withdrew their backing (Vatikiotis, 1998: 229). Although the mobilization around the May 1997 elections did not bring immediate change, it created a popular momentum (Berger, 1997).

Even very restrictive electoral opportunities may provide an opening for emerging opposition. In Taiwan (Formosa), for example, one-party dictatorship and martial law had been imposed on the indigenous population by Chiang Kai-shek and his supporters after they fled mainland China in 1949. Protest and intellectual dissent developed after Chiang's death in 1975, but was crushed in December 1979, through the brutal suppression of a human rights rally and jailing of prominent radical leaders of the Formosa Movement. A more moderate opposition gradually developed, however, in the 1980s, which took advantage of a subsequent degree of liberalization, and fielded the wives of jailed opposition leaders in elections, to create the basis for a new opposition party, the Democratic Progressive Party (DPP). Widespread demonstrations and strikes by students, workers and farmers on a range of issues broke out in 1986–7, and in 1987 martial law and restrictions on opposition parties and the press were gradually lifted (Chou Yangsun and Nathan, 1987; Long, 1991: 66–72). Cheng Tun-jen (1989) has suggested that 1986, whilst it did not mark a Philippine-style people power movement, did represent a 'tacit negotiation' between the opposition and the regime. Eventually the leadership engaged in explicit negotiations with the opposition. The KMT regime relaxed its grip gradually, but the DPP, after winning growing support in the local and parliamentary elections during the 1980s and 1990s, was able to win the presidential election in March 2000. Taiwan can be seen as one of the more successful and peaceful of democratic transitions (Rigger, 2004).

Constitutional reform and electoral opposition in autocracies: sub-Saharan Africa

A different model of political change, which is initiated by strong popular pressure from below, is where demands are focused on constitutional reform and multiparty elections, but the existing government is incorporated into both processes. The goal is for the opposition to unseat the incumbent president and win office through its success in opening up competitive elections. This was the model widely adopted in sub-Saharan Africa from 1989 to 1992. In many francophone states the resistance specifically demanded a specially convoked constitutional conference, which Bratton and van de Walle call a 'major organizational innovation' and suggest was influenced by the precedent of the Estates General from the French Revolution (Bratton and van de Walle, 1997: 172). This constitutional and electoral approach to achieving change met with important, but varying, degrees of success. Richard Joseph has listed seven models of transition in Africa that treat '1. the national conference' and '2. government change via democratic elections' as separate categories; but the first is only a success if followed by the second – as his reference to Benin under both indicates – although the second can stand on its own (Joseph, 1993).

Decolonization in Africa from the 1950s created a large number of independent states with high hopes for the future, but inheriting numerous problems of economic and educational underdevelopment and artificial colonial borders sometimes led to ethnic conflicts. By the late 1980s almost all countries were either one-party states, effectively supporting individual autocrats, or ruled by individual dictators or military leaders. Although one-party states, which quite often emerged out of the struggle for independence, were not necessarily very repressive, and might allow a relatively autonomous civil society to operate, lack of organized political opposition or, in most cases, independent media were conducive to corruption and arbitrariness. After 1990 the collapse of the Soviet bloc tended to discredit both socialist goals and one-party states. As the Zambian trade union leader Frederick Chiluba commented: 'If the owners of socialism have withdrawn from the one-party system, who are the Africans to continue with it?' (Bratton and van de Walle, 1997: 105–6). The Soviet collapse also withdrew one source of aid at a time when Western governments tied aid to 'good governance', including multiparty democracy.

Moves towards multiparty elections were not, however, simply, or indeed primarily, a response to external pressure. There was also an upsurge of popular protests, partially influenced by the example of rebellions in Europe and Asia, but also reflecting immediate economic discontents and political dissent. Bratton and van de Walle (1997: 101–6) argue that regime change in the 1990s 'usually began with popular protests', and opposition to particular policies coalesced into an anger at political leaders and more coherent demands for political change.

Zambian trade unions, for example, which had been struggling to uphold the economic interests of their members and had waged earlier strikes in the public sectors and protests over food prices, demanded a multiparty system in 1989. The regime was also under pressure from a coalition of Christian churches, which had their own independent newspaper, *The Mirror*. President Kenneth Kaunda ceded to the demand for multiparty elections, and when – despite declaring a state of emergency during the campaign, buying votes and scaremongering – he lost, he then accepted defeat (Nugent, 2004: 412–13).

In neighbouring Malawi, long dominated by the personalized and oppressive rule of Hastings Banda, opposition began with the Catholic Church remonstrating in a pastoral letter over the social injustices created by economic policies. It then spread to students, who demonstrated, and to trade unions, who called rolling strikes. Opposition leaders returned from exile, and the army then turned on the paramilitary Malawi Young Pioneers, who acted as Banda's key instrument of social intimidation. Banda and his party were forced to accept constitutional change and multiparty elections, and, although the opposition was split by ethnic and regional divides, Banda gained only a minority of the votes. Ageing and ill, he stepped down (Nugent, 2004: 406–7).

Democratic change in francophone Africa began in Benin, where in January 1989 students took to the streets demanding payment of delayed scholarships and later in the year were joined by teachers and civil servants, who had not been paid for months, and militant market women. The initial focus was on economic demands in an extremely fragile economy, but the wave of popular protest, involving frequent demonstrations in urban areas, turned into a challenge to an incompetent and corrupt government and a demand for democracy (Decalo, 1997; Bratton and van de Walle, 1997: 1) Trade unions in Niger, including the mineworkers, teachers, civil servants and employees of parastatals, backed by youth and student groups, began in 1990 to protest about austerity measures, and the trade unions moved from opposing a wage freeze to bringing 100,000 onto the streets to demand political change (Nugent, 2004: 379; Gervais, 1997).

In both Benin and Niger the ruling regimes accepted that repression was ineffective, and agreed to legalize opposition parties and call national constitutional conferences to debate the principles of a new constitution. Both Benin, which had led the way with this model of change, and Niger after constitutional consultation proceeded to hold multiparty elections, which the opposition managed to win, The People's Republic of Congo (formerly Congo Brazzaville) followed a similar path of popular demonstrations leading to a conference and elections. All three are cited as examples of peaceful regime change in Clark's and Gardinier's (1997) study of reform in francophone Africa.

In Mali, the repressive military government was forced to resign immediately after street protests initiated by market women in the capital spread to other towns and were brutally suppressed, prompting further popular anger. A group within the army then intervened, deposed the government and responded to popular demands for a national conference and elections. In the Ivory Coast, a movement by all sections of the population, including police and soldiers, developed from resistance to austerity measures into demands for an end to one-party rule. The president refused to convene a national constitutional conference, but did concede a multiparty election. He managed, however, to outmanoeuvre a divided opposition and remain in office. Protest movements in Zaire, Togo and Gabon succeeded in forcing the government to hold national constitutional conferences, but did not then achieve any real change.

One of the most notable examples of people power arose in Cameroon, which saw two years of well-organized agitation in 1990–2, encompassing tax refusal and the *villes mortes* (ghost towns) created by transport and commercial strikes and boycotts. Janet Roitman describes a national movement 'of civil disobedience involving a protracted general strike' and notes the role of clandestine alternative services to avoid taxation, for example motor cycles acting as 'hidden taxis' (Roitman, 2004: 24). Despite initial repression, the regime did concede multiparty elections, and there was a strong challenge by the Social Democratic Front in presidential elections in October 1992. The opposition was, however, split between two major parties and many more minor ones; because of these divisions and extensive election fraud, President Paul Biya, who had been in office for ten years, managed to hold on to the presidency with a claimed 40 per cent of the votes. The ruling regime, with French government backing, therefore maintained its control, and the opposition lost ground, though the Social Democratic Front continued to exist (Gros, 1995; Krieger, 2008).

'Electoral revolutions' in 'competitive authoritarian regimes'

The fall of the Soviet bloc, and pressure from Western governments and international organizations after 1991, meant that many regimes of varying degrees of authoritarianism began to go through the motions of holding multiparty elections. This created an opportunity for opposition groups to mobilize, both to try to contest the elections and also to dramatize and resist regime manipulation of the process and challenge false results by large-scale protest. The term 'electoral revolutions' is a convenient label used in the democratization literature – though few if any really count as revolutionary (see Chapter 3). Thompson does, however, allocate Serbia in 2000 to his own category of 'democratic revolutions': peaceful, urban-based cross-class popular uprisings that initiate a transition towards consolidated democracy (Thompson, 2004: 1–17).

Electoral revolutions can be distinguished from 'critical elections' where the government is widely regarded as illiberal, there has been significant popular mobilization, including demonstrations, by the opposition in advance of the elections, and there are fears that the government will try to steal the election. But, in the event, the government accepts a transfer of power (Kalandadze and Orenstein, 2009: 1405). Therefore, no mass protests during or after the electoral process are necessary. There are several examples of 'critical elections' from Eastern Europe: Romania 1996, Bulgaria 1997, Slovakia 1998 and Croatia 2000.

The implications of 'electoral revolutions' for democratization, and the role of people power within them, depends partly on exactly how they are defined. Katya Kalandadze and Mitchell Orenstein (who exclude 'critical elections'), examined 17 such 'revolutions' since 1991 and concluded that failed attempts had 'no discernible impact' and that even the five 'successful' revolutions (Serbia 2000, Madagascar 2001, Georgia 2003, Ukraine 2004 and Kyrgyzstan 2005) 'show little democratic progress in their wake' – although their chart does allocate Serbia and Ukraine an 'improved' democratization score (Kalandadze and Orenstein, 2009: 1403–25). The authors look at the specific politics of the countries involved as well as using broad comparative categories, and indicate pertinently the deeper structural problems. But their polemical focus is to rebut advocates of electoral revolutions and external support for them, and to recommend that 'issues of inter-elite power contestation' should be resolved 'before, rather than during, elections' (ibid.: 1421).

One problem with this comparative analysis is that the authors examine in isolation successive elections under the same regime – the 1996 local elections in Serbia as well as the presidential election in 2000; two elections in Armenia, and three in both Azerbaijan and Belarus. There is, therefore, no sense of a developing and organized movement (from 1996 to 2000 in the case of Serbia), or the possible benefits of mobilizing to protest even if it fails, for example by providing useful experience, creating an organizational base or future opposition leaders. These issues are explored by other authors assessing particular electoral protests: for example Anar Valiyev (2006: 17–35) argued that despite shattered hopes and repression after the opposition failed in the November 2005 parliamentary elections in Azerbaijan, the protests did result in increased political participation; and Vitali Silitsky (2006: 63–97) claimed that protests against the presidential election in Belarus provided an opportunity to learn from defeat and had created a 'network of solidarity' and a 'revolution of the spirit'.

Valerie Bunce and Sharon Wolchik (who define the electoral model of regime change to include critical revolutions) do recognize the opportunities provided to opposition groups in competitive authoritarian regimes by elections, which may have results the government did not anticipate, and which the opposition may be able to turn into a genuine electoral process. They argue that elections encourage strengthening of NGO coordination and movement mobilization, promote electoral participation and provide voter education. They also recognize that partial electoral success (for example in local elections) may be a jumping-off point for a major opposition challenge in national parliamentary or presidential elections (Bunce and Wolchik, 2010: 145).

Questions about the effectiveness of electoral revolutions

Two types of question (both suggested by Kalandadze and Orenstein) can be raised about the role of electoral revolutions in promoting democratization. The first concerns their effectiveness and potential for toppling semi-authoritarian regimes. The second concerns their longer-term contribution to a strengthening of democratic practices and attitudes. Both questions can be usefully addressed in relation to the former Soviet bloc. This region has witnessed a significant number of electoral revolutions, but also a failure (to date) to achieve the same success in other ex-Soviet republics, despite repeated attempts. In addition, the passage of time since the last apparently successful colour revolution, in Kyrgyzstan in 2005, now makes it possible to cast a rather more sceptical eye on long-term results in terms of democratization.

Comparative studies of democratization and electoral revolutions have found a post-communist or post-Soviet framework useful, both because there have been a significant number of electoral revolutions, and because emergence from communist party rule provides a unifying background and there are similar regional influences. Geographical proximity, often including shared borders, the power of example and conscious political attempts to transmit organizational models, strategic lessons and modes of protest (for example by student groups) all encouraged transmission of a model of regime change (Bunce and Wolchik, 2006a; 2006b; Hale, 2005; 2006).

Success in spreading electoral revolutions and limits to model

Scholars writing in 2005, influenced by the euphoria of a 'wave' of successful popular mobilizations using elections in Eastern Europe, the Balkans and some states formerly part of the Soviet Union, could easily overestimate prospects for further rapid success in the ex-Soviet Union. Hale (2006) challenged this optimism on the grounds that it was necessary to bring about real institutional change to end the dynamics of 'patrimonialism'. Writing a few years later, Bunce and Wolchik (2009) also began to stress the limits of the model, noting the significance of economic and social factors, differences in the vulnerability of 'competitive authoritarian' or 'hybrid' regimes, and the ability of such regimes to learn from earlier movements how to prevent effective electoral challenges.

Another perspective on the potential for further electoral revolutions in the ex-Soviet states is provided by the Russian political analyst Dimitri Furman, who suggests a threefold division in terms of stages of political development. He also gives weight to cultural and religious traditions, suggesting the Catholic and Lutheran areas have moved most quickly to representative democracy, Muslim areas remain the most autocratic, and states that are primarily Orthodox are in the intermediate bloc (Furman, 2008).

He does, however, make some exceptions to this correlation with religious influence, notably placing Russia in the group of most authoritarian states, together with Kazakhstan, Turkmenistan and Uzbekistan, where former Communist Party officials have remained in control since 1991 (or control has passed to Party 'comrades in arms'). He notes that in Turkmenistan and Uzbekistan, where no legal opposition is allowed, any protest that erupts (such as the Andijan protests in Uzbekistan in May 2005, where hundreds were killed) are harshly repressed. Uzbekistan is known in Britain as an exceptionally unpleasant regime, due to protests by a former unconventional ambassador there, Craig Murray, who subsequently published *Murder in Samarkand* (Murray, 2006). Furman predicts that in these states, if a widespread uprising occurred spreading from city to city, it could become a more radical revolution, like that in Iran in 1978–9. The Arab rebellions might also now provide a model.

But of most interest in relation to the 'colour revolutions' and possible future transitions is an intermediate category of 'imitation democracies' that Furman identifies: states that geographically span Western Europe, Transcaucasia and Central Asia, and oscillate between authoritarianism and moves towards electoral democracy, where opposition parties have at least nominally been allowed to contest elections, even if under rigged control and semi-repressive conditions. This intermediate group of post-Soviet regimes has been relatively fragile for a number of reasons, including the development of widespread political corruption and nationalist secessions and wars that began in the late Soviet period. The fact that they inhabit a zone of continuing competition between the neighbouring great power Russia and the USA greatly adds to instability (see Chapter 7). Many of these states have seen serious popular protests and attempts at electoral revolution, as noted above. Moldova (categorized by Furman as borderline between the Baltic states, where control has passed to oppositions several times, and the intermediate zone) experienced large-scale but unsuccessful protests in April 2009 against a disputed election (Pipidi and Monteanu, 2009).

Silitsky, who writing in 2006 was still expressing hope for Belarus, has since written an interesting and pessimistic essay on the ability of autocrats in former Soviet states to learn from earlier electoral revolutions and embrace effective strategies of pre-emption. He suggests three elements in this strategy are 'tactical': repressive measures to undermine still weak opposition groups and civil society bodies and remove leaders; institutional measures such as increasing presidential powers and amending electoral rules to favour the government; and cultural measures to manipulate public opinion and collective memory and promote fear and distrust of the opposition (Silitsky, 2010: 276–9). Silitsky is indeed particularly pessimistic about Belarus, by far the most repressive regime still existing in Europe, where President Lukaschenko has been adept and ruthless in maintaining control, and where the security forces still use the old Soviet nomenclature of 'KGB'. Since Silitsky's essay was published, resisters attempted to defeat Lukaschenko in the presidential elections in December 2010 and held a 30,000 strong protest in Minsk on election night. Opposition candidates and protesters have subsequently been imprisoned, hundreds of human rights activists and journalists arrested, some tortured, and individual dissidents have disappeared – the *Independent* has focused on these developments (Taylor, 2011a; 2011b; 2011c).

Have the colour revolutions helped to consolidate a democratic ethos?

A key issue relevant to this chapter is how the 'successful' revolutions in Georgia, Ukraine and Kyrgyzstan should be judged: whether they have resulted in positive moves towards stable electoral democracy, or whether they have simply succeeded in changing the government rather than the nature of the regime. On one interpretation, suggested by Hale (2006), who focuses on regime dynamics, the colour revolutions were in effect simply contests to secure the presidency for the opposition leader, and could consolidate authoritarianism. Hale was prepared, like some other commentators (including Furman), to be rather more optimistic about the Ukraine, where the fact that the deposed Yanukovych soon returned to office, first as prime minister and then in 2010 as president (the two leaders of the coalition against him in 2004 soon quarrelled), can be interpreted either as a backward step or an indication that due process is being established. The 2010 election was, Mary Dejevsky (2010a) reports, judged relatively fair, and the opposition leader took her complaints to the courts and not the streets.

In Georgia, however, Hale pointed to the rapid consolidation of presidential power by Mikhail Saakashvili, the hero of 2003, and the lack of any real change in the practices of the regime (Hale, 2006: 312–13). Saakashvili has been accused of restricting the press, of arbitrary and corrupt rule and of rigging elections. Amnesty International reported in 2005 that torture and ill treatment of prisoners had continued, and political unrest in November 2007 led Saakashvili to declare a state of emergency (Amnesty, 2005; Jones, 2009: 334; Lanskay and Areshidze, 2008). The Georgian president was seen by many as precipitating a disastrous war with Russia when in 2008 he attempted forcibly to re-establish control over the breakaway province of South Ossetia.

The Kyrgyzstan 'Tulip Revolution' of March 2005 was not strictly an 'electoral revolution'. Protests erupted after parliamentary elections in February/March 2005, which OSCE observers had criticized for extensive violations, but was arguably prompted primarily by economic grievances and anger about the corruption and nepotism of President Askar Akayev. The demonstrations, which began in Osh and then spread to the capital Bishek, were more violent than in Georgia and Ukraine, involving the storming and destruction of parliament and the presidential building and looting of shops, leaving several people dead.

There was some organized opposition to Akayev before 2005 – human rights groups and parliamentary deputies tried to launch a popular movement for his resignation and for political reforms in August 2002. Opposition to Akayev was also linked to opposition to the US military base, which provided a source of lucrative contracts to the Akayev family and his political cronies (Khamidov, 2002). Scott Radnitz, who has done field research in the country, has queried comparisons with Georgia and the Ukraine, and suggested several opposition leaders, who formed a temporary coalition with no common ideology, might have fomented unrest in 2005 to gain control of government (Radnitz, 2006; 2010: 301). Mary Dejevsky (2005) compared the protests unfavourably with the Orange Revolution in Ukraine, where there was strict nonviolence and protesters supported an appeal to the Supreme Court about electoral irregularities and participated in a second round of elections.

The longer-term results of the Tulip Revolution were of very doubtful value in promoting a more democratic regime. Radnitz (2010: 116–17) argues that the two bases of Kyrgyz politics, 'localism' and 'clientilism', had not changed, and that the 'Revolution' resulted from a temporary cross-regional agreement between political and business elites. After Akayev fled the country opposition leaders manoeuvred for position, and Kurmanbek Bakiyev, who had been prominent in the protests, emerged as acting prime minister and also as president. He did win a landslide presidential election in July 2005 against five other candidates, pronounced valid by OSCE monitors. But in 2006 opposition groups took to the streets to demand additional reforms, including a revised constitution to limit presidential powers. This was conceded, but at the cost of serious tensions between 'pro-' and 'anti-'government demonstrators. Economic hardship (exacerbated by a rise in utility prices) and anger at presidential corruption prompted a new unarmed uprising against Bakiyev in April 2010. He initially resisted by arresting opposition leaders and authorizing troops to fire on demonstrators, but then like his predecessor fled the country, as protestors seized weapons from riot police, attacked government buildings and turned to widespread looting (Harding, 2010a). It is too early to judge whether the new government will establish a less corrupt and more stable form of representative government.

Much more serious ethnic violence in the south, where Bakiyev had his clan support and where up to 2,000 Uzbeks were killed and many others fled, was – according to the newly created government – orchestrated by Bakiyev from exile. UN observers supported the allegation that the pogrom was deliberately organized, but anti-Uzbek riots then appear to have spread spontaneously (Harding, 2010b; 2010c). These events underlined the political fragility of a country where inter-communal fears and enmities can be aroused.

People power and longer-term democratization in sub-Saharan Africa

Given the mixed success of the people power demands for multiparty democracy in the period 1989–92, and the fact that initial success did not guarantee longer-term democratic stability, it is not surprising that the first decade of the twenty-first century saw a renewed series of protests against political corruption and autocratic rule in many countries of sub-Saharan Africa.

There was, for example a renewal of popular protests in early 2008 in Cameroon, opposing a rise in fuel prices, and also resisting President Biya's proposed abolition of constitutional limits on how often the president could seek re-election. The protests included a road transport strike, youth demonstrations in the main towns and a hunger strike by the artist 'Joe la Conscience'. But a veteran of the *villes mortes* campaign told a *Le Monde* journalist that this time the protesters had no real organization. The regime immediately seized those trying to initiate resistance, and used the military to control the towns and fire on protesters, resulting in over a hundred deaths, according to estimates from the Cameroon human rights organization (*Monde Diplomatique*, 2008).

One generally recognized successful electoral revolution occurred in Madagascar, where the opposition alleged the president had tried in the December 2001 presidential elections to retain office through fraud. After the official results were upheld by the High Constitutional Court, supporters of the opposition candidate launched a series of demonstrations that continued until June 2002. A newly constituted Constitutional Court rechecked the votes and ruled in favour of the opposition leader, and the previous president took refuge in France (Radrianja, 2003; George-Williams, 2006: 75–9). Kalandadze and Orenstein (2009: 1414) argue, however, that the popular protests were as much about economic as political issues, and that, although the new president did tackle economic development, democratic progress judged by press freedom, civil liberties and fair elections has been more questionable.

A number of less successful popular protests about stolen elections have occurred – for example in Togo (2005), Ethiopia (2005 and 2010), Kenya (December 2007–January 2008) and repeatedly since 2002 in Zimbabwe. After the 2007 elections in Kenya, which led to ethnic violence organized by leading members of the governing party and some leaders of the opposition Orange Democratic Movement, and the 2008 elections in Zimbabwe, when the country was in economic chaos, international pressure eventually secured a temporary coalition between the ruling party and the opposition to avoid the dangers of civil war or national collapse.

The record of people power in Africa since 1990 suggests that large numbers of ordinary people are able to mount committed resistance to corrupt and arbitrary governments, and that these movements have fairly often had some immediate success. Unhappily (as in ex-Soviet states) the longer-term outcome has frequently not been stable and genuinely representative government. In the Ivory Coast, for example, where in 1990 popular resistance forced elections, but did not remove the president (see above), the people rose up again in 2000 to oust General Robert Guei, who had staged a military coup the year before in an electoral revolution, but party conflicts reflecting ethnic and regional divisions degenerated into fighting and renewed coup attempts (Nugent, 2004: 478–80). After a disputed election in late 2010, the defeated president was holding on to office, challenged by a rival, internationally supported, government-in-waiting, and by March 2011, despite the presence of an international peacekeeping force, many had been killed in a civil war.

But establishing the broader political, social and economic conditions conducive to democratization is necessarily a slower process. The role of people power in highlighting and trying to end both corruption and tyrannical rule can be seen as one important element in promoting the ideal and reality of representative democracy. It is potentially destabilizing, but the logic of this argument suggests that multiparty elections themselves, which are often misused by ambitious cliques and individuals and can inflame ethnic rivalries, should be avoided. Indeed, for a long time the dangers of a multiparty system were cited as a justification for one-party states in Africa (and elsewhere).

How electoral resistance strategies can contribute to electoral democracy

So far this chapter has engaged with some of the issues raised by scholars of democratization and of electoral revolution, and sketched in very briefly attempts to achieve democratic change in two regions of the world with virtually no experience of representative electoral institutions. The argument now turns to a more general consideration of how popular resistance movements adopting electoral strategies can potentially strengthen their own chances of success and also provide positive precedents for democratic engagement and constitutional checks on elections in the future. In addition they have provided a model for movements elsewhere, and may have lessons for countries that pride themselves on being developed democracies, but often have deficiencies in their electoral practices.

Monitoring and strengthening the electoral process

The main focus of movements which have decided to take advantage of referenda and elections is on encouraging people to turn out and vote for opposition parties or coalitions, and on protecting their electoral rights and trying to ensure fair elections.

The first requirement is to ensure maximum popular participation, through promoting registration of voters and then encouraging them to cast their vote. In Chile, for example, only three million were registered at the beginning of 1988. Seven thousand volunteers, who were part of the Crusade for Citizen Participation, succeeded in registering a further four million, despite fear and official intimidation in poorer neighbourhoods associated with support for the left. The campaign adopted a range of methods, including rock concerts, to attract apathetic younger voters (Ackerman and Duvall, 2000: 296–7). The Serbian resistance strengthened its planning for the election in 2000 through Exit 2000, set up by 30 civil society groups to ensure those opposed to Milosevic did actually vote (Vejvoda, 2009: 312).

Safeguards against regime attempts to rig or steal elections and creation of independent monitoring bodies have also been central to many recent electoral revolutions. In Chile the regime itself set up a constitutional tribunal which appointed poll watchers – with the Philippine example as a warning, Pinochet wanted an internationally credible plebiscite. The opposition organized a parallel monitoring process and, since the people voted openly at polling tables, they also organized a vote count at 20 per cent of the 20,000 tables across the country and relayed the results to a central computer (Ackerman and Duvall, 2000: 299).

Strong civil society bodies created to monitor elections independently were a crucial part of the strategy in both the Philippines and Serbia. The National Movement for Free Elections (NAMFREL) was first created in the 1950s in the Philippines by the Catholic Church and business and veterans' organizations, and was revived for the 1986 elections by the church, business and professional groups. NAMFREL mobilized many thousands throughout the country to monitor the election procedures, document and publicize violations, and try to prevent the seizure of ballot boxes, and was able to show convincingly that the official results had been manipulated (Hedman, 2006: 1; Zunes, 1999: 142). The Centre for Free Elections was created in 1996 in Serbia, and was able to provided effective monitoring, first of the 1996–7 local elections, and then of the 2000 presidential election, and to publicize evidence to counter the official statistics (Vejvoda, 2009: 306).

The opposition groups that promoted the 'colour revolutions' were also well aware of the need to provide independent checks on the electoral process. The elections in Georgia in 2003 were monitored by local civil society groups (43 were registered with the election commission) and by the International Society for Fair Elections and Democracy, which claimed 2,500 individual monitors. They provided an alternative tabulation of votes and conducted exit polls, and so created a context for the popular demonstrations (Jones, 2009: 330). Exit polls also figured prominently in the Ukraine in December 2004. They were conducted by several different civil society organizations, which adopted slightly different methods (some used anonymous polling, but one did not) and came up with slightly different results. The regime countered with its own exit polling, and moreover bought off the president of one the 'independent' organizations, who predicted a clear lead for the official presidential candidate, Yanukovych (Wilson, 2005: 100–11). However, opposition groups were able, through monitoring of the election procedures, to point to a number of blatant forms of fraud, such as open intimidation in some areas, stuffing ballot boxes and bribery of voters, to substantiate their case (Wilson, 2005: 105–10).

There are two immediate strategic reasons for systematic measures to promote electoral participation and electoral checks in contexts where the opposition has a chance of winning, but the regime is likely to use intimidation and fraud. The first is that it puts pressure on the regime to appear to act fairly, and increases the chances of the opposition achieving a peaceful change through the election. The second is that, if the regime tries to steal the election, the opposition can take to the streets with clear evidence of rigging, and will gain legitimacy for its resistance. When the Zimbabwe Movement for Democratic Change managed to organize for the first time a systematic check on voting procedures and vote counts in the March 2008 election, it was able to force a recount of the vote; in this period the opposition organized 'make our vote count' demonstrations (Cherry, 2009: 25).

Creating electoral strategies and electoral competence

Even when the opposition knows it is too weak to win, contesting elections may be part of a longer-term strategy of resistance, and a means of preparing potential voters to exercise their rights effectively in later elections.

Bunce and Wolchik (2010: 145) develop this argument in their comparison of the role of the electoral model of change in Serbia and Slovakia, noting for example growing awareness of methods of election fraud, experience in voter registration and electoral campaigns, and lessons from previous defeats, for example the lack of political unity among the opposition in Slovakia in the 1994 elections.

Rigger suggests that in Taiwan, even at a stage when elections could not overturn the KMT government, once dissident candidates were allowed to stand, they gained 'a platform for mobilizing popular support' and voters were able to indicate backing for opposition demands. Moreover, local elections allowed 'voters to master the art of voting and candidates the art of electioneering' (Rigger, 2004: 288). Encouraging voting could also be seen as part of a process of promoting citizen competence needed to sustain a democratic regime after authoritarianism has been overthrown.

Egypt has since late 2004 seen a combination of street protests and electoral participation by sections of the opposition opposed to Mubarak. Kifaya (Enough!) held its first public silent protest in December 2004 and gained support, especially among the young, despite its protests often being swamped by police (El-Mahdi, 2009: 88–91). The activists also began to use blogs on the Internet. At that stage the protesters hoped to prevent Mubarak gaining a fifth term in office.

Presidential elections were held in 2005 after President Mubarak, responding to US pressure to present a more democratic face, held a 'referendum' on constitutional change to allow more than one candidate to stand. When protesters from Kifaya took to the streets to demand real reform, they were beaten by police and pro-Mubarak mobs (Fisk, 2005). Although two major left-wing groups boycotted the presidential election in September as a farce, many liberal groups did put up candidates and Ayman Nour, a 40-year-old lawyer of the Ghad (Tomorrow) Party, posed a serious threat to Mubarak in the first round, and was cheered by supporters at a rally in Tahrir Square. The Muslim Brotherhood, banned from standing as a political party, condemned the presidential race as 'cosmetic', but it urged its supporters to vote in order that they could gain experience for the forthcoming parliamentary elections in November, when it planned to field its own 'independent' candidates (Phillips, 2005; Brookings Institution, 2005).

The parliamentary elections in November became a focus for people expressing their desire to vote and for a fair process. Novelist and political commentator Ahdaf Soueif (2010) recalled how people climbed through windows to vote after police had blocked the entrances, and how polling officers were 'dragged into open mawed police vans clinging to their ballot boxes'. The judiciary were officially in charge, and individual judges protested about blatant ballot box stuffing and non-residents being brought in to vote; some were beaten by the police. The elections were also a focus for protest by civil society groups: internal monitoring groups published detailed critical reports, leading journalists and intellectuals issued a public statement condemning regime handling of the elections, and the association of judges called for the resignation of the minister of the interior (Howden, 2005). The rigging of the process and the protests were noted in a *Washington Post* (2005) editorial critical of US policy towards Egypt.

When parliamentary elections were held again in November 2010, contested in the first round by liberals and the Muslim Brotherhood through 'independent' candidates, they were ruthlessly manipulated by the regime, which blocked entry to polling stations to likely opposition supporters, stuffed ballot boxes and turned off the lights (in one area would-be voters held up candles to reveal already full boxes). The majority of sceptical voters ignored the elections. The ruling National Democratic Party announced it had won 96 per cent of the vote in early results for the first round, and both the Muslim Brotherhood and the liberal opposition boycotted the second round (Shenker, 2010). There had been growing unrest during 2010, both by workers forming unions and by political reformers – notably the youthful 6 April network, created in 2008 after security forces on that day killed textile workers attempting to strike. Disillusion, but determination to resist, was increased by the blatant election rigging.

It was against this background that the mass demonstrations erupted in January and February 2011. A coalition of opposition groups, including the 6 April movement, but ranging from reformists petitioning for constitutional change (the Mohammed El Baradej campaign) to revolutionary socialists, had already planned demonstrations on 25 January 2011. Instead of a few hundred protesters assembling, they discovered that they had become part of a popular revolution (Ibrahim, 2011). The Egyptian people went to the polls again on 19 March 2011 to vote in a genuine referendum on constitutional change. Many expressed their joy and pride in voting as citizens for the first time, and although the young and more radical members of the protest movement opposed the proposed early elections, which they feared would advantage the ruling party and the Muslim Brotherhood against the new political forces, a majority (of the 70 per cent of the electorate who turned out) voted for early moves to establish a civilian government.

Electoral strategies and a minimum model of democracy

Emphasis on the positive role electoral strategies can often play in promoting the goals of a people power movement suggests that multiparty elections to a representative assembly, often combined with direct election of a president, is the model all states should endorse. It also suggests that there is a minimal model which transcends the varieties of actual constitutions, institutional arrangements and diverse underlying social and economic realities. The veteran theorist of democracy, Robert Dahl, proposed seven basic requirements. In summary these are:

- elected officials to control government;
- regular relatively fair elections;
- more or less universal suffrage; and
- the rights of all citizens to run for office;

- to exercise free speech;
- to access independent political information; and
- to form autonomous associations, interest groups and political parties (Dahl, 1982: 11).

Others have accepted a minimum model focused on elections and provision of basic civil liberties, but elaborated slightly to give concreteness to formal requirement (Schmitter and Karl, 1993: 44–6). Dahl himself has noted, especially in relation to democratization, the importance of developing the political competence of citizens (Dahl, 1992: 45–59).

There are two main possible criticisms. One might be that this presupposes a primarily Western liberal model, not allowing for different historical and cultural traditions, social structure and alternative ideals, for example of participation. One response is that movements of resistance around the world have seen such a minimum model as a way of trying to guarantee the basic political rights and freedoms they seek. A complementary response is that it is precisely the diversity of conditions in states seeking to democratize that makes a minimum model useful. It is then possible to develop varied institutions and procedures and pursue a range of social, economic and cultural policies around the model, just as within the Western tradition there have been varied constitutional forms, political values, degrees of decentralization and participation, state provision of welfare and social democracy.

The other objection to a minimum model is that there is a wide range of issues that arise in consolidating a stable representative democracy, such as an appropriate institutional infrastructure, an autonomous civil society, and establishing the necessary political attitudes of tolerance of opposition and willingness to compromise. The narrowness of an election-focused model as a basis for change is one objection that can be raised by those sceptical about the centrality of electoral revolutions to achieving long-term democracy (Kalandadze and Orenstein, 2009: 1420). The counter-argument is that, whilst free and fair elections are obviously only a starting point and not an end point, this demand does shine a light on many aspects of corrupt and authoritarian regimes and, if at least partially achieved, opens up possibilities for change. There is also a potential role for use of nonviolent action to increase the scope for participation and promote more radical institutions.

A more general point, of international relevance, is that emphasis on proper election procedures, rights of opposition parties and availability of independent sources of information, now increasingly underpinned by transnational NGOs and international governmental organizations, has contributed to creating a much more rigorous standard for elections around the world.

Can people power be a threat to electoral democracy?

The emphasis of this chapter has so far been on the case, in many circumstances, for combining electoral strategies with the methods of people power, such as large and repeated demonstrations, occupation of public spaces, strikes, boycotts and civil disobedience. But it is possible to reverse the line of argument and to suggest that large-scale and prolonged public agitation, even when peaceful on the part of the demonstrators, can threaten electoral norms and undermine constitutional rules and safeguards. Setting precedents for taking to the streets or calling strikes in a political crisis, therefore, can undermine the processes of representative democracy. Doubts about resort to popular demonstrations can be formulated from at least two broad perspectives.

The first gives priority to encouraging respect for constitutional and electoral processes wherever they exist, even if in unsatisfactory or still embryonic form, as the best way to strengthen lawful and representative government in the longer term. Staffan Lindberg (2006), for example, drawing on an analysis of 232 African elections, argues that in Africa holding elections promotes democratization, regardless of fraudulent manipulation and the immediate outcome, because voting for a choice of candidates denotes citizenship and participation in the whole organizational process promotes democratic values. Multiparty elections also provide electoral experience for party organizers and create a new formal role for state institutions.

Belief in the importance of strengthening the role of elections led some observers of the Mexican election of July 2006 to argue that the major demonstrations by Lopez Obrador and his Democratic Revolutionary Party (see Chapter 5) were a threat to the crucial requirement that defeated candidates and parties accept the electoral outcomes. They also argued (contra leftist interpretations) that these elections were, despite irregularities, the best organized and least corrupt in Mexican history, and that there was a judicial process to deal with complaints (Estrada and Poire, 2007).

The second perspective supports popular resistance to blatant government abuses, but is concerned about the implications of frequent resorting to the streets. So analysts might query mass demonstrations when:

- the constitutional justification is debatable;
- they do not command clear majority support and are divisive; or
- they appear to be serving the interests of particular elites or ambitious individual politicians.

In Thailand since 2006 neither the government supporters nor the opposition have been in a position to claim they are acting on clear constitutional principles (though some protesters have seen themselves as either resisting a corrupt and arbitrary political figure or opposing the role of the military in politics). The protests certainly reflect deep social and political divisions, serve the interests respectively of the established elite or the populist figure of Thaksin, and have seriously threatened the stability of the country (see Chapter 5).

Some of these arguments might also apply to what looked like a replay of people power in the Philippines in January 2001, when hundreds of thousands of peaceful demonstrators mustered in Manila in the now iconic Epifanio de los

Santos Avenue (EDSA), backed by protests in other cities, to demand the immediate resignation of President Joseph Estrada. The president, a former film star, had won a populist election when he promised support for poverty programmes. However, it soon became clear that he was incompetent to govern and that he offered business favours to cliques of businessmen and provincial politicians with dubious reputations. He was impeached by the House of Representatives on charges of corruption, but during the trial by the Senate managed to prevent a crucial piece of evidence becoming public by 11 senatorial votes to 10, prompting the prosecution team to resign. This was the crisis that led to the protests. As the crowds on the streets increased, leaders of the opposition pressed Estrada to leave office, and he handed over to Vice-President Gloria Arroyo. Thompson (2004: 32) comments that 'people power II' drew again on the key forces that overthrew Marcos: the Catholic Church, business and the opposition press, backed by students who swelled the crowds.

Commentators debated how far 'EDSA II' could be seen as a genuine triumph of people power, and how far it was orchestrated by a clique behind the scenes, including the military, seeking to regain their control (Lande, 2001; Spaeth, 2001; Liwag Kotte, 2001). Ben Reid (2001), whilst taking issue with Western commentators who criticized the demonstrations, and arguing that they did represent significant mobilization and empowerment, concluded that they were ultimately controlled by an elite. One reason for wondering about the constitutional legitimacy of the overall process was that Estrada still had support among the poor (despite his failure to tackle poverty effectively), and his offer to hold a snap election was turned down, probably in part for fear he might have won it.

The fact that EDSA II reflected the views of only part of Philippine society was soon dramatized by a further episode of 'people power'. Immediately after Estrada was arrested in April 2001, thousands demonstrated over several days to demand his release and the resignation of his successor, and the crowd grew to an estimated 300,000 at a rally. The demonstrators were mostly the urban poor, though some politicians encouraged the protest. Civil society organizations that had supported the resistance to Estrada mobilized their own supporters to surround the presidential palace and to defuse the threat to Arroyo (Liwag Kotte, 2001). But, unlike in Thailand, there has not been a repeated resort to popular mobilization to demand a change of government in the Philippines.

People power: last defence of the constitution?

Despite valid concerns that there is a danger of prolonged mass demonstrations becoming a first, rather than a last, resort, in a context where fragile constitutional rules and electoral procedures need to be respected, there is a strong case that people power can act as a safeguard of the constitution. If rulers bend the rules or try to alter the constitution in their favour, then popular resistance may help to prevent them. Where sections of the armed forces threaten a civilian regime popular backing for the government can be an important factor.

In Africa there has been a tendency for initially elected presidents to try to prolong their personal rule beyond the legally defined term. In some cases they have announced a formal change in the constitution. Popular opposition to constitutional manipulation has had mixed results. As we saw above, the opposition failed in 2008 to prevent President Biya in Cameroon maintaining his grip on government. In Zimbabwe, when Robert Mugabe called a referendum in February 2000 to endorse constitutional changes that included enhancing presidential powers, the newly created Movement for Democratic Change led a successful campaign for a 'No' vote. But through intimidation and fraud Mugabe has managed to manipulate elections and remain in office for the succeeding decade, despite repeated courageous opposition.

In neighbouring Zambia, however, popular resistance prevented President Chiluba, elected in 1991, from amending the constitution to allow him to stand for a third term in office. This was seen as a betrayal of the democratic principles that his party, the Movement for Multiparty Democracy, had endorsed when it ended the one-party rule of Kaunda ten years earlier. There was also public outrage at the scale of corruption during Chiluba's term in office. Resistance came from the trade unions, which he had previously represented, a coalition of women's organizations, church bodies and civil society groups that had earlier been active in ending one-party rule students and the public – several thousand demonstrated in the capital, Lusaka. A key source of opposition came from within his own party, including members of his cabinet – although Chiluba brought in loyalists to attack inner-party opponents at a stage-managed party congress designed to endorse constitutional change. The strength of opposition inside both the party and the country (combined with pressure from international aid donors) persuaded Chiluba to abandon plans for a third term. After Chiluba was convicted of stealing 23 million pounds of public money in May 2007, Isabel Matheson, former BBC correspondent in Zambia, commented on the spirit of the opposition in 2001, quoting a shop assistant who said: 'We don't hate you, Mr President, but please just do the right thing and leave' (BBC, 2007). The protests fell short of full-scale people power – Tim Butcher writing for the *Daily Telegraph* described it as 'the gentlest of African revolutions' – but they did indicate the importance of public resistance (Butcher, 2001; Apawo Phiri, 2008: 121–3).

Threats from sections of the military to a civilian regime can also mobilize the public. After the military junta of Argentina was ousted in the wake of their defeat in the Falklands War, the military remained a threatening presence. When a barracks uprising occurred in April 1987, demanding a stop to trials of those accused of serious human rights abuses during the 'dirty war', the public interpreted this (though perhaps mistakenly) as a threatened coup, and huge numbers poured onto the streets to defend President Alfonsin (Lopez Levy, 2004: 122; Nordern, 1996).

At times civilian governments have explicitly turned to their citizens to help defeat a possible *coup d'état*. When President de Gaulle was faced in April 1961 with rebellious generals in charge of military units that had seized Algiers and threatened to take over Paris, he called on both the French people to resist and loyal members of the armed forces in Algeria to refuse cooperation with the rebels. The civilian population in France mobilized in a token general strike and preparations to blockade the airports peacefully, and many in the armed forces engaged in what De Gaulle later described as 'passive resistance' that successfully thwarted the rebels before they were eventually arrested by military units (Roberts, 1975; Talbott, 1980).

Conclusion

This chapter has charted a variety of ways in which popular protest or rebellion has been linked in recent decades to pressure for constitutional change and also participation in electoral procedures (even when rigged). Two modes of political activity seen as antithetical – electoral and constitutional, and defiantly disobedient and 'unconstitutional' – are therefore often two sides of the same coin. This linkage is especially striking when popular resistance is used to defend legitimate civilian governments against threatened coups. The tension between the two approaches can, however, sometimes threaten constitutional stability.

Two key issues addressed have been the role of people power in using electoral processes to achieve constitutional change and multiparty democracy, and whether change resulting from popular mobilization promotes longer-term effective democratization. Despite impressive success for people power in securing immediate change, this chapter has noted quite frequent failures, in particular in relation to the former Soviet bloc and sub-Saharan Africa. Some of the problems relate to the organization and strategy of the resistance – for example the need for unity. But others reflect the intransigence of rulers and difficulties posed by the wider social context, such as clan or ethnic divisions. An even more mixed picture emerges when looking at the progress in promoting stable constitutions and democratization, especially in the regions which have been the primary focus of this chapter. It is therefore clear why the more ambitious claims for the positive role of people power link it to the existence of strong civic coalitions. Trade unions, women's associations and sometimes religious bodies, which transcend some social divisions and provide an organizational base, can play a valuable role both before and after a change of government. One very important dimension, only touched on so far, is the impact of the international context on developments within individual countries. It is to this dimension we turn in Chapter 7.

A positive conclusion that can be drawn from the exploration of how people power has used elections is not only the great courage, persistence and ingenuity that millions of people in different parts of the world have demonstrated in struggling to achieve electoral democracy, but the contribution of these campaigns to promoting a more rigorous model of truly impartial and effective elections, including in countries which may undervalue their own democratic institutions, or have grown careless about their use.

PART III
Implications of globalization for success of people power

PART III

7 Global trends, transnational solidarity and international politics

The discussion so far has referred briefly to the impact of international politics, both positive and negative, on various resistance movements. This chapter focuses specifically on the international dimension and associated global trends. The importance of international pressures on governments, or of transnational support for resistance, can vary considerably between countries and movements, but the overarching global context necessarily has some impact.

One of the key arguments for adopting nonviolent, as opposed to armed, methods has been that unarmed resistance is more likely to gain sympathy in international public opinion, and that violent repression is more likely to rebound against the regime. Since this is not an automatic process, governments have often been efficient in hiding their worst excesses, recent studies – such as Brian Martin's (2007) *Justice Ignited: The Dynamics of Backfire* and Howard Clark's (2009a) *People Power: Unarmed Resistance and Global Solidarity* – have explored the role of international media, diasporas, transnational organizations and solidarity activists in mobilizing outrage and support. When assessing the causal effectiveness of civil resistance it is important to examine the inherent strength or fragility of a regime, its vulnerability to international publicity and diplomatic pressure, and the potential for economic and political sanctions. These considerations receive weight in *Civil Resistance and Power Politics*, edited by Adam Roberts and Timothy Garton Ash, which includes a wide range of expert case studies (Roberts and Garton Ash, 2009).

One of the obvious questions is how far the changing nature of the international political scene, and the long-term trends associated with globalization, have influenced the prevalence of people power movements and their chances of success. Popular movements have for centuries been promulgating their ideas, methods and symbols of struggle across frontiers, and gaining external support. Diasporas have also a long history of seeking support for national liberation struggles. Nevertheless, the speed and extent of today's global communications, the ability to transmit telling pictures as well as vivid written reports, combined with the proliferation of nongovernmental organizations (NGOs) and networks operating at a transnational level, have created a much greater potential for assisting particular resistance movements. Moreover, the growth of regional and international governmental organizations, the salience of the language of human rights and the ideological weight attached to international law, combined with institutional means of enforcing it, have created a new framework for pressurizing outlaw regimes and their rulers. UN human rights observers, OSCE or African Union (AU) election monitors and the possibility of individual despots being tried by the International Criminal Court (or by some national courts invoking international law) are all potential constraints.

Adherents of the 'realist' school of international relations can argue quite convincingly that, behind the elaborate new structure of international society, the basic economic, military and political interests of states still dominate, and that transnational civil society bodies (and even popular movements of unarmed resistance) can act as direct, or more often de facto, agents for great power politics. These issues are discussed below.

But even granted the considerable importance of the role of national interests and great power imperial ambitions, the differing forms these take over time alter the prospects for resistance movements. Two key shifts in the map of international politics have been the ending of colonial empires in the second half of the twentieth century and the end of the cold war and dissolution of the Soviet bloc. These structural changes in international politics provide the starting point for this chapter. A third structural factor, the evolving nature of the global capitalist economy, and possible implications for the future, provides an end point for the chapter.

The changing great power configuration and increasing role of people power

The dissolution of empires

The general tendency over the past 150 years for the incidence of unarmed resistance and uprising to increase can be charted in relation to the changing structure of international politics. The first examples of people power (noted in Chapter 1) are linked to the demise of the last European empires ruled by autocratic monarchies, challenged both by internal popular movements (as in Russia in 1905) and by national liberation struggles.

The First World War, which ended in defeat and dismemberment for Austria–Hungary and precipitated the Russian Revolutions of February and October 1917, also weakened the European colonial empires in Asia. They were challenged in particular by the impact of the Versailles Treaty on aspirations for nationalist independence and the growing belief in nationalist and democratic principles. A new wave of unarmed national liberation struggles against various forms of European colonialism began with the 1919 May Fourth movement in China for national cultural renaissance and an end to foreign control, although Chinese politics soon disintegrated into warlordism and then became the arena for the guerrilla warfare strategy of the Chinese communists from the 1920s to 1947. The Indian unarmed independence struggle also developed rapidly after 1919.

The Second World War, however, had a more decisive impact on European colonialism, both in terms of the military logic of prosecuting the war, alterations in the international balance of power and changing political attitudes. Arab nationalism was reignited and France ceded independence in North Africa in the 1950s (except in Algeria with its large French settler population), but the former colonial powers retained economic and strategic dominance in the region. Even after the Suez debacle of 1956, Britain maintained a military base in its Protectorate of Aden, until it withdrew in 1967 in the aftermath of serious unrest. In Asia the initial Japanese military success encouraged armed anti-colonial movements but also promoted nationalist resistance to Japanese domination. Unsurprisingly in a context of world war, liberation struggles often took the form of armed resistance, leading after 1945 to rapidly negotiated independence from the Dutch in Indonesia and from Britain in Burma, and to an ongoing guerrilla war against the French in Vietnam.

The Second World War had a more indirect effect on the predominantly unarmed movement against the British Raj in India, resulting in immediate political concessions to gain support against Japan. After 1945 a dominant USA opposed European colonialism and Britain was severely weakened. Judith Brown has stressed the administrative weakness of the Raj after 1945 and Robert Moore has emphasized the economic and diplomatic pressure on the British government and its military overstretch (Brown, 2009: 45–6; Moore, 1983). But the election of a Labour government, already sympathetic to the Indian cause, meant that independence was in any case clearly on the agenda.

During the 1950s both the French and British governments were willing to look towards self-government in their African colonies. Popular resistance movements in Africa, which had started in the inter-war years, gathered momentum in the 1940s and 1950s, and transferred the initiative from traditional leaders to younger radical political activists. The 'positive action' campaigns of marches, strikes and non-cooperation in Nigeria, Kenya (before the violent Mau Mau resistance) and Ghana were important demonstrations of popular nationalist sentiment and political organization, and hastened the pace of change, but could be seen as elements in a wider negotiation with the British government ready to cede independence.

The presence of substantial settler communities controlling land and mineral resources, and the creation of the white-controlled Central African Federation in 1954 required both more sustained unarmed resistance in Malawi and Zambia, and interventions from London – for example the Devlin Report that condemned police-state measures and confirmed African support for independence in Malawi (Baker, 1997). In Southern Rhodesia (now Zimbabwe), when the British failed to support African interests effectively, the liberation movements turned to guerrilla warfare (Ranger, 1968). The intransigence of the Salazar dictatorship in Portugal led to prolonged guerrilla warfare in its African colonies (see Chapter 2), until disillusionment in the armed forces led to the overthrow of Salazar's successor Caetano in 1974.

The long and, for most periods, primarily unarmed struggle against apartheid in South Africa, briefly outlined at the end of Chapter 5, might be seen as the last phase of the resistance to European colonialism. But because of its longevity it became entangled in the logics of the cold war – the ANC was linked to the Communist Party and its guerrilla wing in particular enjoyed strong Soviet bloc support.

The cold war and changing Western attitudes to anti-communist dictators

The ideological struggle between a world communist movement and the capitalist West had become part of international politics after the Bolshevik Revolution. It became an intrinsic element in great power confrontation from about 1947, when the Soviet bloc opposed the Western US-dominated bloc at a military, political and economic as well as an ideological level. The victory of the Chinese communists in 1949 encouraged guerrilla struggles, and created further Western fears of the spread of communism in Asia: both influenced the final process of decolonization, as in Malaya.

The cold war that structured most aspects of international politics from the late 1940s until the end of the 1980s also impacted on choices of resistance and perceptions of resistance in Asia, Africa and particularly Latin America, after the success of Castro in Cuba. The new Cuban government itself became active in promoting Marxist ideas and guerrilla tactics, which were widely adopted by those opposing dictatorship and oppression. The US government was willing to support right-wing regimes, however repressive or corrupt, if they suppressed 'communist' opposition movements, or provided military bases and alliance solidarity.

Nevertheless, a turn towards unarmed resistance to many of these dictatorships began in the 1970s, sometimes as a result of spontaneous protests by students, intellectuals, workers, farmers or women's groups, but also due to the conscious promulgation of nonviolent methods, notably by radical Catholics in Latin America. The active role adopted by the Catholic Church establishment in some key struggles for human rights and democracy in Latin America (as later in the Philippines and East Timor) also promoted civil rather than armed resistance. There was therefore a wave in the 1970s and 1980s of popular unarmed resistance to military rule and individual dictatorship in both Asia and Latin America – some of the more striking examples are cited in Chapters 5 and 6.

A crucial factor was the changing attitudes in the US government. Jimmy Carter's presidency in the late 1970s resulted in a US foreign policy emphasis on the primacy of human rights, which was a marked change from the *realpolitik* associated with the Nixon–Kissinger diplomacy up to 1974. Despite patchy application, and a reversion to extreme cold war ideology and military policies under Reagan's first administration, by the later 1980s the USA was encouraging the emergence of representative democracies and opposing a number of dictators – though, as is typical of US foreign policy, not all sectors of the bureaucracy were necessarily in agreement or acting in concert.

Nevertheless, in Panama, where the 'strong man' General Noriega had long been a CIA protégé, the US government (partly because of his role in drug smuggling into the USA) switched support in 1987 to the opposition, which had launched mass protests in July/August that year. The US administration imposed economic sanctions, together with the World Bank, and backed opposition parties in the May 1989 elections. Noriega stole the election, and demonstrations and a general strike failed to dislodge him – whereupon the USA decided to invade in December 1989 (Scranton, 1991; Calderon, 1987; Weeks and Zimbalist, 1989).

A striking reversal of US policy also occurred in Chile, where US government and corporate backing for Pinochet's 1973 coup against the democratically elected Marxist President Allende turned into support for the opposition, which was campaigning against Pinochet extending his presidency through the 1988 plebiscite. The change in US policy by the late 1980s was in part a response to the thawing of the cold war as a result of Gorbachev's active détente and arms control policies – although the change of direction in Chile was signalled by the appointment of a new ambassador prepared to show support for the opposition as early as 1985 (Huneeus, 2009: 207–8). The US State Department tended to be more doubtful about openly supporting repressive and/or corrupt autocratic rulers against a democratic opposition – for example favouring the political opposition in the Philippines (and the anti-Marcos group in the military) in the mid-1980s, as did some members of Congress. The Pentagon still backed Marcos, and President Reagan was persuaded to abandon him only at the last minute in 1986, when the US government arranged to remove him and his wife from the country (Kessler, 1991: 202, 211; Schock, 2005: 88).

The role of West European governments has also been important. Despite a tendency to follow the US lead, many European governments have been more inclined to emphasize human rights and democratic considerations – central to the Council of Europe and the constitution of the European Union. This was particularly true of Scandinavian governments tending to pursue a rather more independent foreign policy. In the case of Chile the US government was isolated in its backing for Pinochet, and in West Germany in particular, which had long cultural ties with Chile, both Social Democrat and Christian Democrat governments sponsored support to the opposition (Huneeus, 2009: 208–10).

Dissolution of the Soviet bloc

The earlier episodes of people power that occurred within the Soviet bloc – the 1953 uprising in East Germany, the 1956 movements for de-Stalinization in Poland and Hungary (the former unarmed, and the latter only taking up arms to resist Soviet reoccupation), and the 1968–9 Czechoslovak resistance to uphold the 'Prague Spring' against Soviet occupation – were also shaped by the cold war context and US–Soviet great power competition. This polarization for a long time constrained the potential of popular resistance, since concessions to reform movements threatened to undermine Soviet control, and open support from the USA and the West, for example through the Voice of America radio broadcasts, strengthened the case that all movements for internal change were anti-Soviet and anti-socialist. But, as we have seen, opposition groups within the Soviet bloc by the 1970s and 1980s sought to avoid a Soviet military response, became increasingly aware of the potential of widespread unarmed resistance, and in some cases at least were swayed by a moral preference for nonviolent rather than violent methods.

The growing success of this wave of people power can be linked to increasing weakness of individual East European regimes: the Polish government made major concessions to the 1970 and 1976 strikes, and even more to Solidarity in 1980–1 – until responding to counter-pressure and military threats from the Soviet Union – partly because it was comparatively economically and politically weak. Eastern Europe as a whole had as a result of growing détente become increasingly linked economically to the West and more vulnerable to Western economic and diplomatic pressure. Finally, in 1989 the ultimate success of the revolutionary movements was closely linked to Soviet unwillingness to resort again to military force. The success of people power then fed back into the USSR itself, reinforced the movements in the Baltic states and prompted the 1990 popular agitation in the Soviet satellite state of Mongolia.

It is, however, too glib to assume that the Soviet bloc disintegrated solely because of economic weakness, which can in any case be exaggerated. Weakness can spur governments to resort to military violence – a real possibility in both East Germany and Czechoslovakia in 1989. A different kind of Soviet leadership in the late 1980s could have threatened to use its still considerable military might. The policies of détente and internal reform initiated by Gorbachev, and his desire to avoid use of military force, were clearly critical factors in restraining hard-line governments and enabling a peaceful transition. But the crucial weakness of the East European regimes was political and ideological – they had lost the support not only of their people as a whole but many members of the communist parties and sections of the ruling elite. The people power movements manifested and hastened this withdrawal of support.

Both the end of the Soviet Union as a 'superpower' and the discrediting of Soviet-style communist ideology and model of socialist regimes had major repercussions outside Europe. The negotiated end of apartheid in South Africa in the 1990s was facilitated by the disappearance of a perceived 'Soviet threat' as evidenced by the fact that a movement with strong communist support in the past, the ANC, was allowed to take office. In sub-Saharan Africa as whole, as Chapter 6 indicated, the collapse of the Soviet bloc undermined the legitimacy of one-party states and encouraged popular mobilization for multiparty democracy. The economic and political influence of the US- and Western-dominated international organizations also increased – although China had played some role in Africa it has only gradually been extending its sphere of influence to the African continent. The end of the cold war also meant that it became easier to dislodge Suharto as the West ceased to turn a blind eye to human rights abuses in Indonesia, although this factor was probably more important in relation to Indonesian occupation of East Timor (see below).

Continued US–Russian rivalry and the West versus Islamic extremism

As a result of the collapse of the Soviet bloc, and then of the Soviet state itself, into its constituent republics, the military, economic, diplomatic and ideological balance of power has swung decisively in favour of the United States. Nevertheless, Russia retains significant military, economic and political leverage, in particular its energy supplies of oil and gas which can be used to put pressure on neighbouring states reliant on them, such as Ukraine and Georgia, and also strengthen Russia's position vis-à-vis Western states that need these energy supplies. The relationship between the USA and Russia still has strong overtones of the earlier cold war, as the tricky negotiations over renewal of the START (Strategic Arms Reductions Treaty) in 2010 indicated, although the conflict is no longer strictly ideological. The steady encroachment of NATO in the previous Soviet sphere, and conflicts over Western plans for anti-missile missile bases in Eastern Europe, replay military themes and fears from an earlier era.

This context has, as noted in Chapter 6, a considerable impact on governments in former Soviet republics and on the implications of and prospects for people power against authoritarian or semi-authoritarian regimes in that region.

The wave of 'electoral revolutions' that began in the Philippines has spread across Eastern Europe in the 1990s and former Soviet states since 2000. The ousting of Milosevic in Serbia in October 2000 can be seen as the final stage in Eastern Europe. Ivan Vejvoda suggests that the model of voter mobilization that sealed the victory over Vladimir Meciar in Slovakia in November 1988 and over Franjo Tudjman in Croatia in January 2000 provided crucial examples (Vejvoda, 2009: 311). But the Serb example also became a precursor of the 'colour revolutions' in Georgia and the Ukraine, and less successful protests in other post-Soviet states.

In general the Russian regime has tended to bolster established governments who have been amenable to Russian policy aims, against opposition leaders and people power movements seen as more hostile to Russia and inclined to join the Western economic and political sphere. Silitsky (2010: 294–8) argues that the Russian regime is promoting an 'authoritarian international' among former Soviet states that have suppressed attempts at electoral revolution or ruthlessly crushed opposition – even returning Uzbek activists to Uzbekistan after the Andijan massacre in 2005. Conversely, the US governments and West European governments and institutions have tended to favour opposition parties and movements. But the position has often been more nuanced, and varies between different former Soviet republics and precise US and Russian interests in them.

Two important factors have been military bases and energy supplies. Both Russia and the USA have important strategic bases in some states, which impact on internal politics. The Ukraine, for example, which since the 'Orange

Revolution' of December 2004–January 2005 has swung between presidents seen as pro-Western or relatively pro-Russian, has a Russian naval base on the Black Sea. When the agreement by the Ukrainian government to extend the lease on this base for 25 years came before parliament in April 2010 the passionate disagreement between deputies led to smoke bombs and fist fights, but the deal narrowly passed. The USA has what it regards as crucial strategic interests in Uzbekistan – an airbase in the south of the country – because Uzbekistan shares a border with Afghanistan and the US military needs transit rights whilst waging war on the Taliban and Al Qaeda.

As a result, as WikiLeaks distribution of the US embassy cables revealed, although the embassy confirmed UN reports of horrific tortures, and commented on forced labour in the cotton fields and high levels of corruption and criminality within the regime, it also warned that public US pressure could result in the withdrawal of transit rights (Leigh, 2010: 8). The UK government is complicit in covering up the nature of the regime (for example withdrawing, as noted earlier ambassador Craig Murray, who tried to publicize torture) for the same strategic reasons, since it has significant numbers of troops in Afghanistan.

Kyrgyzstan, whose complex and often corrupt and violent politics were briefly surveyed in Chapter 6, is the only former Soviet republic that has both Russian and US military bases on its territory. The US Manas airbase is strategically valuable for supplying troops in Afghanistan. President Bakiyev, who achieved office as a result of the 2005 'Tulip Revolution', threatened to revoke permission for both bases, and secured the offer of a large loan and cheap Russian energy supplies, but also negotiated substantial financial deals to supply the US base for his extended family and friends. When Bakiyev was forced to flee to Kazakhstan after the 2010 popular insurrection, Russia hastened, according to *Independent* reports, to support the new interim government, and the Obama administration began to negotiate for a new agreement over the Manas airbase (Cockburn, 2010: 30; Walker, 2010: 27).

There are other military issues impinging on the politics of the region, for example the Russian military support for South Ossetia's secession from Georgia, and its brief invasion of Georgian territory in 2008, alarmed the Ukraine. The then president Yushchenko publicly argued in the *Washington Post* the need to become part of the 'collective security system of free democratic countries exemplified today by Nato' (Yushchenko, 2008: 26). His more pro-Russian successor Yanukovych backed away from this stance, but has showed some interest in the potential advantages of joining the European Union (Dejevsky, 2010b: 33).

As the reference to bases needed for military operations in Afghanistan indicates, the other major ideological and geopolitical conflict structuring international politics is the US-led struggle to suppress, or at least confine, the spread of Islamic religious extremism, which is in turn extremely hostile to the West and tends to support violence against Western targets. As a result the US government and Western allies have backed or at least tolerated corrupt and ruthless regimes in the former Soviet Union and 'moderate' Islamic autocrats in the Arab world and elsewhere. For example, the West supplied military assistance to the dictatorial ruler of the Maldives, until rising internal opposition by 2007 triggered a change of course (Zunes, 2008). Even where US officials have promoted cosmetic moves towards representative government, as in Egypt in the period 2005–10, the administration has tended in practice to make very low-key protests about infringements of democracy, and Western security services have had their own sinister contacts in Middle Eastern countries, used for example to torture suspected terrorists in the policy of 'extraordinary rendition'.

The unarmed Tunisian uprising in January 2011, and the chain reaction of people power protests across the Middle East suggests (in March 2011) that the nature of at least some Arab governments may be changed. This in turn may fundamentally alter the dynamics of regional politics – for example the role of Syria in Lebanon (see Chapter 5) – and also impinge on the US military presence in the region and on the future position of Islamic extremist organizations. What the 'Arab Spring' – including the military confrontation between the rebels and the Gaddafi regime in Libya – does dramatically illustrate is that, whilst the changing great power rivalries and military confrontations do provide an important framework for popular movements, these movements can in turn alter the nature of these structural 'realities'.

International governmental organizations, the media and transnational pressures

The growth of international governmental organization, commitment to developing international law, concern for human rights, international parliamentary cooperation and an increasing role for professional associations, trade unions and campaigning movements were changing international politics towards the end of the nineteenth century. These forms of globalization intensified in the twentieth century, despite two world wars. The creation of the League of Nations, and then of the United Nations, provided forums for national liberation movements and publicizing abuses of human rights; the growing bloc of newly independent former colonies in the UN gave further backing to anti-colonial movements still trying to achieve their goal, and UN resolutions provided a framework for a range of governmental sanctions and transnational campaigns – most notably in relation to ending apartheid in South Africa. The UN frequently puts pressure on repressive regimes – the Secretary General and representatives of the UN Human Rights Council have for example visited Burma. UN specialized agencies can also play a role: the International Labour Organization has investigated charges that the regime employs forced labour (Moser-Puangsuwan, 2009: 47).

Regional intergovernmental organization has become increasingly important in the architecture of international politics, a trend most pronounced in Europe, which has seen the gradual extension of the membership, range of functions and supranational ambitions of what is now the European Union (EU). The EU has promoted democratization by providing substantial economic and political incentives to countries to apply to join it, by setting democratic and human rights – as well as economic – requirements for entry, by conferring a seal of approval of democratic credentials for countries admitted into the EU, and by locking member states into representative institutions, so that a reversion to dictatorship is extremely unlikely and would incur very substantial sanctions. Other European bodies highlight human rights and election issues. The Council of Europe, which promulgated the European Convention on Human Rights in 1950 and set up the European Court of Human Rights at the Hague, has recently drawn up criteria for judging the fairness of elections. The OSCE regularly provides election monitors and reports on disputed elections. The OSCE – originally the CSCE – arose out of the Helsinki process of the 1970s and the 1975 Helsinki Agreement, which sought to establish détente and was endorsed by both NATO and Warsaw Pact states. It was the Helsinki Agreement (which included a set of clauses on human rights) that provided a legitimating framework for the human rights groups, notably Charter 77 in Czechoslovakia, that arose within the Soviet bloc. Since the end of the cold war European regional organizations, including the Parliament of the EU, provide a potential source of funding and political support at various levels to national opposition movements opposing authoritarian governments.

Regional organizations are important in other parts of the world. The Organization for African Unity, now the African Union (AU), initially backed anti-colonial and anti-apartheid struggles. In recent decades it has tried to resolve conflicts between African states, providing peacekeeping forces and monitoring elections. This latter role potentially provides assistance to opposition movements seeking to unseat 'competitive authoritarian' regimes, although AU leaders, in particular Thabo Mbeki in South Africa, were reluctant to condemn President Mugabe of Zimbabwe, one of the original leaders of the struggles for liberation from white rule. In Asia the primarily economic regional organization, the Association of South East Asian Nations (ASEAN), has not generally provided leverage for opposition in countries like Burma, which was admitted to membership in 1997 (despite some qualms among member states and opposition from the EU, which boycotts the military regime) – partly with the aim of reducing China's influence in Burma (Fink, 2001: 234–5). But both the Philippines and Malaysia have urged the release of Aung San Suu Kyi and Thailand has allowed entry to refugees from Burma (Moser-Puangsuwan, 2009: 47). The Organization of American States (OAS), although it does provide a forum for policy debate, has clearly been dominated by the USA in the past. But it does include the Inter-American Commission on Human Rights, set up in 1959 as a permanent and autonomous body, which has regularly produced national reports, investigated specific individual complaints and recommends policies to protect human rights to governments and the OAS. Since the Inter-American Court of Human Rights was created under the American Convention of Human Rights (which entered into force in 1978) the Commission can submit cases to the Court and request advisory opinions.

International events involving governments or major transnational bodies have offered a focus for resistance movements to publicize their cause. The high profile of sporting events, and the constriction of a government's ability to suppress protest in front of the world's media – although it may lock up its known dissenters in advance, as happened in both Moscow and Beijing – has encouraged movements to try to use the Olympic Games. The 2008 Games in Beijing prompted the Tibetan diaspora and its supporters outside China to hold high-profile demonstrations on the route of the Olympic torch from Athens 2008, especially in London, Paris and San Francisco. Significant resistance also occurred in Tibet and China (see below). The holding of the football World Cup in Argentina in 1978 led journalists to publicize the weekly vigil of the 'Mothers' with their distinctive headscarves walking in the Plaza de Mayo, and some of the European footballers came to the square to demonstrate their support (Ackerman and Duvall, 2000: 276). Sporting boycotts, which may extend to individuals or national teams refusing to attend major international events in repressive regimes, or to play teams from those countries, are also one way to express solidarity with resisters. It is generally agreed to have been an effective means of isolating South Africa and of creating pressure for changes in apartheid (Orkin, 1989).

The growing influence of a range of major transnational civil society bodies such as Amnesty International and Human Rights Watch is linked in part to their intersection with international and regional governmental organizations and appeal to the official human rights declarations and agreements endorsed by them. They lobby intergovernmental organizations on behalf of liberation or democracy movements, as well as national governments and parliaments. They also help to secure media publicity and promote transnational campaigns or boycotts. The International Red Cross Committee can ask to investigate the condition of political prisoners – as in Burma. The role of international election monitoring bodies, both governmental and non-governmental, was noted in Chapter 6. Transparency International highlights national corruption.

The awarding of the Nobel Peace Prize – despite the policy of sometimes rewarding government leaders better known for their adherence to realpolitik, because they have brokered or participated in peace agreements – has quite often provided a publicity focus and legitimacy to leading figures in resistance movements at a time when they need international support. Vaclav Havel and Aung San Suu Kyi are two examples. The prize can also publicize the contribution of less widely known activists, such as Adolfo Perez Esquivel of the Peace and Justice Service, which has promoted nonviolent resistance in Latin America, and Rigoberta Menchu for her activism in the indigenous Peasants' Union in the dangerously violent context of Guatemala in the 1980s.

Long-established international professional associations (and more recent bodies such as Journalists Across Borders) try to exert pressure on governments by highlighting persecution of individual writers, journalists, artists, academics, doctors or lawyers, producing authoritative reports, for example on breaches of international law and promoting professional boycotts. External and international trade unions are specially well placed to promote and ensure implementation of economic boycotts if this policy has been agreed internationally. Where trade unions and workers are important in internal resistance, as the copper miners have been in Chile, they may also attract fraternal cross-border solidarity. The American AFL-CIO threatened a boycott of Chilean goods in 1978 (Ackerman and Duvall, 2000: 283).

The growing significance of transnational advocacy networks in highlighting human rights issues, and sometimes providing a platform for people living under repression who have difficulty in making their voices heard, has been widely recognized in the literature on social movements and globalization. The analysis by Margaret Keck and Kathryn Sikkink, *Activists Beyond Borders* (Keck and Sikkink, 1998), and their concept of 'the boomerang effect' of transnational publicity and pressure returning to target those suppressing rights, is now a standard reference. Despite the greater salience of human rights issues and organizations trying to publicize them, there are, however, still largely hidden struggles against severe repression in many parts of the world. For example, despite the fact that Indonesia now has a more internally democratic system than it did before 1998, the Indonesian military still acts brutally in the occupied territory of West Papua, where they block the roads and exclude all media and NGOs, according to an exiled representative of the Free West Papua campaign. An accidentally leaked military video tape in October 2010 showed troops assaulting and torturing West Papuans and brought the issue into some of the US and British press. Members of the US Congress and Scottish Parliament began to take up the issue in late September 2010 (Lateu, 2010).

Ability to transmit and access detailed information about campaigns of resistance, human rights abuses and other key issues is central to gaining global publicity and eliciting a transnational response, as Keck and Sikkink have argued. Therefore changing communications technology impacts on the role the wider world can play, for example through Internet petititons, protests at embassies or other solidarity demonstrations. But new technology has also had an important impact at national and local levels: the role of mobile phones, texting and the Internet in assisting rapid mobilization of demonstrations or strikes; the importance of exchanging news and photos on the Net in creating a mood of internal anger and determination and in publicizing events within the region have all been demonstrated in recent people power movements. Indonesian students used mobile phones and texting to coordinate demonstrations in 1997. An article on mass protests in Moldova in April 2009 against a disputed election is entitled 'Moldova's "Twitter Revolution"' (Pipidi and Monteanu, 2009). The importance of Twitter in bringing together protesters in Iran's Green Movement in 2009 is also stressed in many of the accounts.

The 'Arab Spring' has also drawn attention to the role of communications technology. Whilst the popular unarmed uprising in Tunisia that culminated in the hated president and his family fleeing the country on 14 January 2011 was a response to economic hardship and political repression, the Internet spread images of the early protests and encouraged further resistance. Tunisian students and middle-class opponents of the regime apparently shared information about the WikiLeaks revelations about the US Embassy assessments of their corrupt 'mafia-like' president. This led some Western reporters and commentators to dub the uprising the 'WikiLeaks Revolution', although, as Mona Eltahawy (2011) has argued, it is extremely patronizing to suppose Tunisians were not already aware of the nature of their own government. It is more important to note that the Tunisian government had been tightly controlling and censoring the Net, but was not able to stop its use to foster resistance. The Egyptian government started to curb Net access after facing major demonstrations on 25 January 2011, organized through Facebook (Harb, 2011).

The role of new communications in protest is still developing, and their potential in repressive contexts such as Burma, Iran, Tunisia and Zimbabwe is being researched (Meier, 2008). But some commentators, for example the Belorussian researcher Evgeny Morozov (2011) in *The Net Delusion*, have cautioned against 'cyber-utopianism' and stressed the potential of regimes not only to block Net communication but to use it to infiltrate resistance and disseminate counter-propaganda. He also notes that in Iran in 2009 there were fewer than 20,000 registered with Twitter at the time of the elections. Using new technology reveals communications problems where the infrastructure is missing: reliance on mobile phones in Tibetan resistance in 2008 effectively excluded western Tibet (see below). Obviously it is the highly educated, more prosperous and the younger generations who are most likely to mobilize using the most recent technologies – both internally and around the globe. In most of the world the urban poor, and those living outside cities or large towns, are unlikely to have computer access. For this reason Amnesty was in 2010 trying to distribute thousands of radios inside Burma, so that people could listen to the Burmese exile station in Oslo or Burmese-language broadcasts by the BBC, Radio Free Asia or the Voice of America (Coyle, 2010). It is arguable that the role of mainstream newspapers and broadcasting outlets remains very important in presenting and interpreting movements of resistance to publics and political actors at an international level. The relatively 'old' technology of television in particular is still central to conveying images of protest. Al Jazeera, for example, certainly helped inspire popular response to Tunisia in the Arab world and continued to be important, even though Mubarak tried to block transmission from Tahrir Square, and the station has been constrained by Qatari government priorities in covering the Bahraini protests.

The East Timor resistance and changing international context

The significance of both the shifting configuration of great power politics and the wider international context of intergovernmental organizations, transnational networks and international media to national struggles is well illustrated by the development of the campaign for national independence in East Timor. This was a Portuguese colony until the Revolution of the Carnations in Portugal in 1974, when by agreement it began to move towards independence. Indonesia, which had already incorporated West Timor, invaded in December 1975, just after the Revolutionary Front for an Independent East Timor (FRETILIN), which had majority support, had declared independence. Some sources suggest that the Australian and US governments colluded with the Jakarta regime, which portrayed its action in terms of preventing the success of a communist independence movement. Ironically an Australian Labor Party prime minister, Gough Whitlam, generally noted for his progressive policies, was supportive of Suharto and declared in September 1975 that East Timor, which then had a population of 600,000, was too small to be an independent state (Martin et al., 2001: 143–56).

Despite two UN Security Council resolutions supporting East Timorese independence and condemning the invasion, and despite the rape, torture and killing of tens of thousands of East Timorese civilians by the Indonesian military in the first few months, Western governments effectively continued to acquiesce in the draconian Indonesian annexation. This policy included suppressing indigenous languages, executing East Timorese teachers and destroying schools, encouraging Indonesian immigration, and herding many into strategic hamlets, which resulted during 1978–9 in tens of thousands more dying of hunger. (Estimates of the numbers of East Timorese who died in the years soon after the invasion vary, but may have been up to a third of the population.) FRETILIN mounted a guerrilla resistance, but the Indonesian military attacked its organization and killed or captured key leaders, so by the late 1980s it was seriously weakened.

From the late 1980s, however, a shift in both ideology and strategy within the East Timorese resistance, which moved away from guerrilla attacks in the countryside towards primary emphasis on unarmed protest in the towns, developing resistance to Suharto inside Indonesia itself, and major changes at an international level, combined to lead to a referendum on independence in 1999 supervised by the UN. Despite a subsequent civil war, fostered by armed groups backed by Indonesia, that prompted the intervention of a UN peacekeeping force, East Timor achieved its independence in May 2002 (Martin, 2007: 23–33; Stephan, 2006; Stephan and Chenoweth, 2008: 25–32).

East Timor's people have been predominantly Catholic, and the Church played an important role in the development of an unarmed movement that gradually won wider support. The East Timorese Council of priests condemned policies leading to 'the ethnic, cultural and religious extinction of the people of East Timor' in January 1985; Bishop Carlos Belo denounced abuse of human rights (as his predecessor had done); and a visit by Pope John Paul II in November 1988 provided the occasion for the first public demonstration, covered by international media, that demanded independence. This led to a strategy of using international visits to organize demonstrations. The initiative for resistance passed to a younger generation, especially students, who created networks to promote information and organize nonviolent protest, not only in East Timor but in Indonesia. East Timorese activists created links to Indonesian intellectual and student opposition and received support from

Indonesian human rights groups (Stephan, 2006: 62). But East Timorese students apparently had some influence on the thinking and organization of the developing student resistance to the Suharto regime – some of the student leaders from both sides met in prison in the late 1980s (Boudreau, 2004: 215). Later, in the 1990s, joint protests between Indonesian and East Timorese students frequently took place, including 'fence jumping' and nonviolent sit-ins at Western embassies in Jakarta, where information about the resistance movements was disseminated.

The catalyst that led to a large-scale movement using nonviolent methods, extensive cooperation with the opposition inside Indonesia and growing international support and solidarity with the East Timorese resistance was yet another atrocity by the Indonesian regime: the Dili massacre of November 1991. The opposition combined a previously planned demonstration for independence with a peaceful funeral procession for a young man shot by troops. When Indonesian troops opened fire at the cemetery, killing over 200, Western reporters were present, some of whom were beaten by the troops, and they became convincing witnesses to the massacre. Particularly crucial was film taken by a British Yorkshire Television photographer, which was smuggled out and shown subsequently in many countries, arousing outrage. Martin (2007: 31) stresses that this time Indonesian repression backfired because the news of it could not be suppressed (as had happened with worse massacres in the past) and Indonesian attempts to denigrate and blame the protesters, or to provide official exoneration of the military were unconvincing. Further violence against East Timorese resisters failed to deter the movement and intensified international anger.

The international response included a UN delegation report on Dili, US Congress demands for withdrawal of US military aid and arms to Indonesia, campaigns supporting East Timor in many countries, and pressure from international human rights groups. The awarding in 1996 of the Nobel Peace Prize to Bishop Carlos Belo and Jose Ramos-Horta, representing the diplomatic wing of the independence movement, focused world attention on East Timor and created an occasion for demanding a referendum on independence. The international context of the 1990s – the end of the cold war, the new emphasis on human rights and democratic self-government, and a growing number of small states granted recognition and represented at the UN – all assisted the East Timorese claim for independence. The switch towards primarily unarmed resistance (although the guerrilla forces were maintained in reserve) highlighted Indonesian troop brutality and removed any excuse for violent repression.

The contribution of transnational civil society groups to the ultimate victory of the East Timorese came partly from the mainstream and 'liberal establishment' end of the spectrum: parliamentarians (an attempt by Portuguese parliamentarians to visit East Timor in 1991 was a prelude to the Dili massacre), major human rights organizations and the Nobel Peace Prize.

But Stephan (2006: 63) argues that there was 'a strong grassroots component orchestrated by East Timorese who traveled round the world' to spread information and encourage pressure from below on governments supporting the Indonesian regime. In particular she credits the East Timor Action Network in the USA, created by a small group of activists, and incorporating human rights and faith-based groups, with effective lobbying of members of the US Congress and the State Department to withdraw forms of military and economic aid. Individuals from the War Resisters' International in the USA and Canada were prominent in this agitation and involved in giving evidence before the UN Committee on Decolonization on East Timor.

Australian activists in particular campaigned hard (though up to the 1990s unsuccessfully) to change their own government's stance, encouraged protest elsewhere, fostered links with the East Timorese resistance – including through a hidden radio transmitter in Darwin – and tried to smuggle Western journalists into the country (Martin et al., 2001; Martin, 2007). Some campaigners elsewhere engaged in radical forms of nonviolent protest, especially against arms sales by Western governments to Indonesia. Four British women, for example, entered a British Aerospace plant and attacked with hammers a Hawk Fighter plane to be exported to Indonesia, and justified their action as an attempt to prevent genocide in East Timor. The trial in Liverpool Crown Court in August 1996 was notable because the judge allowed witnesses from East Timor to speak, and the jury acquitted the women, who had based their legal defence on the international Genocide Convention (Randle, 1996). It also drew attention to the role of Western corporations in supporting the Suharto regime.

But the East Timor struggle highlights the fact that the effectiveness of civil society solidarity campaigns is related to the context of 'power politics' and also geographical factors. Where an oppressive regime is directly imposed by another country, or has political, economic and perhaps military support from the regional great power (as often in the case of the USA and Latin America), then strong opposition from within the dominant state in support of the resistance is especially significant. The most radical form this can take is a refusal to take part in military action that reinforces the oppression. Two examples are initiatives within the Israeli military in the 1980s, which included refusal to support attempts to crush the First Intifada, and the End Conscription Campaign in South Africa, which gained urgency from opposition to the role of the South African Defence Force inside the black townships (Kidron, 2004; Cock, 1992: 75–90).

Regional politics and cultural attitudes can be very important. The opposition in Zimbabwe after 2000, for example, has not benefited much from Western election monitors and human rights organizations (dismissed by the regime as instruments of Western colonialism), although these groups have helped to maintain a fairly high profile for the opposition movement in world media and to undermine President Mugabe's legitimacy at an international level. Citizens in neighbouring southern African states did not offer significant solidarity, with the exception of the South African trade unions backing their fellow unionists, who were central to the opposition movement in Zimbabwe. More dramatically, in April 2008, South African dockers, supported by a coalition of civil society groups inside South Africa and by the International Transport Workers Federation, refused to unload a Chinese arms shipment destined for Mugabe (Carter and Cherry, 2009). Geography also has practical importance – even in an era of instant global communications – since local contacts, knowledge of local languages and being close to borders can all affect ability to communicate with an internal opposition or supply it with material aid. Burmese opposition groups, which maintain offices in Thailand, receive support from Thai civil society (Moser-Puangsuwan, 2009: 47, 49 n.13).

Diasporas: their role in relation to internal resistance and the international context

Many internal resistance movements have links to external diasporas, often composed both of long-term emigrants settled in other countries and more recent refugees and activists who have fled repression. These diasporas have links to internal groups and can negotiate with national governments, represent the cause to international organizations and work with transnational civil society bodies to mobilize support for the internal resistance. They often provide articulate intellectuals able to explain the politics of their country to international media, and create opposition parties or coalition organizations that can claim a degree of legitimacy as an alternative locus of loyalty. Diaspora activity is not always helpful – over time an ideological gap and differing priorities or perceptions may develop between sections of the diaspora and the mainstream internal resistance, there may be some conflict between internal and external leaderships, and diasporas may (as in the case of Burma) be deeply divided. Nevertheless, the campaigning efforts and practical support they offer can be very important, especially in lengthy struggles, as in South Africa and the Palestinian Occupied Territories (Rigby, 2009: 177–83).

Tibetan national resistance to China is a particularly interesting example of diaspora politics, and illustrates some of the potential tensions between internal resistance and external opposition. The role of the Dalai Lama has been central to Tibetan religious and national consciousness. Fears that the Chinese planned to kidnap him led to a popular uprising in Lhasa in the spring of 1959, and precipitated the decision by the fourteenth Dalai Lama to leave the country (Shakya, 1999: 185–211). The scale of the Tibetan exodus, after the Dalai Lama escaped, to be followed by tens of thousands of his supporters, and the effectiveness of Chinese control, which quelled major internal political protest until the late 1980s, have also made the diaspora vital to the Tibetan cause. The Dalai Lama has, moreover, since 1979 been engaged in dialogue with the Chinese government and attempted to negotiate a compromise political settlement after launching a peace plan in 1987.

The Tibetan example is of particular interest in relation to themes of this book because of the Dalai Lama's emphasis on nonviolence. There was a (separate) violent phase of the Tibetan struggle, when imposition of land reform in a region of eastern Tibet sparked armed peasant resistance, which turned into a longer-running guerrilla campaign, backed by the CIA until the 1972 US–China rapprochement, but this was peripheral to the political struggle (Gittings, 2010: 165–6).

The development of the Tibetan diaspora within contemporary global politics has created an interesting tension between a pre-modern form of religious nationalism and today's values and practices. National identity in Tibet has been inextricably linked to the distinctive Tibetan form of Buddhism, with its rituals of prayer wheels and incense, tradition of intense theological debate, and the dominant role of thousands of Buddhist monasteries. The conflict between the Tibetans and the Chinese government has reflected not only opposed historical claims to ownership of the land, but differences between a traditional ('feudal' in Chinese terminology) mode of life and Beijing's emphasis on economic modernization. The Chinese government destroyed many monasteries in the 1950s, but has generally tolerated religious practices (except during the ideological extremism of the Cultural Revolution) although within a framework of strict and often harsh controls. It has also tried to use Buddhist institutions to its own advantage. The Party has, however, deliberately diluted Tibetan distinctiveness by a policy of large-scale Chinese immigration and, more recently, tourism, reducing the potential for mass non-cooperation by ethnic Tibetans.

The Dalai Lama has tried to bridge the gulf between the tradition he represents and a Western version of modernization, and early in his rule expressed a wish to introduce democratic reforms. He has been the centre of a government in exile based on the 100,000 Tibetans living in India (there are also about 20,000 in Nepal and thousands in North America and around the world). Exiles have take part in literacy campaigns, and the younger generation have tended to become well educated and Westernized in their attitudes – women for example now fill a quarter of the seats in the Tibetan Parliament in Exile (Harvey, 2009). Recently the Dalai Lama demonstrated his commitment to democratic principles by announcing on 10 March 2011 in a speech in India (circulated on the Net) that he would step down as political leader of the exile government in favour of a politically elected figure. He would remain as spiritual leader (Burke, 2011).

The Tibetan diaspora has engaged in periodic protests (often supported by international sympathisers and celebrities who have espoused the cause), for example against visiting Chinese government officials in various countries, and (as already noted) at the time of the Beijing March 2008 Olympics. Members of the younger generation have not lost their desire to attain Tibetan independence, indeed some have become more militant, critical of the Dalai Lama for his commitment to his nonviolence and his willingness to offer a compromise to the Chinese government based on national autonomy.

Revived internal resistance was led, in 1987, by nonviolent protests by monks and nuns, but developed momentum until the imposition of martial law, when many were jailed. However, a much more widespread and more secular resistance, which continued for several months, and included attacks on Chinese migrants in Tibet, erupted in March 2008 (after initial protests in monasteries had been suppressed), both in the Tibetan Autonomous Region and among Tibetans in adjacent Chinese provinces. Protesters included, according to the Tibetan historian Tsering Shakya (2008: 18), 'school children, students, intellectuals, city workers, farmers, nomads – as well as Tibetan university students in Beijing and other cities'. The demonstrations spread largely through mobile phones and texts (which limited the amount of dissent in western Tibet, where the necessary mobile network is missing) and resulted in at least 6,000 arrests. The protests were not linked to the official diaspora. Indeed, the Dalai Lama has openly admitted that his own influence and that of the émigré government over internal resistance is now weaker.

Evidence of a significant continuing desire for cultural autonomy and political self-government inside Tibet is clearly crucial to the credibility of diaspora politics. It is doubtful if a national struggle can ever be won primarily from outside the country. The Tibetan movement is, moreover, hampered by China's increasing economic and military great-power status and its relative immunity to external pressures, limiting the leverage of the diaspora. Real progress for the Tibetan cause is probably dependent on significant political change inside China itself, and willingness to end the policy of large-scale Chinese immigration into Tibet.

Transnational civil society bodies and the role of nonviolent protest and intervention

Diasporas often link up with mainstream liberal advocacy networks, which offer support through lobbying, publicity and solidarity demonstrations. But they may also seek support for smuggling in printing and radio equipment, or banned literature, where regimes tightly control access to communications – as the former communist regimes did – or for taking out messages and helping individuals to escape. They may also cooperate with transnational groups trying to apply economic leverage, find dramatic forms of political protest, or promote awareness of the potential of unarmed resistance strategies and methods.

Campaigning for arms or trade boycotts by governments and intergovernmental bodies, and seeking to reinforce the policy of economic boycott through citizen action, such as refusing to buy goods from the country (as in calls for boycotts of South African produce) or operating a tourism boycott (as in the case of Burma) has been a common tactic. Civil society groups may also try to isolate and stigmatize the regime more selectively and symbolically – for example through cultural, academic or sporting boycotts. These are often very controversial and can be in danger of isolating citizens and opponents of the regime without affecting the regime itself, just as economic boycotts can intensify hardship for ordinary citizens. The mounting resistance in the Maldive Islands from 2004 to 2008 to the autocratic and nepotistic rule by President Maumoon Gayoom considered calling for holiday-makers to boycott this 'tourist paradise', but decided that it would destroy the economy and harm ordinary people too much. Instead 'Friends of the Maldives' called for a 'selective boycott' of resorts where commercial interests were most closely tied to the regime (Kunzru, 2006).

But boycotts are sometimes called for by leading individuals and organizations within a resistance, as in South Africa and Burma (although Aung San Suu Kyi since her release from house arrest in 2010 appeared to be reconsidering her support for this policy). Students and radical groups have sometimes embraced the policy of encouraging Western corporation to disinvest in repressive regimes, especially where corporations in order to operate successfully had to have close links to the regime, as in Burma (Fink, 2001: 242). There was a successful movement in universities in the USA and Britain in the mid-1990s demanding such disinvestment – linked in the case of Pepsi Cola to franchises for sales of the product on campus (Klein, 2000: 402–3). Other companies such as Heineken and Levi-Strauss agreed to disinvest. The Free Burma Coalition in the USA successfully persuaded a number of cities and counties, and the state of Massachusetts, to legislate against purchase of goods from companies doing business in Burma, until the Supreme Court ruled against them. Where corporations have colluded in human rights and environmental abuses, solidarity campaigns have brought lawsuits against them: a US court ruled that Unocal should pay compensation to those forced by the Burmese army to work on laying the Yadana gas pipeline, and a French court ruled against the Total Oil corporation (Moser-Puangsuwan, 2009: 47).

Radical transnational groups periodically try to intervene directly inside country to show solidarity and boost the morale of the resistance. For example an international group of 18 from Thailand, Malaysia, Indonesia, the Philippines, the USA and Australia entered Burma as tourists on the tenth anniversary of the 1988 resistance to stage a brief demonstration (Fink, 2001: 244). A much more sustained transnational effort to offer support to Palestinian resistance to Israeli occupation policies in the West Bank has been undertaken by a range of Israeli, leftist and Christian groups since the outbreak of the Second Intifada in 2000 (Dudouet, 2009; Wright, 2009; Zelter, 2009).

Although the Second Intifada has been primarily associated with armed resistance, a significant unarmed resistance has developed. An opposition movement, Al Mubadar (the Initiative), committed to an unarmed strategy and promoting a broad coalition of individuals and civil society groups, was launched in October 2000 with a petition that was signed by 10,000, and founded in June 2002, with the aim of encouraging resistance and forging links both with the Palestinian diaspora and Israeli sympathisers (Barghouti, 2005: 128–9). Since then a 'third intifada' against the Israeli government decision in 2004 to build the 'apartheid wall' between Palestinian territory and Israeli settlements has mobilized residents of some villages losing their olive groves as a result of the wall to make weekly protests – 21 Palestinians had been killed by tear gas, rubber bullets and occasional use of live ammunition by the end of 2010, others injured and many more imprisoned. The Palestinian cabinet in Ramallah has supported the demonstrations, and the EU protested about a year's sentence for a leader of the anti-wall agitation, and Israeli civil rights groups have taken legal action inside Israel to alter the course of the wall in some areas (MacIntyre, 2011a; Carbajosa, 2011).

The rationale for transnational activists is to offer solidarity and promote empowerment of nonviolent resistance within Palestinian territory, and through their presence to deter Israeli security forces from brutal harassment. Some groups emphasize their role as witnesses and subsequent education of public opinion at home. Thousands, especially many Americans of Jewish origin, have taken part in various forms of solidarity action and many have been turned back by the Israeli government. An international presence does not always deter Israeli troops; it has at times exacerbated the situation, leading to an end to the 2002 policy of accompanying Palestinian ambulances (Dudouet, 2009: 131). But the international presence and actions have ensured significant coverage in reputable mainstream media in the West, whilst the killing of several Western volunteers, for example Rachel Corrie, who was trying to prevent a Palestinian home being bulldozed, and Tom Hurndall, who was shot whilst trying to lead Palestinian children to safety, publicized the degree of violence often used by the Israeli occupation forces and in the latter instance led to a court case inside Israel (Dudouet, 2009: 132). Israeli human rights activists who have supported the Palestinians and promoted legal action inside Israel are especially important politically in maintaining links between Palestinians and Israeli citizens in a context of dangerous ideological polarization. The presence of Westerners prepared to risk their lives to support the rights of Palestinians can also, as Barghouti (2005: 129) has argued, be significant in the attempt to combat an Islamic extremism that promotes undifferentiated hatred of the West.

Direct intervention by members of human rights, peace and solidarity movements can take the rather different form of providing protective accompaniment for leading individuals (often human rights defenders) who are at risk of assassination by security services or paramilitary forces, or accompanying refugees. Peace Brigades International is the best-known transnational organization specializing in this approach; others include the US-based Witness for Peace (Mahony and Eguren, 1997; Eguren, 2009: 98–107; Griffin-Nolan, 1991).

A potentially controversial form of transnational intervention by individuals and groups committed to the principle of nonviolent action is disseminating pamphlets (often translated by participants in resistance struggles into their own language) that summarize the strategy and methods of unarmed resistance, organizing training sessions either inside or outside the country where resistance is being mobilized, and conferring with leading activists. The role of the International Fellowship of Reconciliation, and its national section, in nonviolence training in the Philippines was noted in Chapter 5. Some peace organizations have developed expertise in training for confrontational nonviolent action arising out of their own experiences in the Civil Rights movement in the USA or anti-war and green activism – for example the US-based Training for Change and the transnational War Resisters' International (Lakey, 2009: 206–13; War Resisters' International, 2009).

A well-known source of information on unarmed resistance is the Albert Einstein Institution, founded by Gene Sharp, whose pamphlet *From Dictatorship to Democracy*, first written at the request of a Burmese democrat in exile in 1993, has been translated into over 30 languages (Sharp, 1993). The Institution has, when approached for help, discussed the possibilities of nonviolent resistance with movements such as the Palestinian First Intifada, 1987–90, the developing opposition in the Baltic states in 1988–91 and the Serbian students mobilizing against Milosevic. More recently, the International Center on Nonviolent Conflict in Washington has begun promoting knowledge of and support for nonviolent action on a more ambitious scale, and lobbied governments and IGOs. Successful people power movements can potentially provide not only an example, but practical advice, to struggling movements. Individuals from the Serb student resistance OTPOR have been active in advising and encouraging students movements in some of the former Soviet states – notably Georgia, where OTPOR banners appeared in demonstrations, and Ukraine (Kuzio, 2006; Welt, 2010: 178–9). The Ukraine student opposition group, Pora, received considerable support from Slovak organizations that had mobilized to ensure the electoral downfall of Vladimir Meciar in the 1998 elections (Wilson, 2009: 348). Members of the 6 April movement in Egypt (see Chapter 6) had apparently been in contact with OTPOR and some had read Sharp's pamphlet (Jauvert, 2011; Abramsky, 2011).

Potential problems of external support and its limits

There is a paradox that the increasing use of people power across the globe, which is closely linked to the degree of support often available from other governments, IGOs and transnational networks, raises questions about the drawbacks of at least some forms of external support. How far can what looks like a mass popular movement be fostered by external government or unofficial agencies? These problems apply particularly to external funding of an opposition movement – both the sources of the funds and their impact within the country may be questionable. In extreme cases it raises the question whether an opposition movement is being used as a Trojan horse to secure the interests of an external great or regional power.

Accusations by repressive governments that resistance movements are being manipulated by foreign agents is a standard means of trying to delegitimize them, and are frequently ludicrous. When under pressure from the opposition Maldivian Democratic Party (MDP), founded in 2003, the dictatorial President Gayoom, appealed to the strict Islamic sentiments in his country when he attacked the MDP, attacked a small British NGO, Friends of the Maldives, that assisted the MDP, as Christian missionaries who also smuggled in pork and alcohol. Because the founder of the MDP, Mohammed Nasheed, who was jailed for five years after he began calling for political reforms in the late 1980s, had been educated in Britain, he was also accused of acting as a Christian missionary, as well as of drug dealing, terrorism and homosexuality. Ironically, the regime itself employed the British public relations firm Hill and Knowlton – which had worked for the Chinese government after the repression of the Tiananmen demonstrations in 1989 – to provide a more acceptable image to the outside world (Kunzru, 2006: 38–40).

The more frequent accusation, however, from governments facing unarmed resistance, or nervous of the idea spreading to their own country, is that organizations promoting unarmed resistance are acting on behalf of the US government or the West more generally. The concern within the Iranian security services about 'soft coups' was noted in Chapter 2. Iranian officials have a historical precedent for suspecting that foreign security agencies might foster internal unrest, in light of the coup against Prime Minister Mossadeq in 1953, but the Green Movement that arose in 2008 appeared to be entirely generated by anger from within the country. Many of such claims relate, however, to the movements in former Soviet states, where we have noted the continuation of a form of cold war politics between Russia and the West. It is primarily (though not solely) in this context that some of the Western left has seemed eager to take up the accusations. The role of external intervention in movements in Serbia and the former Soviet states has been assessed by analysts of particular movements.

In the case of Serbia, Western governments had generally supported Milosevic and relied upon him to assist in finding solutions to the wars in the Balkans up to 1996, but then changed their assessment and began to offer diplomatic and other support to the opposition. US Radio Free Europe and Radio Liberty, and the BBC, broadcast information about the opposition into the country. A number of well-established Western organizations and funding bodies began to extend practical support, for example technical aid in setting up radio stations and websites for the opposition, and providing funds for electoral monitoring and campaigning (Vejvoda, 2009: 306, 312). Although OTPOR denied it at the time, especially because the Western bombing of Serbia in 1999, in an attempt to halt Serb military action in Kosovo, had created hatred of the West, it received significant Western financial backing (Nenadic and Belcevic, 2009: 32–3). There was also open support for the opposition from the EU, which offered practical technical and financial assistance to municipalities under opposition control, and two smaller European states with good democratic credentials, Norway and Switzerland. Milosevic refused entry to monitors from international organizations for the September 2000 elections, but the OSCE and other bodies published reports on the conduct of the poll.

Vejvoda, Nenadic and Belcevic insist, however, that it was primarily the persistence, courage and organizational skills of the resistance that ousted Milosevic. Given the months of large daily protests in Belgrade in the winter of 1996–7 to challenge the rigging of town hall elections, the build-up of opposition among intellectuals, and the developing campaign by OTPOR from 1997 to 2000, when it had 18,000 members and was able to mobilize large numbers of the electorate to vote for the anti-Milosevic coalition of 18 out of

19 parties, it would be ludicrous to suggest that the resistance was primarily manufactured from outside. Moreover, the final stage of resistance included increasing numbers of journalists in the state-controlled media complaining about bias, and strikes by coal miners and industrial and transport workers. In the culminating demonstration of half a million in Belgrade, political officials and former soldiers from the provinces took part, and even the Belgrade football fans, who were at the forefront of the occupation of parliament and the assault on the television station (Garton Ash, 2009c: 16–17; Vejvoda, 2009: 312). In addition, as noted in Chapter 2, sections of the military and security services refused to carry out Milosevic's orders when the final showdown came.

The case that external intervention played a major role in promoting opposition looks stronger in the case of both Georgia and Ukraine. Despite earlier episodes of courageous protest (for example a protest camp set up in February 2001 in Kiev, and demonstrations throughout the Ukraine demanding impeachment of the then president for alleged complicity in the murder of an investigative reporter), the mass demonstrations that brought about a change in government in both countries were brief (though in Ukraine they stretched over some weeks) and organized with a clear eye to public relations, for example the distribution of orange flags in the Ukraine. There was also ample evidence of Western funding for internal NGOs (Bunce and Wolchik, 2010: 31–2). In Georgia, for example, well-funded new organizations aroused antagonism in their conspicuous display of affluence (Jones, 2009: 329–31). Funds were also supplied for election monitoring and holding opinion polls. McFaul's study of the role played by external assistance, especially by the US Agency of International Development, concludes that outside agencies can only effectively influence a few of the factors contributing to success for the opposition, notably by promoting observation of elections, strengthening civil society groups and funding alternative media (McFaul, 2010: 219).

External intervention was not, however, limited to the West. The Russian government and a range of Russian agencies (with a few exceptions that helped the opposition) gave active support to President Yevtushenko and his electoral campaign in Ukraine in 2004, so external intervention did not decisively advantage one side (Wilson, 2005: 86–96). Moreover, despite the generally tendency of Western agencies to support the opposition and vice versa, the actual position of both the US and Russian governments, when people power movements created a political crisis, was more nuanced. Neither wanted serious instability or violence. In Georgia both the Russian and the US ambassadors were against the immediate overthrow of President Shevardnadze, and would have preferred him to serve out his term (Jones, 2009: 331; Welt, 2010: 186).

Criteria for legitimate intervention

Given the genuine dangers of popular movements being used to promote great power or regional national interests, and the potential for crude forms of intervention to undermine the credibility of internal resistance, there are obvious problems in direct outside intervention by governments. There are also pitfalls for transnational civil society groups if they fail to respect the goals of protesters and impose their own ideological agendas. It can be even more dangerous if 'experts' in campaigning and nonviolent protest do not pay attention to internal knowledge of the complexities of politics and culture within a particular society or encourage risky tactics – considerations given priority by those with long experience in the field.

Nevertheless, as indicated throughout this book, external solidarity, political support in key forums and practical aid can be crucial to resistance movements struggling with minimum resources against repression. Whilst backing for opposition movements from governments of other states is often questionable, governments can give sanctuary to refugees and opposition activists, allow a diaspora to set up offices and organizations to represent the opposition, or provide facilities for external media such as radio stations. Moreover, since foreign offices maintain a network of diplomatic missions round the world, they can influence the policy of their own governments towards a regime, often maintain links with opposition leaders – as in Burma where Aung San Suu Kyi was welcomed on her release from house arrest in 2010 by foreign diplomats – and may even help to arrange that opposition activists or journalists leave the country when at serious risk. Embassies may also facilitate the exit of dictators when people power reaches a climax. In addition, human rights activists have received important support from sympathetic embassies with the official ability to make representations about rights abuses and to encourage external diplomatic action. The work of the Peace Brigades International in accompanying individuals at risk of assassination involves maintaining such diplomatic links (Winstanley, 2009: 108–9). A handbook written by and for diplomats itemizes and illustrates the diplomatic measures available for 'democracy development support' (Diplomats Handbook, 2009). National parliaments representing a range of political parties, and with a role in curbing their own governments, can offer support through fact-finding reports and missions, or parliamentary debates, that are potentially more impartial than government interventions. Individual parliamentarians can also offer moral support or act as observers (if allowed in) at people power demonstrations; for example a young Estonian MP joined the tent city in Kiev in December 2004 for weeks (Krushelnycky, 2006: 293).

The justifiability of governmental, diplomatic or parliamentary support for opposition movements in another country is linked to international law and adherence to principles of human rights. Since these are central to the role of some IGOs, direct forms of intervention to support opposition movements are likely to have greater legitimacy if they are provided through bodies like the UN or OSCE. They are well placed to highlight human rights issues and promote diplomatic or economic sanctions. There may be a particular role for IGOs to assist negotiations between an opposition and the regime – the UN and the Commonwealth, for example, took part in the prolonged negotiations in South Africa leading up to 1994. Where regimes hold elections or referenda there is scope for impartial monitoring and publicity of abuses (Pastor, 1999). The European Parliament has given a public hearing to leading dissidents and offers an annual Sakharov Prize for Freedom of Thought that includes financial support for individuals to continue their campaigning. Analysis of what the EU already does and how it could provide a more consistent support to nonviolent activists is provided in a report to the European Parliament by Veronique Dudouet and Howard Clark, 'Nonviolent Civic Action in Support of Human Rights and Democracy' (Dudouet and Clark, 2009).

Economic globalization and its implications

Judgements about external support for opposition movements are necessarily influenced by ideology. Democracy promotion programmes viewed positively from a Western liberal perspective can be interpreted as political and cultural instruments to extend US and Western hegemony from other perspectives. Since the end of the cold war extending multiparty parliamentary forms of democracy has been closely interlinked with pressure to adopt extreme free market beliefs and policies. The collapse of the Soviet bloc coincided with the apparent defeat of Keynesian economics and social democratic politics in the West, replaced by neoliberal policies promoting an end to many kinds of state regulation and state responsibility for social welfare in favour of minimum restriction on financial institutions and businesses, and privatization of water, energy, transport and other national services. Some leading figures in the former Soviet bloc were happy to embrace a new official ideology – despite the very severe hardships for most of the population in a period of transition. Given the economic problems that these countries were facing, others were persuaded there was no viable economic alternative. In South Africa the Africa National Congress (as noted in Chapter 4) was constrained to accept the rules of the Western economic system as part of the price for abolishing apartheid. As a result, a gulf soon opened up between the party leaders and many poor workers and township residents who had previously supported the ANC (Kingsnorth, 2003: 87–123; Ngwane, 2004).

People power movements are essentially the expression of a popular demand that people should have some direct control over their own lives. Typically, therefore, they are directed against dictatorial or semi-authoritarian regimes and demand democratic political institutions. But anger against political elites is also fuelled by the perception of major economic corruption at the top – especially in countries where the great majority are very poor and governments squander fortunes on private enrichment. People power movements in Africa, in particular, are therefore often directed primarily at corruption, which may be associated with political autocracy, but also quite often flourishes in and distorts at least nominally representative parliamentary regimes (Beyerie, 2010). Popular uprisings are often fuelled by poverty, high prices and unemployment, as in Indonesia in 1997–8 (Vickers, 2005: 204–5). Economic hardship was also the starting point for Burma in 2007 and Tunisia in January 2011.

There are many possible causes of serious poverty. People power movements may be responding to dominant global economic trends and institutions, whilst perceiving them primarily in terms of their own direct experience of economic hardship and government policy. The 'structural adjustment' programmes in Africa in the 1980s and 1990s, which required governments to abolish subsidies for food and other essentials, were one factor in promoting the popular anger and resistance that challenged autocratic governments in the early 1990s (see Chapter 6). These programmes were being imposed by the International Monetary Fund and the World Bank during the 1980s and 1990s, and also by Western governments offering 'aid', but they were at a stage removed.

However, by the 1990s there was increasing popular perception in Africa, Asia and Latin America that international financial and economic institutions, governments signing 'free trade' agreements and multinational corporations were combining to impose on the ordinary people policies which cut state provision of welfare, privatized essential services such as water and fuel supply, allowed pursuit of oil and gas supplies to destroy the lives and environment of indigenous peoples, small farmers and fishing communities, and effectively subjected their countries to forms of alien domination. This perception led to many notable struggles, often using nonviolent methods, against particular projects and corporations – for example the Ogoni movement against Shell in Nigeria and the Cochabamba resistance to water privatization in Bolivia (Kingsnorth, 2003: 71–81; Cooper, 1999; Obi, 2000).

There has been a degree of continuity between some previous people power movements and determined popular resistance to neoliberal policies. In Indonesia, the students who were at the forefront of overthrowing Suharto in 1998 were prominent in 1999 protests against President B.J. Habibe ending food and fuel subsidies. In South Korea, the trade unions and students active in overthrowing military dictatorship, as well as the unemployed and angry farmers, have been engaged in more recent strikes and demonstrations on economic issues. In South Africa, resistance to apartheid by trade unions and township associations in the 1980s was transmuted into strikes and new forms of militant opposition to neoliberal policies, privatization and the local World Bank Office (Desai, 2002; Kingsnorth, 2003: 89–123; Ngwane, 2004). Opposition to the operations of particular multinational corporations involved in arming or providing PR services for dictatorial regimes, or playing a role in their economies, is another thread connecting resistance to political oppression and the Global Justice Movement emerging at the end of the 1990s.

Much of the current resistance to multinational corporations and neoliberal economic agendas can, however, be interpreted in a framework of social movements, rather than people power. But if the definition of a 'people' is extended beyond 'nation states' (or nations seeking an independent state) to encompass indigenous peoples, then many of the struggles which have been part of the Global Justice Movement, where indigenous communities are defending their land and life style against corporate or government policies, would qualify. Often these campaigns can be viewed from multiple perspectives – the rights of indigenous peoples to autonomy and at the same time campaigns to preserve the environment and achieve social justice.

If 'the people' is interpreted in terms of class, rather than 'the body politic' or cultural nationhood, then resistance by peasant farmers and workers, where they form a clear majority, could count as people power. In fact the bias of neoliberal policies tends to mean that many professional groups and public servants may join in resistance, as was demonstrated in major protests in many Latin American and African countries in the 1990s and the first decade of the twenty-first century.

Opposition to economic policies destroying the lifestyle and livelihood of indigenous peoples and small farmers throws into relief the choice between guerrilla or nonviolent strategies of resistance, debated in Chapter 2. The best known example of the guerrilla option is the creation of the Zapatistas in the Chiapas region of Mexico in 1994, in order to protect Mayan land, economic practices and autonomy against the threat posed by the North American Free Trade Association. But the Zapatistas have not followed a typical guerrilla path, minimizing their use of violence, becoming part of the Global Justice Movement, and relying heavily on global communications media (Holloway, 2005).

A more old-fashioned form of guerrilla strategy is represented by the Naxalite movement in India. The Naxalites emerged in 1967, when indigenous people in West Bengal engaged in armed struggle to reclaim their land from local landlords. The movement spread to other states within India and for several years seemed to signal the start of a Maoist-style guerrilla struggle promoted by the (Maoist) Communist Party. But the death of a respected leader, numerous political and ideological splits in the movement and imprisonment of thousands of key communist officials ended this first phase (Kujur, 2008).

Since then the Naxalites have supported the cause of indigenous peoples resisting government-backed corporate exploitation of national resources and maintained an armed presence in remote areas. Government claims of Maoist involvement have been used to justify killing and torturing tribal people (Padel, 2010). The Naxalites have, especially through their political fronts, engaged in a range of nonviolent protests (sit-ins, social boycotts, strikes and encirclements) and promoted forms of direct democracy such as people's courts (Bhatia, 2002: 260). But in India, where there is still a Gandhian movement, there is a clear division between the Naxalites and activists committed to unarmed resistance, which can potentially attract strong transnational support (for example against multinationals) and is likely to cause much less suffering to communities engaged in resistance. There have been quite a few such nonviolent struggles (Mazgaonkar, 2009; Palit, 2003).

The only two nationwide revolts against neoliberal policies which would strictly qualify as examples of nationwide people power, so far, have been the unarmed uprising in Bolivia in 2003 (summarized in Chapter 5) and the popular response to the total breakdown of the economy in Argentina in December 2001. Both took place in nominally representative democracies (which had emerged out of dictatorships in the 1980s), but in both cases the people saw their governments as acting in the interests of alien economic forces. In Bolivia the 2003 uprising, which toppled the government, and further agitation, led in December 2005 to the election of the first indigenous president of the country, Evo Morales, and of his Movimento al Socialismo coalition in parliamentary elections. Morales won an unprecedented 54 per cent of the vote cast by 85 per cent of the electorate (Hylton, 2006: 69). He has since been pursuing an economic and political agenda strongly opposed to the previous 'Washington consensus'.

In Argentina, where in the previous decade governments had enthusiastically pursued neoliberal policies and unregulated privatization, the IMF refusal to provide further loans plunged the ailing economy into crisis. When the government responded to economic desperation and looting by imposing a state of emergency, an angry people rose up and overthrew it (Lopez-Levy, 2004). Protest and popular mobilization from below also led to creative improvisation of social and economic solutions to disaster, and a growing sense of communal empowerment, through street assemblies, squatters' groups, worker seizure of factories and an upsurge of alternative media. Although this popular mobilization was largely dissipated after a return to economic normality, many 'recovered factories' were still being run by workers seven years later (Whyte and Gavernet, 2008; Petras and Veltmeyer, 2005). In May 2003 a new government emerged under President Nestor Kirchner, who was more responsive to social movements than earlier governments had been, and early on initiated a review of all the privatization contracts.

It is unclear how far popular resistance to global economic policies will impinge on national politics in the future. However, the topic raises fundamental questions about the nature of the Western liberal democratic model and the meaning of democracy, as well as reviving the debate about the role and limits of legitimate popular protest within a representative multiparty framework. As more countries move towards a minimal model of electoral democracy, people power may become more closely associated with demands for people to control their economic destiny and their environment.

Conclusion

This book has covered a very wide range of examples of unarmed resistance, but a few key arguments and themes run through the discussion. The initial claim is that people power (including a wide range of methods of nonviolent protest in different cultures and contexts) is not new – unarmed and sustained popular resistance to political repression and injustice is part of our inheritance. This inheritance, has, however, been partially hidden from history, both because of the bias of written records and earlier historians, and because there has been a strong tendency to equate rebellion and revolution with armed violence. Therefore unarmed resistance has often played an important but not fully recognized part in earlier revolutions.

There has, however, been a significant alteration in popular consciousness in recent decades in many parts of the world, and a much greater willingness to embrace nonviolent methods of protest and to be committed to peaceful rebellion. Moreover, whereas in the past resisters often moved from unarmed protests to guerrilla tactics, there is now some tendency for movements that have waged armed struggle to experiment (in some cases successfully) with unarmed resistance. This does not mean, unfortunately, as is obvious from the daily news, that there is a general reduction in the use of violence for political ends. But, whereas a strategy of 'people's war' had important parallels with a long-term unarmed resistance struggle, there is today a much sharper distinction between popular movements seeking to overthrow corrupt and autocratic governments or repressive types of regime through people power, and organizations or groups committed to acts of destructive terrorism. Although people power may sometimes turn into armed rebellion, as in Libya in 2011, this has not been typical of recent movements.

The obvious question is why the incidence of people power has so strikingly increased. This question can be broken down into two separate questions:

- Why have so many people become willing to undertake sustained protests to change their political regime, despite the disruption of their daily lives and often severe risk of arrest, injury or even death?
- Why have they in general been more inclined to adopt consciously peaceful methods and abstain from taking up arms?

The willingness of people to protest is closely linked to, and partly responsible for, the rapid spread of electoral democracy, the 'third wave' of democratization since the 1970s. Economic hardship, forms of blatant social injustice or anger about the scale of political corruption are often triggers for protest, but these grievances have tended to evolve into specifically political demands for constitutional government, individual and political rights, and electoral choice. Moreover, many regimes that have felt constrained to present some appearance of political legitimacy to their populations and the wider world have held plebiscites or rigged elections, often providing a focal point for popular resistance. Hence the interesting combination in many countries of electoral strategies with extra-constitutional forms of political action, such as strikes, occupations and mass demonstrations in defiance of orders to disperse.

Long-term trends transforming traditional forms of society, such as urbanization, economic development, higher education levels, new forms of communication and a raising of individual expectations can be adduced to explain the growing popular demands for democracy over the past two centuries. Earlier Western scholarship on democratization stressed that some cultural milieux and religious beliefs were more favourable to representative democracy. But, although there is some historical basis for this claim, the spread of people power demonstrates that people in all cultures who have bitter experience of arbitrary and repressive forms of government desire basic political rights and democratic choice. Moreover, belief in both popular control over governments and individual human rights has become a significant element in international politics in recent decades, through the role of many international governmental organizations and influential international nongovernmental organizations. International law stressing human rights and seeking to hold those denying these rights to account has become more central. The speed and accessibility of new means of communication have also made it much easier to spread news of human rights violations and of people power uprisings. These developments tend to increase the potential for global support for unarmed resistance movements; examples of transnational networks that seek to provide various forms of solidarity were cited in Chapter 7.

The willingness to adopt modes of resistance that deliberately avoid use of weapons is in some cases a conscious moral and political choice, where groups initiating resistance and national and local leading figures are motivated by religious conviction or by conscious adherence to the tradition of nonviolent resistance associated with Gandhi. More often it is primarily a strategic choice based on awareness that the regime (or an occupying force) can muster overwhelming military might and much more easily justify its use if the resistance takes up arms. Protesters also perceive the political advantages of remaining peaceful in order to encourage sections of the regime to defect, and to maximize international support. But above all popular willingness not only to adopt, but to maintain, an unarmed resistance has clearly been influenced by the success of previous movements and the power of example. There is now an increasing awareness (even in countries where censorship is practised) of major people power movements in other parts of the world, but the demands and ethos of regional movements, and regional styles of protest, have clearly been influential in Latin America, Asia, the former Soviet sphere, Africa and the Middle East. Even ultimately unsuccessful movements can provide tactical inspiration: for example protesters trying in 1990 to change one-party rule in Mongolia looked to Tiananmen Square when they began their own public fast.

Commitment to intrinsically nonviolent means of protest is in many cases influenced by the nature of the goals of the protesters. In the case of the popular organization and demonstrations to counter the rigging of elections, which became widespread in the first decade of this century, the focus on demanding a fair electoral process and respect for constitutional norms, as well as on replacing authoritarian governments by opposition parties, is more congruent with nonviolent than violent modes of popular resistance. Two alternative modes of demonstrating a popular (or at least a majority) will – people power and elections – have been intertwined. This trend has been closely linked to international setting of criteria for fair elections and electoral monitoring.

Even where the aim of people power movements is to bring about a fundamental change, as in 1989 in the Soviet bloc, what the participants mostly aspired to – apart from national independence – was not some totally original brave new world, but the rule of law, civil liberties and representative multi-party democracy. Whilst some disappointed commentators denied that 1989 could be classed as a revolution, others welcomed a model of nonviolent revolution, linked to political moderation, and a willingness to compromise and negotiate where necessary. The Arab revolutions that broke out early in 2011 focused on the demand for constitutional rights and genuine electoral democracy, and initially tended to show a willingness to compromise – their positions hardened and their demands became more uncompromising when the regimes met unarmed protest with widespread arrests and bloodshed.

It is not easy to achieve real political transformation. Even initial success, as in some of the electoral revolutions (such as in the Philippines and Serbia) and recently in the uprisings in Tunisia and Egypt, is only a first stage; further popular pressure, as well as more basic changes in political attitudes and practices, are needed to produce permanent radical change. There are, of course, no guarantees that people power will achieve even initial success. Governments ruling over militarily and economically strong countries, and able to gain regional support or ignore international condemnation, may be able mobilize their full forces of repression to quell for a time even the bravest resistance. Chapter 6 noted debate among scholars about the potential ability of threatened authoritarian regimes in the former Soviet sphere to start learning from example how better to defeat popular protest; the same process may be occurring in parts of the Arab world. The changing configuration of great power politics can also have a double-edged impact: in some cases increasing the fragility of autocratic regimes – for example if previous great power support is transferred to the opposition – but in others bolstering repressive governments due to strategic or economic priorities and the perceived need to contain the latest threat.

The fact that in recent decades the goal of most people power protests has been to replace repressive regimes with basic liberties and electoral democracy does not mean that this will necessarily be true in the future. Chapter 7 noted that in Bolivia and Argentina there were in the past decade examples of popular rebellion based partly on economic demands and resistance to international bodies such as the IMF and major corporations dictating national economic policies. There have also been protests around the world, on a somewhat lesser scale, about the role of oil and mining corporations, privatization of previously public services and enforced austerity measures. The issues are both economic and political, and sometimes environmental. Moreover, desire for popular control (once formal national independence has been won) can logically extend to opposing the dominance of a particular great power or regional power within national politics. But one of the most important features of upsurges of people power is unpredictability.

How 'the people' should be defined and how a particular expression of people power should be understood was explored in Chapter 5. But the key claim here is that people assembling in public squares to demand a better political future often demonstrate the democratic ideal at its best. In the past governments and intellectual commentators have generally viewed large crowds as a potentially dangerous rabble, liable to engage in irrational destruction; some contemporary journalistic comment still reflects this image of the 'mob'. It is of course true that crowds in some circumstances can turn to rioting, looting, arson and attacks on individuals – there are well-known historical examples, and this can still occur. Indeed, the incidence of rioting in Kyrgyzstan in both 2005 and 2010 is one reason for hesitating to describe these protests as 'people power'. But, when people join together to assert their collective political goal of ending repression, they often transcend divisions of religion, class, ideology or ethnicity and display impressive self-discipline.

The central emphasis of this book is on the political importance of people power as a phenomenon: the remarkable fact that ordinary men and women armed with nothing but courage, determination, ingenuity and ability to cooperate can undermine and overthrow regimes defended by ruthless security services and armed with the latest weaponry. The importance of protest is worth asserting because academic analysts, suspicious of immediate impressions, are often reluctant to accept that people power is really significant. There is a strong tendency – especially in retrospect – to minimize the role of the popular protests and emphasize instead the significance of long-term trends, the underlying economic, military or political weaknesses of the regime, the role of international pressures or the importance of elite negotiations. All these factors may indeed influence both the context of resistance and the final outcome – and this book seeks to take them into account. There is, moreover, always room for competing interpretations. But progress towards democracy requires popular commitment to achieve it.

Appendix: People power movements against political repression since 1975

There are many earlier examples of people power (quite a few cited in this book), often arising out of national movements of liberation from European or colonial empires. But the number of unarmed rebellions (against internally dictatorial or authoritarian regimes, or foreign repression) has rapidly increased in recent decades. This list – which includes some movements that may be less familiar than famous historical examples – illustrates this trend.

Most of the examples of unarmed resistance listed below are widely recognized as being significant, even though not all have succeeded. Some, however, have received inadequate publicity and recognition in the West. In certain cases scholars disagree over how important the role of popular resistance was in regime change. Quite a few, despite the centrality of unarmed methods, have been associated with previous or parallel forms of armed resistance, and a few have been superseded by violent tactics. Finally, a few of these movements are controversial because of major divisions within their society, or because of the degree of external support extended to them.

This list is not exhaustive. One criterion for choice is that all these examples are referred to (although at varying length and with varying frequency) in the text.

IRAN 1977–9 Overthrowing the Shah
BOLIVIA 1977–82 Ending military rule
POLAND 'Solidarity' 1980–1; and 1982–9 (underground existence and re-emergence)
URUGUAY 1980–4 'Smile Revolution' and return to democracy
PHILIPPINES 1983–6 'People Power' overthrows Marcos
KOREA (South) 1979–80 and 1986–7 Claiming democracy
CHILE 1983–8 Deposing General Pinochet
TAIWAN 1977–9 and 1987–9 Promoting moves to democracy
PALESTINE (Occupied Territories) 1987–90 The First Intifada
BURMA (Myanmar) 1988 Uprising against the junta leads to elections (1990)
CHINA 1989 Tiananmen Square
EASTERN EUROPE 1989 'Velvet Revolutions' and negotiated transitions in Poland, Hungary, East Germany and Czechoslovakia; protests in Bulgaria

THE BALTIC STATES 1988–91 Movements for national independence and democracy
MONGOLIA 1989–90 Ending the Communist Party monopoly
NEPAL 1990 'Jana Andolan' uprising to restore democracy
SUB-SAHARAN AFRICA 1989–92 Widespread popular protests demanding multiparty democracy and new elected presidents: e.g. Benin, Niger, Malawi and Zambia (successful); Cameroon 1990–2 *Villes mortes* movement; Ivory Coast (achieved elections but not change of president)
THAILAND 1992 Resisting the generals
SOUTH AFRICA 1952–61; 1976–94 Resisting and ending apartheid
INDONESIA 1987–98 Overthrowing General Suharto
EAST TIMOR 1991–9 Achieving referendum for independence from Indonesia
KOSOVO 1990–8 Ethnic Albanian movement for independence from Serbia
SERBIA 1996–2000 Movement to oust Milosevic
ZAMBIA 2001 Protests prevent Chiluba from exceeding constitutional term of office
MADAGASCAR 2001–2 Contesting a rigged election
GEORGIA Dec. 2003 'Rose Revolution' for regime change
UKRAINE Dec. 2004–Jan. 2005 'Orange Revolution' for new president
LEBANON 2005 'Cedar Revolution' against Syrian influence and occupation
NEPAL 2006 The monarchy overthrown
BURMA 2007 Monks lead protest against economic hardship and dictatorship
ZIMBABWE 2000–8 Contesting Mugabe's autocratic rule
MALDIVES 2004–8 Overthrowing an autocrat
TIBET 1959; 1987–8; 2008 Challenging Chinese policies and occupation
IRAN 2009–10 'Green Movement' against stolen election and for political reform
THE 'ARAB SPRING' 2011:
Tunisia and Egypt Jan.–Feb. 2011 Overthrowing autocrats and demanding constitutional change and continued protests for further radical reform;
Bahrain, Yemen and Syria: Prolonged resistance in early 2011 – protests in other Middle Eastern states

NB Some examples quite often cited are excluded from this list:

a) especially contentious examples of popular mobilization:

- Kyrgyzstan 2005 and 2010;
- Philippines 2001;
- Thailand 2006–10.

b) unsuccessful protests to overturn 'stolen elections' in Armenia, Azerbaijan, Belarus and Moldova.

c) popular movements in advance of 'critical elections', where incumbents did stand down after losing election: Romania, Bulgaria, Slovakia and Croatia.
d) widespread but unsuccessful protests in sub-Saharan Africa since 2000 against rigged elections, corruption or presidents exceeding their constitutional term of office.

Bibliography

Abrahamian, E. (2009) 'Mass Protests in the Iranian Revolution, 1977–79', in A. Roberts and T. Garton Ash (eds) *Civil Resistance and Power Politics* Oxford, Oxford University Press, 162–78

Abramsky, S. (2011) 'Gene Sharp: Nonviolent Warrior', *The Nation*, 16 March, http://www.thenation.comarticle/159265

Ackerman, P. and J. Duvall (2000) *A Force More Powerful* New York, Palgrave

Adams, J. (1856) *The Works of John Adams* 10 vols Boston MA, Little, Brown & Co. Online Library of Liberty http://oll.libertfund.org/index

Albert, D.H. (ed.) (1980) *Tell the American People: Perspectives on the Iranian Revolution* Philadelphia PA, Movement for a New Society

———(1985) *People Power: Applying Nonviolence Theory* Philadelphia PA, Movement for a New Society

Alternative Defence Commission (1983) *Britain Without the Bomb* London, Frances Pinter

Amnesty (2005) 'Georgia: Torture and Ill-treatment Still a Concern after the "Rose Revolution"', *Report* London, International Section, 62

Antal, D. (1994) *Out of Romania* London, Faber & Faber

Apawo Phiri, I. (2008) 'President Frederick Chiluba and Zambia: Evangelicals and Democracy in a "Christian Nation"', in T. Ranger (ed.) *Evangelical Christians and Democracy in Africa* Oxford, Oxford University Press, 93–130

Arato, A. (1993) 'Interpreting 1989', *Social Research* 60(3): 610–46

Arendt, H. (1958) *The Origins of Totalitarianism* 2nd rev. edn, London, George Allen & Unwin

———(1970) *On Violence* Harmondsworth, Allen Lane

———(1973) *On Revolution* Harmondsworth, Penguin

Aristotle (1948) *The Politics of Aristotle* trans. E. Barker, Oxford, Clarendon Press

Atack, I. (2006) 'Nonviolent Political Action and the Limits of Consent', *Theoria* 53(111): 87–197

Baker, C. (1997) *State of Emergency: Crisis in Central Africa, Nyasaland, 1959–60* London, Tauris Academic Studies

Balfour, S. (1989) *Dictatorship, Workers and the City: Labour in Greater Barcelona Since 1939* Oxford, Clarendon

Barghouti, M. (2005) 'Palestinian Defiance: Interview by Eric Hazan', *New Left Review* 32: 117–31

BBC (2007) 'Chiluba's Legacy to Zambia', by Isabel Matheson, BBC News, 4 May, www.bbc.co.uk/1/hi/world/africa

———(2009) 'The Reunion: Nelson Mandela Release', 13 September, BBC Radio Four

Becker, J. (1992) *The Lost Country: Mongolia Revealed* London, Hodder & Stoughton

Beer, M.A. (1999) 'Violent and Nonviolent Struggle in Burma: Is a Unified Strategy Workable?', in S. Zunes, L.R. Kurtz and S.B. Asher (eds) *Nonviolent Social Movements* Oxford, Blackwell, 174–84

Beissinger, M.R. (2009) 'The Intersection of Ethnic Nationalism and People Power Tactics in the Baltic States, 1987–91', in A. Roberts and T. Garton Ash (eds) *Civil Resistance and Power Politics* Oxford, Oxford University Press, 231–46

Belden, J. (1973) [1949] *China Shakes the World* Harmondsworth, Penguin

Bellow, W. (1986) 'Aquino's Elite Populism: Initial Reflections', *Third World Quarterly* 8(3): 1020–30

Benson, M. (1994) *Now is the Time: A Personal Account of South Africa's Historic Transition from Apartheid to Democracy* Sydney, Australian Broadcasting Corporation, ABC Books

Berger, M.T. (1997) 'Old State and New Empire in Indonesia: Debating the Rise and Decline of Suharto's New Order', *Third World Quarterly* 18(2): 321–61

Berlin, I. (1969) 'Two Concepts of Liberty', in *Four Essays on Liberty* Oxford, Oxford University Press

Best, G. (1982) *War and Society in Revolutionary Europe, 1770–1870* London, Fontana

Beyerie, S. (2010) 'Resisting Corruption: Recent Progress in Indonesia and Kenya', 19 November, http://opendemocracy.org

Bhatia, B. (2002) 'The Naxalite Movement in Central Bihar', in M. Randle (ed.) *Challenge to Nonviolence* Bradford, University of Bradford, 255–63

Binnendijk, A.L. and I. Marovic (2006) 'Power and Persuasion: Nonviolent Strategies to Influence State Security Forces in Serbia (2000) and Ukraine (2004)', *Communist and Post-Communist Studies* 39: 411–29

Bleiker, Roland (2000) *Popular Dissent, Human Agency and Global Politics* Cambridge: Cambridge University Press

Blickle, P. (1981) *The Revolution of 1525: The German Peasants' War from a New Perspective* trans. T.A. Brady and H.C.E. Midelfort, Baltimore, Johns Hopkins University Press

Boetie, de la, E. (1997) [1550s] *The Politics of Obedience: The Discourse of Voluntary Servitude* Montreal, Black Rose Books

Boga, D. (2010) 'Curfew in the Vale', *New Internationalist* October: 46–7

Bondurant, J. (1958) *The Conquest of Violence: The Gandhian Philosophy of Conflict* London, Oxford University Press

Boorstin, D.J. (1969) *The Americans, Vol. 2: The National Experience* Harmondsworth, Penguin

Boots, W.T. (1991) 'Miracle in Bolivia: Four Women Confront a Nation', in P. McManus and G. Schlabach (eds) *Relentless Persistence: Nonviolent Action in Latin America* Philadelphia PA, New Society Publishers

Boserup, A. and A. Mack (1974) *War Without Weapons* London, Frances Pinter.

Boudreau, V. (2004) *Resisting Dictatorship: Repression and Protest in Southeast Asia* Cambridge, Cambridge University Press

Boulding, K.E. (1999) 'Nonviolence and Power in the Twentieth Century', in S. Zunes, L.R. Kurtz and S.B. Asher (eds) *Nonviolent Social Movements: A Geographical Perspective* Oxford, Blackwell, 9–17

Bratton, M. and N. van de Walle (1997) *Democratic Experiments in Africa* Cambridge, Cambridge University Press

Bromke, A. (1981) *Poland: The Last Decade* Ontario, Mosaic Press

Brookings Institution (2005) 'The 2005 Egyptian Elections: How Free? How Important?', Middle East memo No. 8, 24 September, www.brookings.edu/papers/2005

Brown, A. (1997) 'Locating Working Class Power', in K. Hewison (ed) *Political Change in Thailand: Democracy and Participation* London, Routledge, 163–78
Brown, J.M. (1989) *Gandhi: Prisoner of Hope* New Haven, Yale University Press
——(2009) 'Gandhi and Civil Resistance in India, 1917–47: Key Issues', in A. Roberts and T. Garton Ash (eds) *Civil Resistance and Power Politics* Oxford, Oxford University Press, 43–57
Buchan, J. (2009) 'A Bazaari Bonaparte?', *New Left Review* 59: 73–88
Bunce, V. and S. Wolchik (2006a) 'Favourable Conditions and Electoral Revolutions', *Journal of Democracy* 17(4): 5–18
——(2006b) 'International Diffusion and Postcommunist Electoral Revolutions', *Communist and Post-Communist Studies* 39(3): 283–304
——(2009) 'Postcommunist Ambiguities', *Journal of Democracy* 20(3): 93–107
——(2010) 'A Regional Tradition: The Diffusion of Democratic Change under Communism and Postcommunism', in V. Bunce, M. McFaul and K. Stoner-Weiss (eds) *Democracy and Authoritarianism in the Postcommunist World* Cambridge, Cambridge University Press, 30–56
——(2011) *Defeating Authoritarian Leaders in Postcommunist Countries* Cambridge, Cambridge University Press
Burke, E. (1973) [1790] *Reflections on the Revolution in France* Conor Cruise O'Brien (ed.) Harmondsworth, Penguin
Burke, J. (2011) 'It's Time for a New Generation, Says Dalai Lama as He Drops Political Role', *Guardian*, 11 March
Burrowes, R. (1996) *The Strategy of Nonviolent Defense: A Gandhian Approach* Albany NY, State University of New York Press
Butcher, T. (2001) "Opposition Cheered by Chiluba's Climbdown', *Telegraph*, 7 May, www.telegraph.co.uk/news/worldnews/africaandindian ocean/zambia/1329461/
Calderon, R.A. (1987) 'Panama: Disaster or Democracy', *Foreign Affairs* 66: 328–47
Callahan, M. (2009) 'Riddle of the Tatmadaw', *New Left Review* 60: 27–63
Camus, A. (1962) [1951] *The Rebel* Harmondsworth, Penguin
Canovan, M. (2005) *The People* Cambridge, Polity
Carbajosa, A. (2011) 'Mother Tells of Fresh Tragedy in Family's Battle with Occupation', *Observer*, 9 January
Carter, A. (2009) 'People Power and Protest: The Literature on Civil Resistance in Historical Context', in A. Roberts and T. Garton Ash (eds) *Civil Resistance and Power Politics* Oxford, Oxford University Press, 25–42
——and J. Cherry (2009) 'Worker Solidarity and Civil Society Cooperation: Blocking the Chinese Arms Shipment to Zimbabwe, April 2008', in H. Clark (ed.) *People Power* London, Pluto Press, 191–2
——, H. Clark and M. Randle (2006) *People Power and Protest Since 1945: A Bibliography of Nonviolent Action* London, Housmans Bookshop. Revised and updated version available at www.civilresistance.info
Casey, M. (2009) 'Protests Wreck Asian Summit in Thailand', *Independent on Sunday*, 12 April
Chamberlain, G. (2010) 'Booker Novelist Faces Arrest for "Seditious" Kashmir Comments', *Guardian*, 27 October
Chandra, B. (1989) *India's Struggle for Independence* New Delhi, Penguin Books
Chassay, C. (2006) 'Huge Protest Brings Beirut to a Standstill', *Guardian*, 2 December
Cheng Tun-jen (1989) 'Democratizing the Quasi-Leninist Regime in Taiwan', *World Politics* 41(4): 471–99

Cherry, J. (2009) 'Zimbabwe: Unarmed Resistance, Civil Society and Limits of Solidarity', in H. Clark (ed.) *People Power: Unarmed Resistance and Global Solidarity* London, Pluto Press, 50–63

Chou Yangsun and A.J. Nathan (1987) 'Democratizing Transition in Taiwan', *Asian Survey* 27(3): 277–99

Clark, D.N. (ed.) (1987) *The Kwangju Uprising: Shadows Over the Regime in South Korea* Boulder CO, Westview Press.

Clark, H. (2000) *Civil Resistance in Kosovo* London, Pluto Press

——(ed.) (2009a) *People Power: Unarmed Resistance and Global Solidarity* London, Pluto Press, 1–20

——(2009b) 'The Limits of Prudence: Civil Resistance in Kosovo', in A. Roberts and T. Garton Ash (eds) *Civil Resistance and Power Politics* Oxford, Oxford University Press, 277–94

——(2010) 'Conscription, Movements Opposed to', in N.J. Young (ed.) *The Oxford International Encyclopedia of Peace* New York, Oxford University Press, Vol. 1, 468–73

Clark, J.J. and D.E. Gardinier (eds) (1997) *Political Reform in Francophone Africa* Boulder CO, Westview Press

Clausewitz, C. von (1968) [1832] *Clausewitz on War* A. Rapoport (ed.) Harmondsworth, Penguin

Cobban, A (1961) *A History of Modern France* 2nd edn, Vol. 1, Harmondsworth, Penguin

Cock, J. (1992) *Women and War in South Africa* London, Open Letters

Cockburn, P. (2010) 'Analysis', *Independent*, 10 April

Cohn, S.K. (2004) *Popular Protest in Late Medieval Europe* Manchester, Manchester University Press

Cole, G.D.H. and R. Postgate (1949), *The Common People (1746–1946)* London, Methuen

Conser, W.H., R.M. McCarthy, D.J. Toscano and G. Sharp (eds) (1986) *Resistance, Politics and the American Struggle for Independence* Boulder CO, Lynne Rienner

Cooper, J. (1999) 'The Ogoni Struggle for Human Rights and Civil Society in Nigeria', in S. Zunes, L.R. Kurtz and S.B. Asher (eds) *Nonviolent Social Movements* Oxford, Blackwell, 189–202

Coyle, V. (2010) 'Breaking the Silence', *Amnesty Magazine*, November/December

Crabtree, J. (2005) *Patterns of Protest: Politics and Social Movements in Bolivia* London, Latin American Bureau

Crawshaw, S. and J. Jackson (2010) *Small Acts of Resistance: How Courage, Tenacity and Ingenuity Can Change the World* New York, Sterling Publishing Company

Cressy, D. (2006) *England on the Edge: Crisis and Revolution, 1640–1642* Oxford, Oxford University Press

Dahl, R.A. (1982) *Dilemmas of Pluralist Democracy* New Haven CT, Yale University Press

——(1992) 'The Civic Problem of Competence', *Journal of Democracy* 3(4): 45–59

Dajani S. (1994) 'Between National and Social Liberation: The Palestinian Women's Movement in Israeli Occupied West Bank and Gaza', in T. Mayer (ed.) *Women and the Israeli Occupation* London, Routledge, 33–61

——(1999) 'Nonviolent Resistance in the Occupied Territories: A Critical Re-evaluation', in S. Zunes, L.R. Kurtz and S.B. Asher (eds) *Nonviolent Social Movements* Oxford, Blackwell, 52–74

Dale, G. (2006) *The East German Revolution of 1989* Manchester, Manchester University Press

Dalton, D. (1993) *Mahatma Gandhi: Nonviolent Power in Action* New York, Columbia University Press

Daly, M.W. (1998) 'The British Occupation 1882–1922', in M.W. Daly (ed.) *The Cambridge History of Egypt* Cambridge, Cambridge University Press, Vol. 2, 239–51

Debray, Regis (1967) 'Revolution in the Revolution? Armed Struggle and Political Struggle in Latin America', *Monthly Review Press* 19(3) Special issue
Decalo, S. (1997) 'Benin: First of the New Democracies', in J.F. Clark and D.E. Gardinier (eds) *Political Reform in Francophone Africa* Boulder CO, Westview Press, 43–61
Dejevsky, M. (2005) 'Kyrgyzstan Questions', www.openDemocracy.net, 30 March
——(2010a) 'Ukraine is At Last Throwing Off the Shackles of the Cold War', *Independent*, 9 February
——(2010b) 'Ukrainian Leader Tacks Back towards EU from Russia', *Independent*, 2 October
Deming, B. (1971) *Revolution and Equilibrium* New York, Grossman
Desai, A. (2002) *We Are the Poors: Community Struggles in Post-Apartheid South Africa* New York, Monthly Review Press
Diplomat's Handbook (2009) 'Diplomat's Handbook for Democracy Development Support', 2nd edn, http://www.diplomatshandbook.org/
Dobson, R.B. (ed.) (1970) *The Peasants' Revolt of 1381* London, Macmillan
Donald, M. (2001) 'Russia 1905: The Forgotten Revolution', in M. Donald and T. Rees (eds) *Reinterpreting Revolution in Twentieth Century Europe* Basingstoke, Macmillan, 41–54
Dudouet, V. (2009) 'Cross-Border Nonviolent Advocacy during the Second Intifada: The International Solidarity Movement', in H. Clark (ed) *People Power* London, Pluto, 125–34
——and H. Clark (2009) 'Nonviolent Civic Action in Support of Human Rights and Democracy', Brussels Directorate-General for External Policies of the Union, EXPO/B/DROI/2008/69 PE407.008, http://www.europarl.europa.eu
Dunn, J. (1989) *Modern Revolutions* 2nd edn, Cambridge, Cambridge University Press
Ebert, T. (1969) 'Nonviolent Resistance against Communist Regimes', in A. Roberts (ed.) *Civilian Resistance as a National Defence* Harmondsworth, Penguin, 204–27
Economist, The (2010) 'Briefing Myanamar's Election: Slowly the Army Eases Its Grip', 6 November, 29–32
Eguren, L.E. (2009) 'Developing Strategy for Accompaniment', in H. Clark (ed.) *People Power* London, Pluto Press, 98–107
El-Mahdi, R. (2009) 'The Democracy Movement: Cycles of Protest', in R. El-Mahdi and P. Marfleet (eds) *Egypt: The Moment of Change* London, Zed Press, 87–102
Eltahawy, M. (2011) 'The First Arab Revolution', *Guardian*, 17 January
Estrada, L. and A. Poire (2007) 'Taught to Protest, Learning to Lose', *Journal of Democracy* 18(1): 73–87
Fanon, F. (1965) *The Wretched of the Earth* London, MacGibbon & Kee
——(1970) *A Dying Colonialism* Harmondsworth, Penguin
Feher, F. (1995) 'The Evergreen de Tocqueville (on the occasion of the Hungarian publication of *Democracy in America*)', *Thesis Eleven* 42: 69–86
Finch, H. (1985) 'Democratization in Uruguay', *Third World Quarterly* 7(3): 594–609
Fink, C. (2001) *Living Silence: Burma Under Military Rule* London, Zed Books
——(2009) 'The Moment of the Monks: Burma, 2007', in A. Roberts and T. Garton Ash (eds) *Civil Resistance and Power Politics* Oxford, Oxford University Press, 354–70
Fischer, L. (1954) *Gandhi: His Life and Message for the World* New York, New American Library (Signet Key Book)
Fisher, J. (1989) *Mothers of the Disappeared* London, Zed Books
Fisk, R. (2005) 'Protesters Beaten as Egypt Votes on Electoral Reform', *Independent*, 26 May
——(2007) 'Hizbollah Warns PM there is Worse to Come', *Independent*, 25 January
Foucault, M. (1990) *Politics, Philosophy, Culture: Interviews and Other Writings* L.D. Kritzman (ed.) London, Routledge
——(1991a) [1975] *Discipline and Punish: The Birth of the Prison* Harmondsworth, Penguin

——(1991b) 'Truth and Power', in P. Rabinow (ed.) *The Foucault Reader: An Introduction to Foucault's Thought* Harmondsworth, Penguin
Furman, D. (2008) 'Imitation Democracies', *New Left Review* 54: 29–48
Galtung, J. (1989) *Nonviolence and Israel/Palestine* Honolulu HI, University of Hawaii Institute for Peace
——(1996) *Peace by Peaceful Means: Peace and Conflict, Development and Civilization* London, Sage
Garton Ash, T. (1983) *The Polish Revolution: Solidarity 1980–82* London, Jonathan Cape
——(1989) 'Revolution: The Springtime of Two Nations', *New York Review of Books* 36(10): 3–10
——(2009a) '1989!', *New York Review of Books* 56(17): 1–7
——(2009b) 'Velvet Revolution: The Prospects', *New York Review of Books* 56(21): 20–4
——(2009c) 'The Strange Toppling of Slobodan Milosevic', in T. Garton Ash, *Facts Are Subversive: Political Writing from a Decade Without a Name* London, Atlantic Books, 3–24
——(2009d) 'A Century of Civil Resistance: Some Lessons and Questions', in A. Roberts and T. Garton Ash (eds) *Civil Resistance and Power Politics* Oxford, Oxford University Press, 371–90
Gellner, E. (1995) 'The Price of Velvet: Thomas Masaryk and Vaclav Havel', *Czech Sociological Review* 3(1): 45–57
George-Williams, D. (ed.) (2006) *Bite Not One Another: Selected Accounts of Nonviolent Struggle in Africa* Addis Ababa, University of Peace, Africa Programme
Gervais, M. (1997) 'Niger: Regime Change, Economic Crisis and Perpetuation of Privilege', in J.F. Clark and D.E. Gardinier (eds) *Political Reform in Francophone Africa* Boulder CO and Oxford, Westview Press, 86–108
Giordano, A. (2006) 'Mexico's Presidential Swindle', *New Left Review* 41: 5–27
Gittings, J. (2010) 'Tibet, Resistance to China in', *The Oxford International Encyclopedia of Peace* Vol. 4, New York, Oxford University Press, Vol. 4, 163–6
Golan, G. (1971) *The Czechoslovak Reform Movement* Cambridge, Cambridge University Press
Goldman, M. (2009) 'The 1989 Demonstrations in Tiananmen Square and Beyond', in A. Roberts and T. Garton Ash (eds) *Civil Resistance and Power Politics* Oxford, Oxford University Press, 247–59
Goldstone, J.A. (1991) *Revolution and Rebellion in the Early Modern World* Berkeley, University of California Press
Gorbachev, M. (1991) *The August Coup: The Truth and the Lessons* London and New York, Harper Collins
Gray, J. (1990) *Rebellions and Revolutions: China from the 1800s to the 1980s* Oxford, Oxford University Press
Gregg, R.B. (1960) [1935] *The Power of Nonviolence* London, James Clarke
Griffin-Nolan, E. (1991) *Witness for Peace: A Story of Resistance* Westminster, John Knox Press
Groom, A. (2009) 'Bows, Arrows and a Dream of Liberation', *Independent*, 14 August
Gros, J.-G. (1995) 'The Hard Lessons of Cameroon', *Journal of Democracy* 6(3): 112–27
Grynspan, D. (1991) 'Nicaragua: A New Model for Popular Revolution in America', in J.A. Goldstone, T.R. Gurr and F. Moshiri (eds) *Revoutions of the Late Twentieth Century* Boulder CO, Westview Press
Guevara, Ernesto 'Che', (2009) [1961] *Guerrilla Warfare: The Authorised Edition* London, Harper Perennial
Gurr, T.R. and J.A. Goldstone (1991) 'Comparisons and Policy Implications', in J.A. Goldstone, T.R. Gurr and F. Moshiri (eds) *Revolutions of the Late Twentieth Century* Boulder CO, Westview Press, 324–52

Guttridge, L.F. (1992) *Mutiny: A History of Naval Insurrection* Annapolis MD, US Naval Institute Press
Habermas, J. (1986) 'Hannah Arendt's Communicative Concept of Power', in S. Lukes (ed.) *Power* Oxford, Blackwell, 75–93
——(1990) 'What does Socialism Mean Today? The Rectifying Revolution and the Need for New Thinking on the Left', *New Left Review* 1(183): 7–18
Hale, H.E. (2005) 'Democracy, Autocracy and Revolution in Post-Soviet Eurasia', *World Politics* 58(1): 133–65
——(2006) 'Democracy or Autocracy on the March? The Colored Revolutions as Normal Dynamics of Patronal Presidentialism', *Communist and Post-Communist Studies* 39(3): 305–29
Harb, Z. (2011) 'Ammar 404', *Red Pepper* 12
Harding, L. (2010a) 'Blood, Chaos and Looting as Kyrgyzstan Overthrows "Tyrannical" Government', *Guardian*, 9 April
——(2010b) 'UN Official Accuses Outside Groups of Planning Kyrgyzstan Violence', *Guardian*, 16 June
——(2010c) 'Survivors Tell of "Attempted Genocide" as Lenin's Ethnic Timebomb Explodes', *Guardian*, 17 June
Harris, H. (1988) 'Women and War: The Case of Nicaragua', in E. Isakson (ed.) *Women and the Military System* Hemel Hempstead, Harvester/Wheatsheaf, 190–209
Harvey, N. (2009) '50 years from Home', *New Internationalist* 17–24
Havel, V. (1987) 'The Power of the Powerless', in J. Vladislav (ed.) *Living in Truth* London, Faber & Faber, 36–122
Haynes, V. and T. Semyonova (1979) *Workers Against the Gulag: The New Opposition in the Soviet Union* London, Pluto Press
Hedman, E.-L. E. (2006) *In the Name of Civil Society: From Free Election Movements to People Power in the Philippines* Honolulu HI, University of Hawaii Press
Helie-Lucas, M.-A. (1988) 'The Role of Women during the Algerian Liberation Struggle and After', in E. Isaksson (ed.) *Women and the Military System* Hemel Hempstead, Harvester/Wheatsheaf, 171–89
Hirschmann, A.O. (1993) 'Exit, Voice and the Fate of the German Democratic Republic: An Essay in Conceptual History', *World Politics* 45(2): 173–202
Hobbes, T. (1985) [1651] *Leviathan* C.B. Macpherson (ed.) Harmondsworth, Penguin
Holloway, J. (2005) *Change the World without Taking Power: The Meaning of Revolution Today* 2nd edn, London, Pluto Press
Holmes, L. (1997) *Postcommunism: An Introduction* Cambridge, Polity
Howden, D. (2005) 'Egyptian Police Fire on Opposition Voters', *Independent*, 2 December
Huneeus, C. (2009) 'Political Mobilization against Authoritarian Rule: Pinochet's Chile, 1983–88', in A. Roberts and T. Garton Ash (eds) *Civil Resistance and Power Politics* Oxford, Oxford University Press, 197–212
Huntington, S.P. (1991) *The Third Wave: Democratization in the Late Twentieth Century* Norman OK, University of Oklahoma Press
——(1993a) 'The Clash of Civilizations', *Foreign Affairs* 72: 22–49
——(1993b) 'Democracy's Third Wave', in L. Diamond and M.F. Plattner (eds) *The Global Resurgence of Democracy* Baltimore, Johns Hopkins University Press, 3–25
Hylton, F. (2006) 'The Landslide in Bolivia', *New Left Review* 37: 69–72
Ibrahim, G. (2011) 'Revolt Like an Egyptian', *Red Pepper* 18–20
Ignatieff, M. (1993) *Blood and Belonging: Journeys into the New Nationalism* London, BBC Books and Chatto & Windus
——(1999) *The Warrior's Honor: Ethnic War and the Modern Conscience* London, Vintage

International Crisis Group (2008) 'Nepal's Election: A Peaceful Revolution?', Asia Report No. 155, www.crisisgroup.org
Jaffe, P. (ed.) (1947) *Chiang Kai-shek: China's Destiny* London, Dennis Dobson
Jaleel, M. (2008) 'Kashmir's New Generation', openDemocracy.net, 13 October
Jancar, B.W. (1975) 'Religious Dissent in the Soviet Union', in R.L. Tokes (ed.) *Dissent in the USSR: Politics, Ideology and People* Baltimore MD, Johns Hopkins University Press, 191–230
——(1988) 'Women Soldiers in Yugoslavia's National Liberation Struggle, 1941–45', in E. Isakson (ed.) *Women and the Military System* Hemel Hempstead, Harvester/Wheatsheaf, 47–67
Jauvert, V. (2011) 'Egypte: les faiseurs de révolution', *Le Nouvel Observateur*, 24–30 March
Johnson, B. (1987) *The Four Days of Courage: The Untold Story of the People who Brought Marcos Down* New York, Free Press
Johnston, H. (2005) 'Taking the Walk: Speech Acts and Resistance in Authoritarian Regimes', in C. Davenport, H. Johnston and C. Mueller (eds) *Repression and Mobilization* Minneapolis MN, University of Minnesota Press, 108–37
Jones, S. (2009) 'Georgia's "Rose Revolution" of 2003: Enforcing Peaceful Change', in A. Roberts and T. Garton Ash (eds) *Civil Resistance and Power Politics* Oxford, Oxford University Press, 317–34
Joseph, R. (1993) 'Africa: The Rebirth of Political Freedom', in L. Diamond and M.E. Plattner (eds) *The Global Resurgence of Democracy* Baltimore MD, Johns Hopkins University Press, 307–20
Kalandadze, K. and M.A. Orenstein (2009) 'Electoral Protests and Democratization: Beyond the Color Revolutions', *Comparative Politics* 42(11): 1403–25
Kaldor, M. and Z. Kavan (2001) 'Democracy and Civil Society in Central and Eastern Europe', in R. Axtmann (ed.) *Balancing Democracy* London, Continuum, 239–54
Kaminski, B. (1991) *The Collapse of State Socialism* Princeton NJ, Princeton University Press
Kantorowicz, E. (1957) *The King's Two Bodies: A Study in Medieval Political Theology* Princeton NJ, Princeton University Press
Kapcia, A. (2008) *Cuba in Revolution: A History Since the Fifties* London, Reaktion Books
Kapuscinski, R. (2006) *Shah of Shahs* trans. W.R. Brand and K. Moroczkowska Brand, 'Introduction' by C. de Bellaigue, London, Penguin Books
Karatnycky A. and P. Ackerman (2005) *How Freedom is Won: From Civic Resistance to Durable Democracy* Washington DC, Freedom House Research Study
Kasian, Tejapira (2006) 'Toppling Thaksin', *New Left Review* 39: 5–70
Keane, J. (ed.) (1988) *Civil Society and the State: New European Perspectives* London, Verso
——(2009) *The Life and Death of Democracy* London, Simon & Schuster
Keck, M. and K. Sikkink (1998) *Activists Beyond Borders* Ithaca NY, Cornell University Press
Kessler, R.J. (1991) 'The Philippines: The Making of a People Power Revolution', in J.A. Goldstone, T.R. Gurr and F. Moshiri (eds) *Revolutions of the Late Twentieth Century* Boulder CO, Westview Press, 194–217
Khamidov, A. (2002) 'Clan Politics at the Base of Kyrgyzstan's Political Crisis', *CACI Analyst*, 9 November, Central Asia Caucasus Institute, Johns Hopkins University
Kidron, P. (ed.) (2004) *Refusenik: Israel's Soldiers of Conscience* London, Zed Books
King, M.E. (2007) *A Quiet Revolution: The First Palestinian Intifada and Nonviolent Resistance* New York: Nation Books
Kingsnorth, P. (2003) *One No, Many Yeses: A Journey to the Heart of the Global Resistance Movement* London, Free Press (Simon & Schuster)

Kinzer, S. (2003) *All the Shah's Men: An American Coup and the Roots of Middle East Terror* Hoboken NJ, John Wiley & Sons

Klein, N. (2000) *No Logo* London, Flamingo

Kluver, A.R. (1998) 'Student Movements in Confucian Societies', in G.J. De Groot (ed.) *Student Protest: The Sixties and After* London, Addison Wesley, 219–31

Kohn, H. (1945) *The Idea of a Nation* New York, Macmillan

Konrad, G. (1984) *Anti-Politics: An Essay*. London, Quartet

Krieger, M. (2008) *Cameroon's Social Democratic Front: Its History and Prospects as an Opposition Political Party, 1990–2001* Langaa Cameroon, Research and Publishing Common Initiative Group

Krushelnycky, A. (2006) *An Orange Revolution* London, Harvill Secker

Kujur, R. (2008) 'Naxal Movement in India: A Profile', New Delhi, Institute of Peace and Conflict Studies, Research Paper No. 15

Kumar, K. (2001) 'The Revolutionary Idea in the Twentieth Century World', in M. Donald and T. Rees (eds) *Reinterpreting Revolution in Twentieth Century Europe* Basingstoke, Macmillan, 177–97

Kunzru, Hari (2006) 'Welcome to Paradise', *Guardian Weekend*, 16 December

Kuper, L. (1956) *Passive Resistance in South Africa* London, Jonathan Cape

Kuzio, T. (2006) 'Civil Society, Youth and Societal Mobilization', *Communist and Post-Communist Studies* September: 365–86

Laba, R. (1991) *The Roots of Solidarity: A Political Sociology of Poland's Working Class Democratization* Princeton NJ, Princeton University Press

Lakey, G. (2009) 'Nonviolence Training and Charges of Western Imperialism: A Guide for Worried Activists', in H. Clark (ed) *People Power* London, Pluto Press, 206–13

Lande, C.H. (2001) 'The Return of "People Power" to the Philippines', *Journal of Democracy* 12(2): 88–102

Lanskay, M. and G. Areshidze (2008) 'Georgia's Year of Turmoil', *Journal of Democracy* 19(4): 154–68

Laqueur, W. (1978) *Terrorism* London, Sphere Books

Lateu, J. (2010) 'Leaked Video of "Indonesia's Abu Ghraib " Raises International Awareness', *New Internationalist* December

Lawrance, A. (ed.) (2004) *China Since 1919 – Revolution and Reform: A Sourcebook* London, Routledge

Lefort, C. (1986) *The Political Forms of Modern Society: Bureaucracy, Democracy, Totalitarianism* Cambridge, Polity

Leiden, C. and K.M. Schmitt (1973) *The Politics of Violence: Revolution in the Modern World* London, Prentice Hall

Leigh, D. (2010) 'The US Embassy Cables: Central Asia – A President, His Hated Daughter, and Why the US Keeps Them Sweet', *Guardian*, 13 December

Levitsky, S. and L.A. Way (2002) 'The Rise of Competitive Authoritarianism', *Journal of Democracy* 13(2): 51–65

Lewis, P., B. Lomax and G. Wightman (1994) 'The Emergence of Multi-Party Systems in East-Central Europe: A Comparative Analysis', in G. Pridham and T. Vanhanen (eds) *Democratization in Eastern Europe: Domestic and International Perspectives* London, Routledge, 151–88

Liddell Hart, B.H. (1969) 'Lessons from Resistance Movements: Guerrilla and Non-violent', in A. Roberts (ed.) *Civilian Resistance as a National Defence* Harmondsworth, Penguin, 228–46

Lieven, A. (1993) *The Baltic Revolution: Estonia, Latvia and Lithuania and the Path to Independence* New Haven, Yale University Press

Ligt, de B. (1989) [1937] *The Conquest of Violence: An Essay on War and Revolution* London, Pluto

Lindberg S. (2006) 'The Surprising Significance of African Elections', *Journal of Democracy* 17(1): 139–51

Lipset, S.M. (1993) 'The Centrality of Political Culture', in L. Diamond and M.E. Plattner (eds) *The Global Resurgence of Democracy* Baltimore MD, Johns Hopkins University Press, 134–37

Lipsitz, L. and H. Kritzer (1975) 'Unconventional Approaches to Conflict Resolution', *Journal of Conflict Resolution* 19(4): 713–33

Liwag Kotte, E. (2001) 'People Power in the Philippines: Civil Society Between Protest and Participation', *D+C Development and Cooperation* 6: 21–2

Lodge, T. (2009) 'The Interplay of Non-violent and Violent Action in the Movement Against Apartheid in South Africa, 1983–94', in A. Roberts and T. Garton Ash (eds) *Civil Resistance and Power Politics* Oxford, Oxford University Press, 213–30

Long, S. (1991) *Taiwan: China's Last Frontier* Basingstoke, Macmillan

Lopez-Levy, M. (2004) *We Are Millions: Neo-liberalism and New Forms of Political Action in Argentina* London, Latin American Bureau.

Lukes, S. (2005) *Power: A Radical View* 2nd edn, Basingstoke, Palgrave Macmillan

Lukowski, J. and H. Zawadzki (2006) *A Concise History of Poland* 2nd edn, Cambridge, Cambridge University Press

MacAskill, E. (2005) 'Grieving Lebanese Round on Syria', *Guardian*, 17 February

McFaul, M. (2002) 'The Fourth Wave of Democracy and Dictatorship: Noncooperative Transitions in the Postcommunist World', *World Politics* 54(2): 212–44

——(2010) 'Importing Revolution: Internal and External Factors in Ukraine 2004', in V. Bunce, M. McFaul and K. Stoner-Weiss (eds) *Democracy and Authoritarianism in the Postcommunist World* Cambridge, Cambridge University Press

McGirk, J. (2006) 'Advance of the Dharma Army', *Independent*, 15 March

McGuinness, K. (1993) 'Gene Sharp's Theory of Power: A Feminist Critique of Consent', *Journal of Peace Research* 30: 101–15

Machiavelli, N. (1988) [1532] *The Prince* Q. Skinner and R. Price (eds) Cambridge, Cambridge University Press

MacIntyre, D. (2011a) 'Unarmed Demonstrators Fight against the Odds: Analysis', *Independent*, 9 January

——(2011b) 'Quiet Heroines Whose Courage Has Helped Keep Uprising Going', *Independent*, 5 February

MacLeod, J. (2009) 'The Role of Strategy in Advancing Nonviolent Resistance in West Papua', in L. Rechler, J.F. Deckard and K.H.R. Villanueva (eds) *Building Sustainable Futures: Enacting Peace and Development* Bilbao, University of Deusto

——(2010) 'West Papua: From Morning Star to Mourning', openDemocracynet, 16 December

Mahony, L. and E. Eguren (1997) *Unarmed Bodyguards: International Accompaniment for the Protection of Human Rights* West Hartford CT, Kumarian

Maier, C.S. (2009) 'Civil Resistance and Civil Society: Lessons from the Collapse of the German Democratic Republic in 1989', in A. Roberts and T. Garton Ash (eds) *Civil Resistance and Power Politics* Oxford, Oxford University Press, 260–76

Majd, H. (2010) *The Ayatollah's Democracy: An Iranian Challenge* London, Allen Lane

Mandela, N. (1995) *Long Walk to Freedom: The Autobiography of Nelson Mandela* London, Abacus

Martin, B. (1989) 'Gene Sharp's Theory of Power', *Journal of Peace Research* 26(1): 213–22

———(2007) *Justice Ignited: The Dynamics of Backfire* Lanham MD, Rowman & Littlefield
———(2009) 'Making Accompaniment Effective', in H. Clark (ed.) *People Power* London, Pluto
———, W. Varney and A. Vickers (2001) 'Political Jiu-Jitsu Against Indonesian Repression: Studying Lower Profile Nonviolent Resistance', *Pacifica Review* 13(2): 143–56
Maxwell, K. (2009) 'Portugal: "The Revolution of the Carnations", 1974–75', in A. Roberts and T. Garton Ash (eds) *Civil Resistance and Power Politics* Oxford, Oxford University Press, 144–61
Mazgaonkar, M. (2009) 'India – Macro Violence and Micro Resistance: Development Violence and Unarmed Grassroots Resistance', in H. Clark (ed.) *People Power* London, Pluto, 76–85
Meier, P.P. (2008) 'Communication Technology, Repressive Hierarchy and Defiant Networks: Is the State or Civil Society Winning the Information Race?' Paper presented to American Political Science Association annual conference
Mendoza, A., Jr (2009) '"People Power" in the Philippines, 1983–86', in A. Roberts and T. Garton Ash (eds) *Civil Resistance and Power Politics* Oxford, Oxford University Press, 179–96
Merrington, J. (1977) 'Theory and Practice in Gramsci's Marxism', in New Left Review (ed.) *Western Marxism: A Critical Reader* London, New Left Review, 140–75
Meyer, M. (2012) 'Civil Resistance in Liberation Myths: Resistance Strategies in Mozambique's Independence Struggle', in M. Barkowski (ed.) *Rediscovering Nonviolent History and Nation-Making Liberation Struggles* Boulder, co, Lynne Reinner
Michelet, J. (1847) *History of the French Revolution* trans. C. Cocks, London, H.G. Bohn (reproduced by Bibliobazaar)
Milani, A. (2009) 'Cracks in the Regime', *Journal of Democracy* 20(4): 11–15
Miniotaite, G. (2002) *Nonviolent Resistance in Lithuania: A Story of Peaceful Liberation* Boston, Albert Einstein Institution
Mok Chiu Yu and J. Harrison (eds) (1990) *Voices from Tiananmen Square: Beijing Spring and the Democracy Movement* Montreal, Black Rose Books
Monde Diplomatique (2008) 'Triste bilan au Cameroun', www.monde-diplomatique.fr/carnet/2008-03-04-Cameroun, 4 March
Mondlane, E. (1969) *The Struggle for Mozambique* Harmondsworth, Penguin
Moore, B., Jr (1978) *Injustice: The Social Bases of Obedience and Revolt* White Plains NY, M.E. Sharpe
Moore, R.J. (1983) *Escape from Empire* Oxford, Clarendon Press
Morozov, E. (2011) *The Net Delusion: How Not to Liberate the World* London, Allen Lane
Morriss, P. (1980) 'The Essentially Uncontestable Concept of Power', in M. Freeman and D. Robertson (eds) *The Frontiers of Political Theory* Brighton, Harvester, 198–232
Moser-Puangsuwan, Y. (2009) 'Burma – Dialogue with the Generals: The Sound of One Hand Clapping', in H. Clark (ed.) *People Power* London, Pluto, 39–49
Moshiri, F. (1991) 'Iran, Islamic Revolution against Westernization', in J.A. Goldstone, T.R. Gurr and F. Moshiri (eds) *Revolutions of the Late Twentieth Century* Boulder CO, Westview Press
Murray, C. (2006) *Murder in Samarkand* London, Mainstream Publishing
Nagle, J.D. and A. Mahr (1999) *Democracy and Democratization* London, Sage
Nenadic, D. and N. Belcevic (2009) 'Nonviolent Struggle for Democracy: The Role of OTPOR', in H. Clark (ed.) *People Power* London, Pluto Press, 26–35
Ngwane, T. (2004) 'Sparks in the Township', in T. Mertes (ed.) *A Movement of Movements* London, Verso, 111–34

Nordern, D.L. (1996) *Military Rebellion in Argentina: Between Coups and Consolidation*, Lincoln NE, University of Nebraska Press

Nugent, P. (2004) *Africa Since Independence* Basingstoke, Palgrave Macmillan

Nye, J.S. (2004) *Soft Power: The Means to Success in World Politics* New York, Public Affairs (Perseus Books)

——(2008) 'Soft Power and Public Diplomacy', British Council, www.britishcouncil.org

Obi, C.J. (2000) 'Globalization and Local Resistance: The Case of Shell versus the Ogoni', in B.K. Gills (ed.) *Globalization and the Politics of Resistance* Basingstoke, Macmillan, 280–94

O'Connor, W. (1978) 'A Nation is a Nation, is a State, is an Ethnic Group, is a … ', *Ethnic and Racial Studies* 1(4): 379–88

O'Donnell, G. and P.C. Schmitter (1986) *Transitions from Authoritarian Rule: Tentative Conclusions about Uncertain Democracies* Baltimore MD, Johns Hopkins University Press

Orkin, M. (ed.) (1989) *Sanctions Against Apartheid* New York, St Martins Press

Padel, F. (2010) 'Movements for Mountains', *Peace News*, April

Palit, C. (2003) 'Monsoon Risings: Megadam Resistance in the Narmada Valley', *New Left Review* 21: 80–100

Parker, N. (1999) *Revolutions and History* Cambridge, Polity Press

Partos, G. (1993) *The World that Came in from the Cold* London, Royal Institute of International Affairs and the BBC World Service

Pastor, R.A. (1999) 'The Third Dimension of Accountability: The International Community in National Elections', in A. Schedler, L. Diamond and M.F. Plattner (eds) *The Self-Restraining State: Power and Accountability in New Democracies* Boulder CO, Lynne Rienner, 123–42

Petras, J. and H. Veltmeyer (2005) *Social Movements and State Power: Argentina, Brazil, Bolivia and Ecuador* London, Pluto Press

Phillips, J. (2005) 'Egypt's First Presidential Election is Too Close to Call', *Independent*, 5 September

Pike, D. (1966) *Viet Cong: The Organization and Techniques of the National Liberation Front of South Vietnam* Cambridge MA, MIT Press

Pipidi, A. and I. Monteanu (2009) 'Moldova's "Twitter Revolution"', *Journal of Democracy* 20(3): 136–42

Popper, K.R. (1962) *The Open Society and its Enemies* 2 vols, 4th rev. edn, London, Routledge

Preston, P. (1986) *The Triumph of Democracy in Spain* London, Routledge

Price, R.M. (1991) *The Apartheid State in Crisis: Political Transformation in South Africa 1975–1990* Oxford, Oxford University Press

Prins, G. (ed.) (1990) *Spring in Winter: The 1989 Revolutions* Manchester, Manchester University Press

Radnitz, S. (2006) 'What Really Happened in Kyrgyzstan?', *Journal of Democracy* 17(2): 132–46

——(2010) 'A Horse of a Different Colour: Revolution and Regression in Kyrgyzstan', in V. Bunce, M. McFaul and K. Stoner-Weiss (eds) *Democracy and Authoritarianism in the Postcommunist World* Cambridge, Cambridge University Press, 300–24

Radrianja, S. (2003) 'Be Not Afraid, Only Believe: Madagascar 2002', *African Affairs* 102(407): 309–29

Randle, M. (1991) *People Power: The Building of a New European Home* Stroud, Hawthorn Press

——(1994) *Civil Resistance* London, Fontana

——(1996) 'Ploughing a Deep Furrow', *Guardian Society*, 7 August

Ranger, T. (1968) 'African Politics in Twentieth-century Southern Rhodesia', in T. Ranger (ed.) *Aspects of Central African History* London, Heinemann, 210–45

Reddaway, P. (1978) 'The Development of Dissent and Opposition', in A. Brown and M. Kaser (eds) *The Soviet Union Since the Fall of Khrushchev* 2nd edn, London and Basingstoke, Macmillan, 121–56

Reich, J. (1990) 'Reflections on Becoming an East German Dissident, on Losing the Wall and a Country', in G. Prins (ed.) *Spring in Winter* Manchester, Manchester University Press, 65–98

Reid, B. (2001) 'The Philippine Democratic Uprising and the Contradictions of Neoliberalism: EDSA II', *Third World Quarterly* 22(5): 777–93

Rigby, A. (1991) *Living the Intifada* London, Zed Books

——(2009) 'Diasporas: Potential Partners in Struggle', in H. Clark (ed.) *People Power* London, Pluto, 177–83

——(2010) *Palestinian Resistance and Nonviolence* Jerusalem, Palestinian Academic Society for the Study of International Affairs

Rigger, S. (2004) 'Taiwan's Best-Case Democratization', *Orbis* 48(2): 285–92

Roberts, A. (1975) 'Civil Resistance to Military Coups', *Journal of Peace Research* 12(1): 19–36

——(2009) 'Introduction', in A. Roberts and T. Garton Ash (eds) *Civil Resistance and Power Politics: The Experience of Non-violent Action from Gandhi to the Present* Oxford, Oxford University Press, 1–24

——and T. Garton Ash (eds) (2009) *Civil Resistance and Power Politics: The Experience of Non-violent Action from Gandhi to the Present* Oxford, Oxford University Press

Roberts, K. (1991) 'Uruguay: Nonviolent Resistance and the Pedagogy of Human Rights', in P. McManus and G. Calabash (eds) *Relentless Persistence* Philadelphia PA, New Society Publishers, 100–17

Roitman, J. (2004) *Fiscal Disobedience: An Anthropology of Economic Regulation in Central Africa* Princeton NJ, Princeton University Press

Rousseau, J.-J. (1968) *The Social Contract* trans. Maurice Cranston, Harmondsworth, Penguin

Roy, A. (2009) *Listening to Grasshoppers: Field Notes on Democracy* London, Hamish Hamilton

Rubio, L. and J. Davidow (2006) 'Mexico's Disputed Election', *Foreign Affairs* 85(5): 75–85

Rude, G. (1959) *The Crowd in the French Revolution* New York, Oxford University Press

——(1980) *Ideology and Popular Protest* London, Lawrence & Wishart

Sakwa, R. (2001) 'The Age of Paradox: The Anti-revolutionary Revolutions of 1989–91', in M. Donald and T. Rees (eds) *Reinterpreting Revolution in Twentieth Century Europe* Basingstoke, Macmillan, 159–76

Sanguinetti, J.M. (1993) 'Present at the Transition', in L. Diamond and M.F. Plattner (eds) *The Global Resurgence of Democracy* Baltimore MD, Johns Hopkins University Press, 53–60

Satha-Anand, C. (1999) 'Imagery in the 1992 Nonviolent Uprising in Thailand', in S. Zunes, L.R. Kurtz and S.B. Asher (eds) *Nonviolent Social Movements* Oxford, Blackwell, 158–73

Saxonberg, S. (2005) *The Fall: A Comparative Study of the End of Communism in Czechoslovakia, East Germany, Hungary and Poland* London, Routledge

Schell, J. (2004) *The Unconquerable World: Power, Nonviolence and the Will of the People* London, Allen Lane

Schock, K. (2005) *Unarmed Insurrections: People Power Movements in Nondemocracies* Minneapolis MN, University of Minnesota Press

Schmitter, P.C. and T.L. Karl (1993) 'What Democracy is … and Is Not', in L. Diamond and M.F. Plattner (eds) *The Global Resurgence of Democracy* Baltimore MD, Johns Hopkins University Press, 39–52

Schram, Stuart (1966) *Mao Tse-Tung*, Harmondsworth, Penguin
Scott, J.C. (1985) *Weapons of the Weak: Everyday Forms of Peasant Resistance* New Haven CT, Yale University Press
——(1990) *Domination and the Arts of Resistance: Hidden Transcripts* New Haven CT, Yale University Press
Scranton, M. (1991) *The Noriega Years: US–Panama Relations 1981–1990* Boulder CO, Lynne Rienner
Shakya, Tsering (1999) *The Dragon in the Land of Snows: A History of Modern Tibet since 1947* London, Pimlico
——(2008) 'Trouble in Tibet', *New Left Review* 51: 5–26
Sharp, G. (1973) *The Politics of Nonviolent Action* Boston MA, Porter Sargent
——(1979) *Gandhi as a Political Strategist* Boston MA, Porter Sargent
——(1993) *From Dictatorship to Democracy: A Conceptual Framework for Liberation*, Boston MA, Albert Einstein Institution
——(2005) *Waging Nonviolent Struggle* Boston MA, Porter Sargent
Shehadi, N. (2005) 'Lebanon: Battle Resumes', *World Today* 61(4): 7–9
Shenker, J. (2010) 'Egypt's Rulers Tighten Grip on Power Amid Claims of Election Fraud and Intimidation', *Guardian*, 1 December
Shin, D.C. and R.F. Tusalem (2007) 'The Cultural and Institutional Dynamics of Global Democratization', *Taiwan Journal of Democracy* 3(1): 1–28
Shorrock, T. (1986) 'The Struggles for Democracy in South Korea in the 1980s and the Rise of Anti-Americanism', *Third World Quarterly* 8(4): 1195–218
Showstack Sasson, A. (1987) *Gramsci's Politics* Minneapolis MN, University of Minnesota Press
Silitsky, V. (2006) 'Belarus: Learning from Defeat', *Journal of Democracy* 17(4): 138–52
——(2010) 'Contagion Deterred: Preemptive Authoritarianism in the Former Soviet Union (the Case of Belarus)', in V. Bunce, M. McFaul and K. Stoner-Weiss (eds) *Democracy and Authoritarianism in the Postcommunist World* Cambridge, Cambridge University Press, 274–99
Sisk, T. (1995) *Democratization in South Africa* Princeton NJ, Princeton University Press
Skinner, Q. (1978) *The Foundations of Modern Political Thought* Vol. 2, Cambridge, Cambridge University Press
Slovo, G. (2009) *Every Secret Thing: My Family, My Country* rev. edn, London, Virago
Smith, A.D. (1991) *National Identity* Harmondsworth, Penguin
Smolar, A. (2009) 'Towards "Self-Limiting Revolution": Poland 1970–89', in A. Roberts and T. Garton Ash (eds) *Civil Resistance and Power Politics* Oxford, Oxford University Press, 127–43
Snow, Edgar (1972) [1937] *Red Star Over China* Harmondsworth, Penguin
Soueif, A. (2010) 'The Regime Can Fix the Elections – But It Can't Fix the Egyptian People', *Guardian*, 16 September
Spaeth, A. (2001) 'Oops, We Did It Again: Ousting Presidents by Revolutions Has Become a Bad National Habit', *Time Asia* 157(4), 29 January, http://www.time.com/time/asia/magazine/2001
Spence, J. (1996) *God's Chinese Son: The Taiping Heavenly Kingdom of Hong Xiuquan* New York, Norton
Steele, J. (1994) *Eternal Russia: Yeltsin, Gorbachev and the Mirage of Democracy* London, Faber & Faber
Stephan, M.J. (2006) 'Fighting for Statehood: The Role of Civilian-based Resistance in the East Timorese, Palestinian, and Kosovo Albanian Self-Determination Movements', *Fletcher Forum of World Affairs* 30(2): 57–79
——and E. Chenoweth (2008) 'Why Civil Resistance Works: The Strategic Logic of Nonviolent Conflict', *International Security* 33(1): 7–44

——and J. Mundy (2006) 'A Battlefield Transformed: From Guerrilla Resistance to Mass Nonviolent struggle in the Western Sahara', *Journal of Military and Strategic Studies* 8(3): 1–32
Sternstein, W. (1969) 'The *Ruhrkampf* of 1923: Economic Problems of Civilian Defence', in A. Roberts (ed.) *Civilian Resistance as a National Defence* Harmondsworth, Penguin, 128–61
Stirner, M. (1977) 'The State and the Sacred', in G. Woodcock (ed.) *The Anarchist Reader* London, Fontana, 81–7
Strathern, P. (2005) *The Medici: Godfathers of the Renaissance* London, Pimlico
Summy, R. (1994) 'Nonviolence and the Case of the Extremely Ruthless Opponent', *Pacifica Review* 6(1): 1–29
Talbott, J. (1980) *The War Without a Name: France in Algeria 1954–1962* New York, Alfred Knopf
Talmon, J.S. (1952) *The Origins of Totalitarian Democracy* London, Secker & Warburg
Tarrow, S. (2005) *The New Transnational Activism* Cambridge and New York, Cambridge University Press
Taylor, J. (2011a) 'In Europe's Last Dictatorship, All Opposition is Mercilessly Crushed', *Independent*, 8 March
——(2011b) 'Belarus Dictator Mocks Plan to Prosecute Him', *Independent*, 10 March
——(2011c) 'My Husband Phoned to Say he was Going to the Sauna ... We Never Saw Him Again', *Independent*, 12 March
Te Brake, W.H. (1993) *A Plague of Insurrection: Popular Politics and Peasant Revolt in Flanders, 1323–1328* Philadelphia PA, University of Pennsylvania Press
Thompson, M.R. (2004) *Democratic Revolutions: Asia and Eastern Europe* London, Routledge
Tilly, C. (1978) *From Mobilization to Resistance* Reading, Adison Wesley
——(1993) *European Revolutions, 1492–1992* Oxford, Blackwell
Tolstoy, L. (1966) [undated] 'Letter to a Noncommissioned Officer', in P. Mayer (ed.) *The Pacifist Conscience* Harmondsworth, Penguin, 160–5
Trapans, J.A. (ed.) (1991) *Towards Independence: The Baltic Popular Movements* Boulder CO, Westview Press
Trotsky, L. (1959) [1930] *The Russian Revolution* trans. M. Eastman, selected by F.W. Dupee (ed.) New York, Doubleday Anchor
Urban, J. (1990) 'Czechoslovakia: The Power and Politics of Humiliation', in G. Prins (ed.) *Spring in Winter* Manchester, Manchester University Press
Vali, F.A. (1961) *Rift and Revolt in Hungary* Cambridge MA, Harvard University Press
Valiyev, A.M. (2006) 'Parliamentary Elections in Azerbaijan: A Failed Revolution', *Problems of Post-Communism* 53(3): 17–35
Vallance, E. (2009) *A Radical History of Britain* London, Little, Brown
Vanaik, A. (2008) 'The New Himalayan Republic', *New Left Review* 49: 47–76
Varney, W. and B. Martin (2000) 'Lessons from the 1991 Soviet Coup', *Peace Research* 32(1): 52–68
Vatikiotis, M.R.J. (1998) *Indonesian Politics Under Suharto: The Rise and Fall of the New Order* 3rd edn, London, Routledge
Vejvoda, I. (2009) 'Civil Society versus Slobodan Milosevic: Serbia, 1991–2000', in A. Roberts and T. Garton Ash (eds) *Civil Resistance and Power Politics* Oxford, Oxford University Press, 295–316
Vickers, A. (2005) *A History of Modern Indonesia* Cambridge, Cambridge University Press
Vishwakarma, R.K. (2006) *People's Power in Nepal* New Delhi, Manak Publications
Wade, R.A. (2008) *The Russian Revolution, 1917* 2nd edn, Cambridge, Cambridge University Press
Walker, S. (2010) 'Analysis', *Independent*, 12 June

War Resisters' International (2009) *Handbook for Nonviolent Campaigns* London, War Resisters' International

Washington Post (2005) 'Egypt's Ugly Election', (editorials) 10 December, http://www.washingtonpost.com/wp-dyn/content/article/2005/12/09/AR20051209018

Weber, M. (1978) *Economy and Society* 2 vols, G. Roth and C. Wittich (eds) Berkeley CA, University of California Press

Weeks, J. and A. Zimbalist (1989) 'The Failure of Intervention in Panama: Humiliation in the Backyard', *Third World Quarterly* 11(1): 1–27

Weinstein, M. (1988) *Uruguay: Democracy at the Cross Road* Boulder CO, Westview Press

Welt, C. (2010) 'Georgia's Rose Revolution: From Regime Weakness to Regime Collapse', in V. Bunce, M. McFaul and K. Stoner-Weiss (eds) *Democracy and Authoritarianism in the Postcommunist World* Cambridge, Cambridge University Press, 155–88

Whitaker, B. (2005) '500,000 Mass for Hizbullah in Beirut', *Guardian*, 9 March

White, S. (2003) 'Rethinking Postcommunist Transition', *Government and Opposition* 38(4): 417–35

Whitehead, L. (2007) 'The Challenge of Closely Fought Elections', *Journal of Democracy* 18(2): 14–28

Whyte, D. and L. Gavernet (2008) 'Ocupar, Resistir, Producir', *Red Pepper* 160 (June/July): 31–3

Williams, K. (2009) 'Civil Resistance in Czechoslovakia: From Soviet Invasion to "Velvet Revolution", 1968–69', in A. Roberts and T. Garton Ash (eds) *Civil Resistance and Power Politics* Oxford, Oxford University Press, 110–26

Wilson, A. (2005) *Ukraine's Orange Revolution* New Haven CT, Yale University Press

——(2009) 'Ukraine's Orange Revolution of 2004: The Paradox of Negotiation', in A. Roberts and T. Garton Ash (eds) *Civil Resistance and Power Politics* Oxford, Oxford University Press, 335–53

Winstanley, L. (2009) 'With Peace Brigades International in Colombia', in H. Clark (ed.) *People Power* London, Pluto Press, 108–11

Wintle, J. (2007) *Perfect Hostage: A Life of Aung San Suu Kyi* London, Hutchinson

Wolf, E.R. (1973) *Peasant Wars of the Twentieth Century* London, Faber & Faber

Wright, A. (2009) 'The Work of the Ecumenical Accompaniment Programme in Palestine and Israel (EAPPI)', in H. Clark (ed) *People Power* London, Pluto Press, 135–7

Wydra, H. (2008) 'Revolution and Democracy: The European Experience', in J. Foran, J.D. Lane and A. Zivkovic (eds) *Revolution in the Making of the Modern World* London, Routledge, 27–44

Yushchenko, V. (2008) 'Ukraine's Atlantic Future', *Guardian*, 26 August (reprinted from *Washington Post*)

Zelter, A. (2009) 'Women's International Peace Service in Palestine', in H. Clark (ed.) *People Power* London, Pluto Press, 138–42

Zielonka, J. (1986) 'Strengths and Weaknesses of the Polish Case', *Orbis* 30(1): 91–110

Zinn, H. (1980) *A People's History of the United States* New York, Harper & Row

Ziolkowski, J. (1990) 'The Roots, Branches and Blossoms of Solidarnosc', in G. Prins (ed.) *Spring in Winter* Manchester, Manchester University Press, 39–64

Zizek, S. (2009) *Violence* London, Profile Books

Zunes, S. (1999) 'The Origins of People Power in the Philippines', in S. Zunes, L.R. Kurtz and S.B. Asher (eds) *Nonviolent Social Movements: A Geographical Perspective* Oxford, Blackwell, 129–57

——(2008) 'The Power of Protest in the Maldives', openDemocracy.net, 2 December

——and J. Mundy (2011) *Western Sahara: War, Nationalism and Conflict Resolution* Syracuse NY, Syracuse University Press

Index

Ackerman, P. 119–20
Adams, J. 55, 66
advocacy networks 156, 163
Africa 1, 3, 19, 150, 176; creating a 'body politic' 104, 113–14; decolonization 147–8, 170–2; demanding electoral democracy 116, 124–6, 131–2, 138, 140–1; guerrilla warfare in 23, 26–8; role of women, 33
African National Congress (ANC) 19, 38, 45, 85, 114–15, 119, 148, 150, 170; Spear of the Nation, 32
African Union (AU) 146, 154
Afrikaans language, 35, 114
Afrikaner National Party, 38
Afrikaner Resistance Movement 115
age (of resisters) 33, 35–8, 97, 103
agents provocateurs 89
Ahmedabad mill strike 31
Akayev, A. President, 130–1
Albania 65
Albanians (see Kosovo)
Albert Einstein Institution 166
Alfonsin, R. President 140
Algeria 35, 43–4, 52, 147; rebel generals in 140–1
All Burma Monks' Alliance 103
Allende, S. President 51–2, 149
Ambedkar, B.R. 33
American Convention of Human Rights 154
American Revolution 22, 50, 54, 66–7, 93; role of unarmed resistance in 15, 55–6
Amnesty International 130, 155, 157
Amritsar massacre 42
anarchists 78
anarchosyndicalists 17
Andijan protests and massacre 128, 151
Angola 85, 114

apartheid 2, 85, 114, 120, 148, 150, 153–5, 171–1
Aquino, B. 99–100
Aquino, C. 34, 37, 100–1
Arab independence 147
Arab uprisings (2011), 1, 7–8, 40, 72, 89, 129, 153, 156, 176
Arato, A 63
Arendt, H. 22, 50, 55, 65–7, 76, 78–9, 88
Argentina 14, 20, 33, 155; opposing feared coup 140; resisting neoliberal economic policy 172–3, 177
aristocracy 54, 56, 92–3, 104
Aristotle 91
armed resistance 22–48 (see also guerrilla warfare)
Armenia 126
Arroyo, G. 139
Asheed, M. 166
Asia, 1, 18; decolonization 146–8; electoral struggles 116–18, 122–4; people power in 176
Association of South East Asian Nations (ASEAN) 112, 154
Aung San Suu Kyi, 9, 19, 34, 64, 91, 97, 120–1, 154–5, 164, 169
Australia, 158, 160, 164
Austria (Austrian Empire) 18, 26, 107, 146
Ayatollahs 69–71
Azerbaijan 126

Babeuf, F-N, 64
backfire theory 43, 145
Bahrain, 20, 72, 88–9
Bakiyev, K. President 131, 152
Balkan states 128, 167
Baltic states 1, 11, 49, 62–3, 68, 97, 105–8, 129, 150
Banda, H. President 80, 125

banks 30, 84, 100, 102, 110
Banzer, H. General 30
El Baradej, M. 136
Barghouti, M. 165
barricades 49, 54
Bastille, 52, 54, 56, 58–9, 64
Batista, F. President 38, 45
Belarus, 126, 129,157
Belden, J. 38
Belgian general strike, 17
Belo, C. Bishop, 158–9
Ben Ali, Z. President 79–80
Benin 80, 113, 125
Berlin Wall 12, 37, 59–60, 64–5, 107
Bhose, S.C. 19
Biko, S. 114
Biya, P. President, 126, 131, 140
Black Consciousness Movement, 114
Black Sash 114
Black Sea naval base, 152
Bleiker, R. 79, 83
blogs, 21, 135
'body politic' 91–115, 172
Boetie, E. de la 76, 76–81
Bohley, B. 107
Bolivia, 16, 30, 109–10, 171–3, 177
Bolsheviks 52, 58, 62–3, 71, 148
'boomerang effect' 156
Bouazizi, M. 7
Boudreau, V. 122
Boulding, K. 77
Bratton, M. 113, 124
Brazil, 118
Britain, protests in 159–60, 164
British empire 17–19, 22, 33, 42–3, 147; Gandhi on 'English' 75;
British government policy 52, 152
Buddhists 9, 14, 34, 98, 101–3, 111, 162
Bulgaria 105–6, 108, 126
Bunce, V. 120, 126, 134
bureaucracy 69, 79, 148
Burke, E. 54, 92
Burma, 2, 9, 29, 32, 42–3, 45, 70, 92, 97–8, 102, 103, 120, 153–5, 157, 161, 163–4, 166, 169–70; independence 147
Burrowes, R. 80

Caetano, M. President
Calvinists 13, 15
Cameroon 83, 126, 131, 140
Camus, A. 53
capital cities (significance of) 27, 57, 103, 106, 112

capitalism 39, 63, 84, 87, 107, 109, 130, 146, 148
Caravan of the Poor and Democracy-Loving Village People 111
Carter, J. President 69, 99, 148
Castro, F. 26, 32, 148
Catholics, 9, 11, 13–15, 37, 39, 55, 71, 100, 106–7, 112, 125, 128, 133, 139, 148, 158; Peace and Justice Service 155
Ceausescu, N. President 59–60, 83, 108
Cedar Revolution 20, 112–13
Central African Federation 147
Central Asia 129
Central Eastern Europe 9, 20, 65, 67–8, 79, 105, 108
Chad 83
Chamlong Srimuang Major General 101, 111
Chang Hsi-jo Professor 31
charismatic leadership 62–5, 71
Charter 77 12, 39, 65, 79, 154
Chiang Kai-shek General 22, 26, 31, 38, 123
children 35, 83, 97, 163, 165
Chile 14, 20, 51, 83, 98, 120–1, 149, 156; Pinochet's referendum 133
Chiluba, F. 124, 140
China 150, 154; Cultural Revolution 162; May Fourth Movement 146; peasant rebellions 15, 53, 62; people's war 26, 31, 34–6, 38, 40–4; revolution (1949) 53–5, 64; Tibet 155, 161–3
Christians 12–13, 53, 112–13, 125, 164, 166
Chronicle of the Lithuanian Catholic Church 106
Chun Doo Hwan General 118
CIA 52, 149, 162
Cicero 92
citizenship 63, 93, 113–14, 138
Civic Forum, 12, 59–61, 67
civic nationalism 105–9
civil disobedience 9, 12, 19, 28, 30, 55, 57, 77, 100, 126, 138
civil liberties 132, 137, 176
civil resistance 10–11, 16, 27, 29, 32, 36–8, 45–7; comparison with guerrilla warfare 22–3, 27–44; concepts of power 76–9 see also nonviolent resistance
Civil Rights Movement (USA) 11, 13, 19, 87, 165
civil servants 80, 125
civil society 76, 86–7, 168; created from below 79, 89; and electoral democracy

120, 129, 133–5, 137, 139–40; transnational 146, 155, 159–61, 163–6, 169
civil wars 40, 49, 54–5, 58, 94, 111–12, 132, 158
clans 94, 141
Clark, H, 10, 41, 80, 145
'Clash of Civilizations' 118
class structure 3, 17–18, 31, 45, 91–115, 157, 172, 177; and concepts of power 82, 87; electoral democracy 117–18; revolutionary theory 50, 56, 62–6 *see also* peasants, workers
Clausewitz, C. von 25, 44, 47, 80
Cold War 148–9, 151, 154, 159
Cole, G.D.H, 109
colonialism, 8, 18–19, 23, 25–7, 35, 44–5, 47, 55, 113, 146–8, 153–4, 160; and nationalism 104
colour revolutions 1, 47, 52, 68, 117, 151; 'electoral revolutions' 119, 128–31, 134 *see also* Georgia, Ukraine, Kyrgyzstan
Comecon 68
COMELEC 100
'common people' 109–13
'competitive authoritarianism' 126–8, 154 *see also* 'semi–authoritarianism'
Communist Party rule 11–12, 39, 49, 53, 59–5, 67–8, 86, 105, 106–7; former officials 128; transition from 68
communists in opposition 25–6, 31, 34, 36, 38, 40–1, 44, 85, 99, 100, 114, 122, 146, 148, 150, 172
Confucianism 12–13, 118
Congress Party (India) 14, 30
conscription 17; conscientious objection to 17
consent theory of power 75–6, 78, 80–4, 86–7 (see also
Coptic (Christians) 89
corporations (multinationals) 84–5, 110, 149, 160, 164, 171–2, 177
Corrie, R. 165
Cossacks 24, 53
Council of Europe 149, 154
coups d'etat 51–3, 69, 77, 91, 95, 101, 122, 132, 140
'critical elections' 126
Croatia 126, 151
Cromwell, O. 64
Cuba, 26–7, 32, 38, 45, 148
Cyprus 26
Czechoslovakia 10, 12, 39, 60–6, 65, 67–8, 78–9, 97, 108, 118, 149–50, 154

Dahl, R. 136–7
Dalai-Lama 161–3
De Gaulle, C. General 140–1
De Ligt, B. 57, 78
Debray, R. 30, 32
democracy 3–4; electoral model 116–41; minimum model 136–7; participatory model 3, 66–7; rule of the people 8, 91 *see also* civil society, created from below; 'general will'
'democratic revolutions' 126
democratization 116–41, 153, 175
demos 91, 113
Deng Xiaoping 36
Devlin Report 147
diasporas 80, 145, 155, 161–4, 169
dictatorships 1, 4, 7, 9–11, 23, 30, 44–5, 51, 69–70, 77, 80, 88, 116, 118, 120–3, 147–9, 153–4, 169–72
Dien Bien Phu 44
Dili massacre 38, 43, 159
diplomacy 43, 56, 68, 80, 145, 147–6, 150–1, 159, 169
Dirty War 33 *see also* Argentina
Djindic, Z. 37
dominant narrative 52–5, 58, 63, 68
domination 77, 81–4, 86–7, 147
Druze 113
Dubcek, A. 60
Dudouet, V. 170
'duplicitous organization' 88
Duvall, J. 120

East Germany 10–12, 53, 59–61, 63, 65, 67, 83, 95, 97, 107–8, 149–50
East Timor 24, 38, 43, 46, 80, 151, 157–61
East Timor Action Network 160
Egypt (2011) 20, 36, 42, 48, 72, 79–80, 84, 88–89, 103, 153, 157, 166, 176; movement of 1919 33; Mubarak regime 118, 135–6, 153; Nasser coup 51–2
El Salvador, (1944) 10
electoral competence 134–7
electoral resistance strategies 133–7
'electoral revolutions' 116–17, 126–33, 137, 151, 176
End Conscription Campaign 160
English language 78, 14
English Revolution 51, 54–6, 64
Enrile, J. General 37, 52
environmental protests 106, 110, 164, 171–3, 177
EOKA 26

Epifanio de los Santos Avenue (EDSA) *see* Philippines
Estates General (1789) 56
Estonia 62, 106; Estonians 169; Tallinn 11
Estrada, J. President
Ethiopia 132
ethnic divisions 3, 31, 36, 44–5, 92, 103, 108–9, 113, 125, 131–2, 141, 177; ethnicity and nationalism 32, 103–9 *see also* nationalism
European Convention on Human Rights 154
European Parliament 170
'everyday resistance' 76, 81, 83–4
exit polls 134
'extraordinary rendition' 153

Facebook 8, 21, 157 *see also* Internet
Falklands War 140
'false consciousness' 84
Fanon, F. 35, 41, 43–4
fascism 63, 86
Feher, F. 87
feminism 11, 18, 33, 35, 81–2
Finland (1899–1906) 18
First Intifada *see* Intifada
First World War 16, 25, 146
Flanders (peasant revolt) 15–16, 53
Flying University 39
food prices 15, 102, 125, 171
Formosa Movement 123 *see also* Taiwan
Foucault, M. 51, 70–1, 76, 82–4, 96
'fourth wave' of democratization 117
free trade agreements 109, 171
Free West Papua 156
Freedom House 119
FRELIMO 26–8, 34, 40
France 92; French colonialism 35, 44, 147; French government policy 113, 126; French partisans 25; peasant and worker resistance 15–17; resisting coup attempt 140–1 *see also* Ruhr
French language 124–5
French Revolution 50–1, 54, 56, 58, 62, 64, 66–7, 69, 92
Friends of the Maldives 163, 166
Froissart, J. 54
Fugitive Slave Act 18
Furman, D. 128–30

Gabon, 126
Gaddafi, M. General 80, 153
Galtung, J. 85, 87

Gandhi, M.K. 7–9, 12, 18–20, 22, 29–34, 41, 53, 57, 64, 75, 80–1, 175; film of 20
Garibaldi, G. 54
Garton Ash, T. 50, 60, 62, 98, 145
Gayoom, M. President 163, 166
Gaza 80 *see also* Palestine
Gdansk 11, 39, 98
Gellner, E. 50, 67
general strikes 16–17, 30–1, 39, 56, 60, 65, 101, 109, 119, 122, 126, 141
'general will' 95–102
Genocide Convention 160
Georgia 10, 20, 36, 119, 129–30, 134, 151–2, 166, 168
Germany 25; German forces in World War II, 23, 26; German Peasants War 15, 62; German unification 63, 107; West Germany 149 *see also* Kapp *Putsch*, Ruhr
Ghana 147
Giap, V.N. General 28, 44
'glasnost' 61
Global Justice Movement 171–2
global trends 145–73
globalization 3, 145, 153, 156, 170–3
Gorbachev, M. President 52, 61, 68, 106, 149–50
Gramsci, A. 76, 86–7
great powers 105, 129, 146–53, 166
Greek city republic 79
Greek colonels 52, 98
Greek partisans 26
green (environmental) movement, 2, 11, 71, 110, 156, 167
Gregg, R. 42
Griffiths, A. 18
Grivas, G. General 26
Guatemala, 10, 155
Guei, R. President, 132
guerrilla warfare 1–2, 19, 22–48, 54–70, 146–8, 174; comparison with civil resistance 27–30; East Timor 158–9; in newly-created states 92; Philippines 99–100; recent trends 172; scales of destruction 44–5; Tibet 162;
Guevara, E. (Che) 26–8, 31–2, 34, 41, 43
Guinea Bissau 23

Habermas, J. 58, 78, 88
Habibe, B.J. President 171
'Harijans' (Dalits) 32–3
Hariri, R. 112–13
Havel, V. 14, 39, 41, 59–60, 67, 76, 79, 155
Hegel, G.W.F. 94

hegemony 170; concept of 76, 84, 86–7
Helsinki Agreement 154
'hidden resistance' 76, 83 *see also* Scott, J.C.
'hidden transcripts' 87
Hindus, 31–2
Hirschamn, A. 60
Hizbollah, 112–13
Hobbes, T. 78–9, 94
Honecker, E. General Secretary 60
human rights, 3–4, 14, 24, 39, 46. 69, 79, 85 102, 111, 175; and electoral democracy 122, 129–31, 140; and international politics 146, 148–9, 151, 153–4, 156, 158–60, 164–5, 169
Human Rights Watch 155
Hungary (1867), 18; (1956) 61; (1989) 11, 50, 60; intellectual dissent in 39, 78, 86–7, 149
Huntingdon, S. 116–18
Hurndall, T. 165
Hus, J. 108
Husak, G President 60
'hybrid regimes' *see* 'competitive authoritarian'

Ignatieff, M. 105
imperialism 23–6, 30, 43–5, 47, 51, 75, 80–1, 92, 107, 146–8; and nationalism 104 *see also* colonialism
India 162; *see also* Naxalites
Indian independence movement 7, 14, 18–20, 22, 30–3, 75, 146
Indians in South Africa 8, 18, 114
indigenous people 16, 80, 110, 155, 158, 171–3
Indonesia 92, 164; anti-Suharto 36, 89, 120, 123, 150–1; and East Timor 38, 43, 151, 157–60; economic unrest 170, 171; and West Papua 46–7, 156;
Inkatha 114–15; Kawzulu homeland 114
insurrection 53 *see also* rebellion
Inter-American Commission on Human Rights 154
Inter-American Court of Human Rights 154
International Center on Nonviolent Conflict 166
International Court of Justice 109
International Criminal Court 146
International Fellowship of Reconciliation 100, 165
international governmental organizations 153–7, 175
International Labour Organization 153
international law 146, 153, 155, 175

International Monetary Fund (IMF) 171, 173, 177
International Transport Workers Federation 161
Internet 20–1, 42, 89, 118, 135, 156–7, 162 *see also* Facebook, Twitter
Intifada 9, 16, 29, 33–4, 39, 41, 46, 80, 85, 97, 160, 166 *see also* Palestine, Second Intifada
Iran 13; CIA coup 52, 167; Green Movement 2, 110, 71–2, 156, 157, 167; and Lebanon 112; revolution 1, 10, 13, 36, 42, 88, 96–7, 108, 129; and revolutionary theory 50, 62, 69–71; security services 47, 77
Ireland 18, 53; and English Civil War 55
Irish Republican Army (IRA) 30
Islam, political role of, in Iran 51, 69–72; in Maldives 166; in Philippines 99; in Syria 72; Islamic culture and electoral democracy 118; Islamic extremism and West 47–8, 151–3, 165; Koran 14
Israel 112–13; and Occupied Territories, 9, 29, 39, 46, 81, 85, 97, 164–5; Israeli support for Palestinians, 160, 164 165
Italy, 25, 26; city states in 16
Ivory Coast 135, 132

Jacobins, 58, 64, 95
Japan 19, 147; forces in China 22, 40, 154
Jasmine revolution 7 *see also* Tunisia
Al Jazeera 157
Jefferson, T. 55
jiu-jitsu theory 42–3
John Paul II, Pope 158
Jordan 72
Journalists Across Borders 155

Kaminski, B. 84
Kapp Putsch 52
Kapuscinski, R. 69, 88
Kashmir 46
Kaunda, K. 125, 140
Kazakhstan 128, 152
Keane, J. 121
Keck, M. 156
Kenya 132, 147
KGB 106, 129
Khameni, Ayatollah 72
Khomeini, Ayatollah 70–1
King, M. 29, 59
Kirchner, N. President 173
Kissinger, H. 148
Kohn, H. 105

KOR (Committee for the Defence of Workers' rights) 39
Korea, South 13, 118, 171
Kosovo 9, 23, 37, 40–1. 80, 104, 109, 167
Kuomintang 38
Kurds 70
Kuron, J. 9, 39
Kyrgyzstan 126, 128–31, 152, 177

Lagos, R. 83
land seizures 16
Landauer, G. 78
Laos 44
Latin America 1, 9, 24, 30, 45, 86; electoral strategies and democratic transition 116–17, 119, 121–2; regional style of protest 16, 98, 176; resisting neoliberalism 109–10, 172; and USA 148, 160
Latvia 62, 106
Lawrence, T.E. 25
lawyers 80, 89, 135, 155
leadership of movements 62–5, 92, 119, 122
League of Nations Lebanon
Lebanon 112, 153; Palestinians in 112
Lefort, C. 95
Leipzig 11, 13, 37, 61, 107 *see also* East Germany
Lenin Shipyards 11 *see also* Solidarity
Levellers 64
Libya 2, 49, 80, 90, 153, 174
Liddell Hart, B. 23
Lipset, S. 118
Lithuania 62, 105–6, 108
Locke, J. 79 94
Long March 55 *see also* China, revolution
looting 70, 69, 130–1, 173, 177
Louis XVI 52, 58
Lukashenko, A. President 129
Lukes, S. 75, 78, 81, 84
lustration system 68
Lutherans 13, 128
Luxemburg, R. 17, 57

McFaul, M. 117, 168
Machiavelli, N. 86–8
Madagascar 132
Malawi 16, 80, 125, 147; Malawi Young Pioneers 80, 125
Malaysia 154, 164; Malaya 148
Maldives 153, 163
Mali 125
Manas airbase (Kyrgyzstan) 152

Mandela, N. 28, 64, 86, 114–15
Mao Tse-tung 22, 26, 28, 30–3, 38, 41
Maoists 46, 172
Marcos, F. President 8, 37, 51–2, 79, 99–100, 101, 116, 139, 149
Maronites 112
martial law 36, 69–70, 98–100, 121, 123
Martin, B. 43, 145
martyrdom, 13–14, 70
Martyr's Square (Beirut) 113
Marx, K. 84
Marxism–Leninism 32, 43
Marxists (in opposition) 148 *see also* communists
Marxist theory 17, 31, 56, 64, 86, 95
Masaryk, T. 67
Mau Mau 147
Mbeki, T. President 154
Meciar, V. President 151, 166
Men of Zimbabwe Arise 34
Menchu, R. 155
messianism 50, 62, 71
Mexico 16, 27, 110, 138, 172
Michelet, J. 56, 92
Michnik, A. 9
Middle East 1, 18, 48–9, 84, 153, 176
military (armed forces) 13, 17; *coups d'etat* 51–2, 139–40; in government 24, 102, 116, 118, 122–3, 148; and guerrilla warfare 22–5, 43–5; role abroad 85–6, 113, 156, 158–60; supporting resistance 10, 20, 100; suppressing resistance 14, 20, 102, 112; winning over 23, 36–8, 56–7, 58, 59, 80
military power 65, 77, 146–53
Mill, J.S. 108
Milosevic, S. President 1, 11, 35, 37, 40, 78–80, 133, 151, 166–8
mobile phones 20, 89, 156–7, 163
Moldova, 129, 156
Molotov–Ribbentrop Pact 107
monarchy 51, 54, 80, 92, 101, 109
Mondlane, E. 28
Mongolia 49, 62, 150, 176
monitoring of elections 133–5, 146, 154, 160, 167–8, 170
Moore, B. 81
Morales, E. President 173
Morocco 46, 72
Morozov, E. 157
Mossadeq, M. Prime Minister 52, 167
Mothers of the Plaza de Mayo 14, 20, 33, 155

Mothers of Tiananmen 20
Movement for the Restoration of
  Democracy (Nepal) 46
Mozambique 23, 26, 34, 40, 85, 114
Mubarak, H. President 79–80, 103,
  135, 157
Mueda massacre 23
Mugabe, R. President 34, 37, 140, 154,
  160–1
Murray, C. 129, 152
Muslim Brotherhood 135–6
Muslims, 31, 35, 46, 69–70, 89, 108,
  111–13, 118, 122, 128 *see also* Islam
mutiny 17, 38, 52, 56
Myanmar 42 *see also* Burma

Napoleon 25, 51; Napoleonic Wars 57
Nasser, G.A. Colonel 51
nation, people as 91–115
nation states, 3, 44, 92, 104, 171
nationalism 25, 32–3, 62–3, 71, 92, 94,
  103–9, 129, 146–7, 162; national
  liberation movements 18, 28, 44
NATO 37, 151–2, 154
Naxalites 45, 172
Nazis 88, 114
'negative liberty' 66
neoliberalism 68, 109, 170–3
Nepal, 23, 46, 80, 162
nepotism 79, 130, 163
New Forum 59–60, 67, 107 *see also* East
  Germany
Nicaragua 30, 34, 44
Niger, 125
Nigeria 147, 171
Nixon R. President 148
Nobel Peace Prize 155, 159
nomenklatura 65, 68
Non-Cooperation Campaign (1920–22)
  19, 42
nonviolent resistance 1–2, 12–18, 20–1,
  100, 107, 148, 16–2, 163–6, 172 *see also*
  civil resistance
nonviolent revolution, 49–50, 53, 58–62
Noriega, M. General 149
North Africa 26, 147
North American Free Trade Association
  (NAFTA) 172
North Vietnamese 28, 44
North-West Frontier Province 14
Norway 15, 167; Oslo, Burmese radio
  station in 157
Nour, A. 135
nuclear weapons 24, 44, 71

Oaxaca 110
Obama, B, President 77, 152
Obrador, L. 110, 138
October Revolution *see* Russian
  Revolution
Ogoni movement 171
oil 69, 110, 151, 164, 171, 177
Olympic Games 155, 162
Operation Ajax 52 *see also* CIA
Orange Revolution 20, 130, 151–2 *see also*
  Ukraine
oratory 64, 92
Organization for African Unity (OAU) 154
  see also AU
Organization of American States (OAS) 154
Organization for Security and Cooperation
  in Europe (OSCE) 106, 130–1, 146,
  154, 167, 169
Orthodox Church 62, 81, 109, 112, 128
Oslo Accords 29
Ottoman Empire 26

'pacted transitions' 118–20
Pakistan 31, 47, 80
Palach, J, 14
Palestine, 161, 164–5 *see also* Intifada,
  Second Intifada
Panama 149
paramilitaries 125, 165
Paris Commune 66
'passive resistance' 8, 18
patriarchy 34, 82
Peace Brigades International 165, 169
peace movement 11
Pearl Roundabout (Manama) 20, 89
peasants 15–17; and 'everyday resistance'
  83; and guerrilla warfare 25–6, 31, 40,
  44, 45, 104; rebellions 51, 53–4, 62; in
  revolutions 56–7, 64–5, 172 ; rural
  versus urban 110
Peasants' Revolt (England) 15
Peng Teh-huai 31
Pentagon 149
people *passim* concept of 'the people'
  91–115 *see also* common people, nation
people power *passim* definition of 1–4,
  7–12 *see also* civil resistance, nonviolent
  resistance, unarmed resistance
People's Republic of Congo (formerly
  Congo Brazzaville) 125
'people's war' *see* guerrilla warfare
perestroika 61–2, 106
Perez–Esquivel, A. 155
Peru 16

Peterloo massacre 75
Petofi Circle 86 *see also* Hungary
Philippines 1–2, 8, 14, 24, 32, 34, 37, 52, 79, 87, 100–1, 149, 151, 154, 164–5; and 'electoral revolutions' 117, 133; EDSA II (2001) 138–9
Pinochet, A. General 51, 83, 121, 133, 149
Poland 26; 9, 78–9; Catholic Church in 14, 71, 107; civil society in 39, 67, 78–9, 86; intellectuals in 9, 78–9; and nationalism 104, 108; 1956 uprising 61, 65, 86, 149; 1970 and 1976 strikes 12, 150; 1989 50, 65 *see also* Solidarity
police (security forces) 7, 12, 14, 16, 35, 42, 59, 68, 135, 151; benefiting from regime change 68; defecting 23, 36–8, 61; files of 68; relation with military 79–80; resisting 10, 125; target of violence 19, 27, 45
'political defiance' 9
political prisoners 98, 102, 1201, 155
Popes 71, 107, 158
populism 100, 139
Portugal 20, 52, 147, 157
Portuguese colonies, 23, 26–7, 45, 157, 159
'positive action' 9
'post-structuralism' 76
Postgate, R. 109
power, concepts of 3, 75–90 *see also* consent theory of power, domination, hegemony, post-structuralism, soft power, structuralism
Prague Spring 14, 60–1. 149
Presbyterians 55
prices 15, 102, 125, 131, 170
privatization 109–10, 171, 173
Probowo S. General 89
Protestants 13, 59, 100
Public Against Violence 59, 67
'public transcripts' 87
Pugachev, Y. 53

Al Qaeda 47, 152
Qatar 157
Quakers 13
Quit India 19

racism 85, 87, 114
Radio Free Asia 157
Radio Free Europe 167
Radio Liberty 167
Radnitz, S. 130–1
Ramos, F. General 100

Ramos-Horta J. 159
rape 89, 158
Razin, S. 53
Reagan, R. President 148–9
'realism' 77, 146
'realpolitik' 148, 155
Red Cross 155
Reformation 13, 15, 56, 62, 105, 108
refugees 34, 112, 1t54, 161, 165, 169
regime change 79–80, 82, 84
Reich, J. 67, 107
'relentless persistence' 9
religion 9, 12–14; and nationalism 92–3, 103, 108, 109, 162; and political culture 117–18, 128; and political divisions 31, 97, 113; and revolutionary fervour 62, 70–1
Renaissance 93, 105
Revolution of the Carnations 20, 45, 52, 157
Revolutionary Guard Corps (Iran) 47–8
revolution 15, 17, 36, 39, 109; Arendt on 65–7; concept of 2, 51–3; and fearlessness 42, 88; new models 58–67; theory of 49–51, 62–5 *see also* American, colour, English, French, Russian and velvet revolutions
rhetoric 87, 91–4, 109
Rigby, A. 29
riots 89, 177
Roberts, A. 77, 145
Robespierre, M. 66
Roitman, J. 83, 126
Romania 2, 50, 59, 65, 83, 84, 108, 126
Roman republic 92
Rose Revolution 20 *see also* Georgia
Rousseau, J-J, 94–6, 99, 102
Rowlatt Bills 19
Roy, A. 46
Rude, G. 15–16, 69
Rugova, I. 9
Ruhr (1923) 80
rural warfare 26–7
Russia (before 1917) 15, 18, 25–6, 39, 52–3, 86, 146; since 1991 68, 109, 128–30, 151–3, 167–8; Russian minorities in post-Soviet states, 107, 108 *see also* Soviet Union
Russian Revolution 50–1, 54, 56–8, 62, 98, 14, 148

Saakashvili, M. 130
Sahwari movement 23, 46
Sakharov Prize 170

Salazar, A. President 147
Salt March 19, 30
samizdat 39, 98, 106
sanctions 39, 43, 77, 79, 85, 145, 149, 153, 169
sanctuary 14
Sandinistas 30, 44
Sanguinetti, J.M. 122
satyagraha 8, 18–19, 32
Saudi Arabia 72, 112
Schell, J. 24, 44, 55, 57
Schock, K. 10, 24, 120
Scotland 55, 156
Scott, J.C. 76, 81, 83–4, 87
Second Intifada 9, 46, 164
Second World War 8, 19, 23, 25, 34, 106, 147
self-immolation 13
'semi-authoritarianism' 117, 126, 151, 170
Serbia 1, 10–11, 35, 37, 40, 79–80, 109, 126, 133–4, 166, 167–8, 176 see also Kosovo
Serbianization 40, 80
Shah of Iran 1, 10, 13, 35–6, 42, 51, 69–72, 96–7
Sharp, G. 10, 15, 43, 80–1, 166
Shelley, P.B. 75
Shevardnadze, E. President 168
Shia (Muslims) 69, 71, 112
Sieyes, Abbe 92
Sikhas, 33
Sikkink, K. 156
Silitsky, V. 126, 129, 151
Sin, Cardinal J. 100
Singing Revolution 106 see also Estonia
Sinn Fein 18, 30
slavery 13, 18, 93
Slovakia 108, 126, 134–5, 151
Slovaks 59, 67, 108, 166
Slovo, J. 85
Smile Revolution 121 see also Uruguay
Snow, E. 31
social contract 79, 99
Socialist Internationals 17
'soft power' 77; 'soft coups' 167
Somoza, A. President 30, 34, 44
soldiers see military, mutiny
Solidarity Movement 11–12, 39, 59–61, 64–5, 67–8, 97–8, 150
Soueif, A. 135
South Africa 13, 28, 34, 35 114–15, 120; 'armed propaganda' 32, 43, 45, 114; Gandhi in 7, 8, 18–19, 57; in international context 85–6, 150, 153, 155, 163, 164, 170, 171; negotiated transition 38, 85–6, 119; and Zimbabwe 160–1
South Korea see Korea
South Ossetia 130, 152
South Vietnam 28, 32, 44
Soviet Union 10, 36, 88, 105–6; dissolution of 1, 49, 106–7; dissolution of bloc 126, 149–51; during 1989 60, 61, 62, 68, 84; former Soviet states 3, 47, 62, 69, 117, 128–31, 141; Soviet-style system 65, 84–5, 124
'soviets' (councils) 39, 57–8, 66, 98
Spain 25–6, 44, 47, 86, 118–19
Sri Lanka 44
states of emergency 125, 130, 173
Stephan, M. 23, 38, 80, 159
Stirner, M. 53
Strategic Arms Reductions Treaty (START) 151
structural adjustment programmes 171
structuralism (theory of power) 75–6, 78, 84–6
Sub-Saharan Africa 3, 116, 124–6, 131–2, 141, 150
Suchinda Kraprayoon General 101–2
suffrage 16, 93, 136
Suharto General 89, 122–3, 150, 158–60, 171
Sukarno A. President 122
Sukarnoputri, M. 122–3
Sukhanov, N.N. 57
Sunni (Muslims) 70, 112–13
Switzerland 167
Syria 20, 72, 88, 153; and Lebanon 112–13

Tahrir Square (Cairo) 20, 42, 89, 103, 135, 157
Taiping Rebellion 53, 62
Taiwan 120, 123, 135
Taliban 152
Tallinn see Estonia
Tamil Tigers 44
Tarrow, S. 11
taxation 12, 15–16, 18, 30, 39, 55, 77, 83, 110, 126
technology 24, 43–4, 47, 71, 78, 84, 89, 156–7
television 1, 7, 20, 42, 87, 95, 98, 100, 157, 168
terrorism 23–4, 28, 43–4, 47, 87, 121, 153, 166, 174
texting 156, 163

Thailand 14, 71, 101–2, 110–12, 138–9, 154, 161, 164
Thaksin Shinawatra, 111–12, 138
Thich Nhat Hanh 14
third wave (of democratization) 116–20, 175
Thompson, M. 120, 126, 139
Thoreau, H.D. 78
Tiananmen Square (Beijing) 2, 20, 36, 167, 176
Tibet 81, 104, 161, 162–3; diaspora protests 20, 155, 161–3; internet in 157
Tilly, C. 11, 64
Timisoara 60, 83, 108 see also Romania
Tocqueville, A. de 61, 87
Togo 126, 132
Tolstoy, L. 78, 80–1
torture 43, 77, 123, 129–30, 152–3, 156, 158, 172
totalitarianism 77–8, 88, 95
tourism and boycotts 162–4
trade unions 16, 89; leading role in resistance 10, 11, 30, 45, 63, 97, 101, 109–10, 124–5, 140–1, 171; regime unions subverted 86, 87, 97; transnational solidarity 153, 156, 160 see also civil society, strikes, workers
transnational support 153–61, 163–66; criteria for 168–70; limits and problems 166–8
Transparency International 155
tribune (of the people) 92, 98
troops see military
Trotsky, L. 56–8, 64, 66
Truth and Reconciliation Commission 115
Tsars 53, 57, 81
Tudjman, F. President 151
Tulip Revolution 130–1, 152 see also Kyrgyzstan
Tunisia 1, 7–8, 20, 36, 48, 72, 79–80, 84, 88–9, 118, 153, 156–7, 170, 176
Turkmenistan 128
Twitter 8, 21, 156–7 see also Internet
Twitter Revolution (Moldova) 156

Ukraine 3, 20, 37, 119, 126, 129–30, 151–2, 166, 168–9
unarmed resistance passim as a definition 1–3, 10
United Kingdom (UK) see Britain
United Nations Committe on Decolonization on East timor 160
United Nations (UN) 106, 113, 131, 146, 152–3, 158–9, 169

UN Human Rights Council 153
UN Security Council 158
United States (USA) 77, 109, 148–50, 151–3, 170; and Chile 149; and Egypt 135–6; and ex-Soviet states 129–30, 167 and Indonesia 158; and Iran 52, 69, 71; and Latin America 109, 121–2, 148–9; and Lebanon 112–13; and Philippines 99; and Palestine 29; in Vietnam 28, 44
US civil resistance 17, 18, 55 see also American Revolution, Civil Rights Movement
US State Department 149
untouchables see harijans
urban warfare 26–7
urbanization 50, 62–5
Uzbekistan 128, 131, 151–2

Van de Walle, N. 113, 124
Vejvoda, I. 35, 151, 167
velvet revolutions 12, 47, 50, 60, 67–9, 118
Versailles Treaty 114, 146
Vietnam 14, 28 44
villes mortes 126, 131 see also Cameroon
violence 10; concept of 3, 10, 41; and peasant rebellion 15–16; and power 76–8, 87–90; rebounding 42–4; and repression 42, 97, 119; and revolution 49–50, 52, 53–8 see also Fanon, guerrilla warfare
Voice of America 150, 157
voter registration 1e33
Vykom Temple 32 see also harijans

Walesa, L. 59, 64, 98
War Resisters' International 160, 165
Warsaw Ghetto 53
Warsaw Pact 68, 154
'Washinton consensus' 173
Weber, M. 64, 77–80, 103–4
Wenceslas Square (Prague) 64
West Bank 80, 164 see also Palestine
West Germany 59, 60, 67, 107, 149
West Papua 46, 156
West Timor 158
Western Europe 54, 129, 149, 151
Western Sahara 23, 46
WikiLeaks 152, 157
will of the people 91, 95, 97, 99–103
Winter Palace 54, 58
Witness for Peace 165
Wolchik, S. 120, 126, 134

women 92, 93, 103, 115, 141; and cultural restraints 93, 97, 162; and guerrilla warfare 34–5; in national movements 18, 46, 56, 69, 102, 114, 123, 140; in unarmed resistance 30, 33–4, 97 *see also* Mothers of the Plaza de Mayo
Women of Zimbabwe Arise 11, 34
workers 16–17, 109, 156; in earlier revolutions 39, 56–7, 64; and guerrilla warfare 45–6; in national movements 39, 69, 118, 136, 163; resisting neoliberalism 170, 173 *see also* strikes, trade unions
World Bank 149, 171

Xu Qinxian 36

Yanukovych, V. 130, 134, 152
Yemen, 72, 88
Yenan 31 *see also* China, revolution
Yugoslavia 25, e34, 40–1
Yushchenko, V. 152

Zaire 126
Zalavskaya, T. 68
Zambia 10, 32, 34, 124, 140, 147
Zapatistas 47, 172
Zimbabwe 11, 34, 37, 113, 132, 134, 147, 154, 157, 160
Zinn. H. 109
Ziolkoswki, J. 59, 65
Zizek, S. 87

Routledge Paperbacks Direct

Bringing you the cream of our hardback publishing at paperback prices

This exciting new initiative makes the best of our hardback publishing available in paperback format for authors and individual customers.

Routledge Paperbacks Direct is an ever-evolving programme with new titles being added regularly.

To take a look at the titles available, visit our website.

www.routledgepaperbacksdirect.com

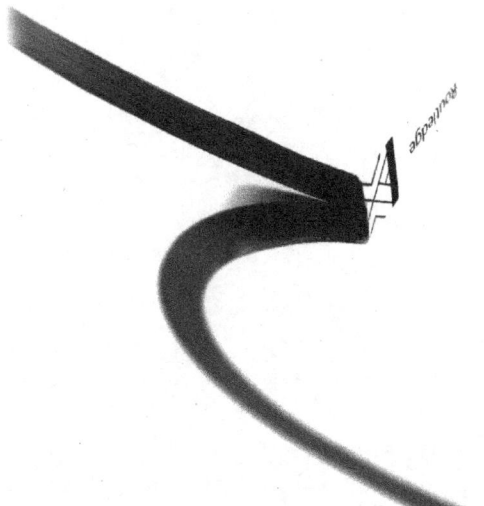